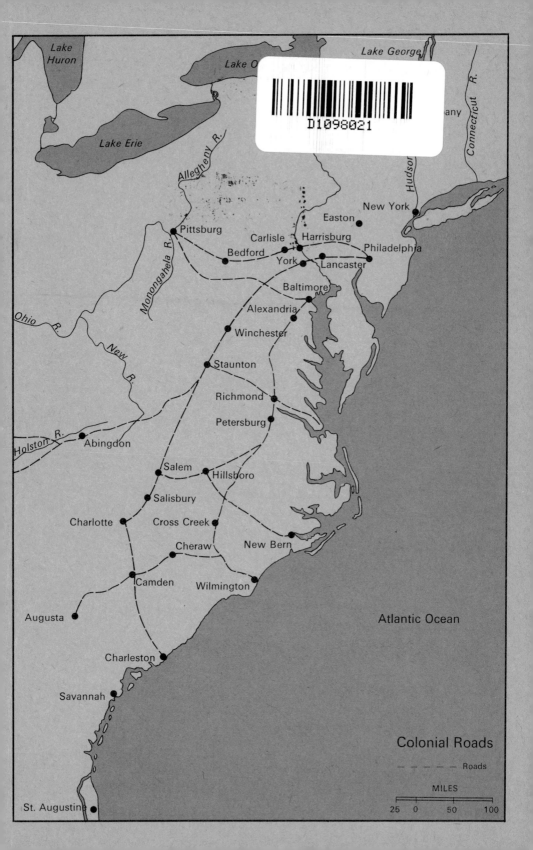

Lake Huron

Lake Erie

Lake O[ntario]

Lake George

Allegheny R.

Connecticut R.

Hudson [R.]

[Alb]any

D1098021

New York

Easton

Pittsburg

Monongahela R.

Carlisle

Harrisburg

Bedford

York

Lancaster

Philadelphia

Baltimore

Ohio R.

New R.

Alexandria

Winchester

Staunton

Richmond

Petersburg

Holston R.

Abingdon

Salem

Hillsboro

Salisbury

Charlotte

Cross Creek

Cheraw

New Bern

Camden

Wilmington

Augusta

Atlantic Ocean

Charleston

Savannah

Colonial Roads

– – – – – Roads

MILES

St. Augustine

25   0   50   100

THE REVOLUTIONARY FRONTIER

HISTORIES OF THE AMERICAN FRONTIER

Edited by

RAY ALLEN BILLINGTON

Each volume in *Histories of the American Frontier* offers a lively but authentic account of one period in the occupation of the North American continent. Prepared by recognized authorities, they are designed to be read separately, for each tells the complete story of one phase of westward expansion. Together they will form the first integrated, multivolume history of the American frontier.

America's Frontier Heritage

The Spanish Borderlands, 1492–1846

The French-Canadian Borderlands, 1604–1763

The Southern Colonial Frontier, 1607–1763

The Northern Colonial Frontier, 1607–1763

The Revolutionary Frontier, 1763–1783

The Trans-Appalachian Frontier, 1783–1815

The Frontier of the Old Northwest, 1815–1860

The Frontier of the Old Southwest, 1815–1860

Traders of the Far Western Frontier, 1803–1840

The Overland Migrations, 1840–1860

Mining Frontiers of the Far West, 1848–1880

The Frontier of the Far Southwest, 1850–1890

The Expulsion of the Red Men, 1865–1890

The Transportation Frontier: Trans-Mississippi West, 1865–1890

The Frontier of the Cattlemen, 1865–1890

The Farmers' Frontier, 1865–1900

The Closing of the Frontier, 1890–1960

THE REVOLUTIONARY FRONTIER

1763-1783

△

JACK M. SOSIN
University of Nebraska

HOLT, RINEHART AND WINSTON

New York • Chicago • San Francisco • Toronto • London

To Kim

FOREWORD

HISTORIANS writing of epoch-making periods of the past are inclined to focus on the events that captured the public imagination at the time and leave in the shadowy background the less spectacular social changes that have an even greater long-range effect on society. Such has been the fate of the period of the American Revolution. Every schoolboy today can recite the names of the heroes whose sacrifices won independence for the colonists, from James Otis to John Jay and Benjamin Franklin. Every literate citizen can recall the chronology of events that led the thirteen colonies to rebellion—the Stamp Act, the Townshend duties, the Tea Act, the Intolerable Acts—and most boast some knowledge of the military and diplomatic achievements of the Patriots as they struggled toward victory. These were men and happenings of heroic stature, and students of the era have understandably fastened upon them to the neglect of others less glamorous or less immediately important.

Yet the years between 1763 and 1783—between the Treaty of Paris that closed the French and Indian War and the Treaty of Paris that ended the American struggle for independence—had a significance not entirely related to the Revolutionary War. During those two decades pioneers first breached the Appalachian mountain barrier to plant Anglo-American civilization in the interior valley of the continent.

This was an event of major importance. The frontier was already nearly a century and a half old when backwoodsmen began raising their cabins at Boonesborough, Harrodsburg, and Boiling Springs Station in the Kentucky Bluegrass, but expansion in this period differed markedly for that preceding it. In early colonial times the horizons of the westward-moving settlers had been bounded by the mountain chain that rimmed the coastal lowlands. Thus restrained, the pioneers had advanced slowly, and in relatively orderly fashion, building their settlements near older communities and keeping in touch with the civilization in which they had been reared. But the Daniel Boones and James Robertsons and Evan Shelbys of the newer generation felt no such psychological restraints. As they crossed the mountain barrier, they saw that a limitless new world awaited their conquest. This exciting realization inspired an urge for pioneering that was to affect generations to come. Westward expansion was to become a way of life for a sizable segment of the nation's people from that time on.

The Revolutionary generation was the first to face the problems stemming from uncontrolled migration. How could lands be surveyed and distributed in an orderly fashion? What kind of legal restraints could be imposed on the frontiersmen? What governmental institutions should be established? How were churches and educational institutions to keep pace with the expanding population in the back country? These were irksome questions, simply because they had not been asked before. When Great Britain controlled the interior in the years following the Peace of Paris in 1763, she tried to solve some of these problems but largely failed; the resulting discontent along the frontiers contributed to the unrest that found expression in revolution. The new government born of that revolution sought answers after 1776, with little more success. The period, in other words, was one of trial and experimentation, as an emerging nation began to establish the conditions that would allow the peopling of the United States.

This book fills a real need in providing an account and interpretation of the many complexities of western expansion during this period. The author, Jack M. Sosin, established himself as a perceptive and original student of the Revolutionary frontier with his study, *Whitehall and the Wilderness: The Middle West in British Colonial Policy, 1760–1775* (1961), a book that forced scholars to revise many of their previous notions of the chain of events leading to rebellion. That work, and his subsequent writings, established him as a historian's historian, one dedicated to the truth and willing to seek it out whatever the effect on past reputations.

The present volume illustrates both the depth of Professor Sosin's learning and the freshness of his vision. It is built on an impressive body of evidence, taken from the extensive printed sources and secondary literature of the period, but it rests as well on research in archival depositories in the United States, Great Britain, and Canada. Some of the most original information has been found in local histories seldom used by historians; a glance at the footnotes will reveal the dependence on antiquarian investigations too often ignored by scholars. The work provides a wealth of illustrative material to substantiate the views presented and suggests new insights that revise our understanding of the period.

The author's grass-roots studies reveal the extent to which cooperative enterprise, rather than individual effort, pushed back the frontier during the Revolutionary era. His account examines the confusion that prevailed in the back country as men chose sides at the start of the war, thus suggesting that the clear-cut lines between Tories and Patriots postulated by an earlier generation of students must be radically redrawn. The land cessions that founded the public domain and the origins of the national land system are given detailed treatment. The importance of county courts in the government of the West and the reasons why they did not respond to democratizing forces are clarified. A meaningful analysis is presented of the frontier social order, stressing its complexity, the rapidity with which stratification occurred, the persistence of a gentry class, and the stubborn determination of the elite to transplant unchanged the culture they had known in the East.

This book is a work of sound scholarship, carefully wrought, and clearly presented. The reader will be richly rewarded with new information, fresh insights, and the shattering of outworn viewpoints.

This volume is one of eighteen in the Holt, Rinehart and Winston *Histories of the American Frontier.* Like other books in this series, it tells a complete story; it may also be read as part of the broader history of westward expansion told in connected form in these volumes. Each is written by a leading authority who brings to his task an intimate knowledge of the period that he covers and a demonstrated skill in narration and interpretation. Each will provide the general reader with a sound but readable account of one phase of the nation's frontier past, and the specialized student with a documented narrative that is integrated into the general story of the nation's growth. It is the hope of the authors and editor that this full history of the most American phase of the American past will help the people of the United States to understand themselves and thus be better equipped to face the global problems of the twentieth-century world.

Ray Allen Billington

The Huntington Library
August 1966

PREFACE

It was the trans-Appalachian region Frederick Jackson Turner had in mind when he posed his famous frontier thesis: the peculiarity of American culture stemmed in part from the necessity to repeatedly adapt to a continually advancing frontier. However loosely and imprecisely he defined it, for Turner the frontier promoted the formation of a composite American nationality; it furthered democracy and at the same time it produced both individualism and an inquisitive, coarse character. In a less famous work, Turner pointed to the existence of a previous, less emphasized frontier region, the Old West. Settled in the years between 1676 and 1763 this region included the back country of New England, the Mohawk Valley, the great valley of Pennsylvania, the Shenandoah Valley, and the upcountry of the South between the mountains and the fall line of the rivers flowing into the Atlantic. In the Old West he saw the beginnings of what later characterized the transmontane West: democratic, self-sufficient agricultural communities, more primitive and individualistic than the seaboard societies and differing from them in language, religion, economic life, social structure, and ideals. Isolated from the coast, the Old West began the movement of internal trade that later developed home markets and diminished American dependence on Europe for industrial goods. Moreover, the interior was in sharp conflict with the coastal region on many issues: debts, taxation, defective local government, legislative apportionment, and internal improvements. Turner found that along the entire frontier, from New England to Georgia, the "familiar struggle of West against East, of democratic against privileged classes," existed. As a result of this conflict the settlers of the Old West played an important role during the Revolutionary era in providing for the separation of church and state, promoting religious liberty, democratizing and reforming state constitutions, fostering monetary legislation for the relief of debtors, limiting slavery, providing precedents for liberal land legislation, and in contributing the social conditions and democratic ideals for the later trans-Allegheny frontier.[1]

Turner's distinction between the Old West and the trans-Allegheny West presents certain problems for a study of the frontier during the Revolutionary period inasmuch as he considered the settlement of the Old West to be fairly complete by 1763, but felt that the transmontane region was only in the initial stage of settlement during the decade 1773 to 1783. Actually, much of the Old West—the Holston region and the back country of Pennsylvania, as well as New York and the southern Piedmont—was still being settled between 1763 and 1783. In these years the Old West could be considered an inner, or secondary, frontier while the region beyond the mountains could be thought of as an outer, or primary, frontier.[2]

Turner himself considered the frontier from various viewpoints. He took into account population density and the mental attitudes of the settlers and saw the frontier as a line between civilization and barbarism. In this book the frontier will be studied as a region recently settled, indeed still in the process of settlement, where social and political forms have not as yet crystallized. This is not a study of frontier expansion alone, but of the process of settlement and of the embryonic economic, social, political, and cultural forms evident in the newer regions of the Old West and in the trans-Allegheny settlements during the Revolutionary era. Turner's thesis on the significance of the transmontane frontier and his analysis of the contribution of the Old West are two themes for investigation. But we might also study the extent to which established institutions were continued as the frontier was advanced. The more complex a culture, the less susceptible it may be to modification by the wilderness, and the more likely it is to transform the primitive environment. Finally, we might ask to what extent, if any, did the availability of land modify a society in which land was the prime requisite for social and political status?

Jack M. Sosin

Lincoln, Nebraska
June 1966

---

[1] Frederick Jackson Turner, *The Frontier in American History* (New York, 1925), pp. 1–4, 22–37; and Frederick Jackson Turner, "The Old West," Wisconsin State Historical Society, *Proceedings*, LVI (1908), pp. 185–186, 194–195, 218–233.
[2] These concepts are used by Miles S. Malone in his work, "The Distribution of Population on the Virginia Frontier in 1775" (Ph.D. dissertation, Princeton University, 1935), pp. 1–2.

CONTENTS

LIST OF MAPS

◁ **1** ▷

Background and Setting

The early history of America is the story of the peopling of a continent: a few score pioneers at Jamestown in 1607, a few thousand a generation later, over 200,000 by 1689, and a million 75 years later. As the settlers increased in number, they moved, inexorably it seemed, from the Atlantic coast up the valleys of the rivers flowing from the mountain barriers in the west. Restricted at first to a precarious hold in the coastal basins and the Tidewater region, they firmly established themselves and then in the course of a century surged inland, checked only by the intermittent wars with the French, the Spanish, and the Indian tribes who resisted their advance, particularly after 1689. By the middle of the eighteenth century they were ready to cross the mountains and occupy the Ohio Valley. In an effort to retain the great North American interior and to restrict the English to the narrow coastal shelf, the French seized control of the Forks of the Ohio, touching off the last of the great intercolonial wars, known traditionally as the French and Indian War, or the Seven Years' War, and more recently as the Great War for the Empire. After years of bloody conflict the British

1

emerged victorious, and by the Peace of Paris in 1763 they eliminated the French. The Union Jack now flew over all of North America east of the Mississippi River. West of the Great Father of Waters, Spain ruled uncontested.

Once more the British colonists could resume the march into the hinterland. But how were they to placate the Indians whose resentment against white expansion often led many to side with the French, bringing death and destruction to the frontier? How was land to be distributed equitably so as to pacify both the settlers and the natives? How could the pioneers hope to cope with the warriors and conquer the mountain barriers now before them?

Conquest of the mountain barrier was the pioneers' immediate problem. The western Piedmont and the Appalachian Highland, a region of rugged mountains, plateaus, and valleys, extends in a great arc from northern New England to central Georgia and Alabama. By the end of the French and Indian War in 1763 settlement had not yet reached all of the southern Piedmont, a rolling land rising from several hundred to 2000 feet and extending from some 50 to 200 miles in the south. Great portions of this fertile upcountry in Georgia and the Carolinas were still unoccupied. Beyond the Piedmont is the formidable barrier of the Appalachian Highlands. The Older Appalachian chain runs from Pennsylvania south to Georgia and Alabama; its eastern portion is rolling upland; its western half is higher and more mountainous, extending from southern Pennsylvania to Virginia at a height of 2000 feet. South and west of Roanoke the mountain barrier broadens to a width of seventy miles in the Great Smoky and Unakas mountains of North Carolina. More formidable are the Newer, or Folded, Appalachians, stretching from the St. Lawrence south through Lake Champlain and the Hudson River Valley, diagonally across Pennsylvania, Maryland, Virginia, eastern Tennessee, and into Georgia and Alabama. The eastern portion is essentially a great corridor or longitudinal depression. For over a thousand miles the Appalachian Valley fringes the base of the old Appalachian Highland from the foot of the Green Mountains of central Vermont to Tennessee where a wide natural gap allows passage through the Cumberland plateau of the southern Appalachians.

The Appalachian plateaus, commonly called the Allegheny or the Cumberland Mountains in the south, were the most formidable natural barriers to westward expansion. From the Catskills and Allegheny escarpment of western New York to the mountains of western Pennsylvania and eastern Kentucky and Tennessee, the horizontal structure of the Newer Appalachians is almost unbroken. Consequently, in an age of primitive transportation, the topographical features of the terrain forced settlers to follow the rivers that dissected and penetrated the mountain barriers. In the north is the 300-mile-long Hudson River and its tributary, the Mohawk, whose southern tributaries, the Schoharie River and Cobleskill Creek, along with the nearby Charlotte River, originate near the headwaters of the Susquehanna River flowing southwest into Pennsylvania. The Susquehanna and its tributaries provided two routes west from Philadelphia: one by the west branch, the other by the southern tributary, the Juniata. Further south, travelers using the Monongahela and its larger branches, the Youghiogheny, Cheat Valley Fork, Buckhannon, and the West Fork, could reach the upper Ohio. Or by ascending the James, Potomac, or Roanoke rivers in Virginia, they could reach the Great Valley of the Appalachians extending south from the Potomac for 300 miles. Flowing north and west, the Kanawha, formed by the Greenbrier and New rivers, cuts through the Allegheny front and joins the Ohio, while the Holston, Clinch, and Powell rivers run southwest to the Tennessee. In western North Carolina and the valley of East Tennessee a series of streams flow from the Blue Ridge across a high plateau, through the Great Smoky Range to the Appalachian Valley. These rivers all contribute their waters directly or indirectly to the Tennessee which, with the Cumberland, is the major lateral tributary of the Ohio from the south. In the South Carolina Piedmont flow the Catawba, Broad, and Saluda rivers. The sources of the Savannah are also in this region. Since transportation facilities were technologically limited, these river systems directed the pattern of expansion.

The land watered by these streams—the areas of major settlement—varied in nature. The western portions of the southern Piedmont consisted of rolling hills with fertile soil composed of limestone or stiff clays and covered with a variety of vegetation. Enjoying a superior climate and being well suited for settlement, this area attracted thousands of pioneers who poured into the back country of the Carolinas and Georgia during the 1760s. No other region in the vast complex of hills, valleys, and mountains, except the Kentucky Basin and Mohawk Valley, offered so much rich land. At the opposite end of the scale was Vermont, where great numbers of immigrants found granite mountains and sandstone hills, and relatively little land suitable for cultivation. Except for the Champlain Valley, a narrow strip along the Connecticut River, and a few other valleys, Vermont was a poor agricultural region. Despite the initial optimism of the first settlers, primitive cultivation was possible only as long as the stratum of vegetable mold was not washed away or exhausted following the clearing of the land.[1] In the regions to the south and west, the Mohawk and Susquehanna valleys received many pioneers, but much of the land lining the Susquehanna was too steep and hilly for cultivation. Farther south the Great Valley of the Appalachians, about thirty miles wide and running for hundreds of miles to the southwest, provided room for settlement and access to the Kentucky Basin through the Cumberland Gap. Lined by mountains and dissected by ridges, this valley was filled with rich soil that had washed down from the limestone heights.

By the middle of the eighteenth century the British Atlantic frontier had advanced in some regions to the mountain barriers; in other areas—the Carolinas 'and Georgia where the Piedmont was widest—it had not yet reached the mountains. In New England the last of the western Connecticut and Massachusetts townships were being filled, but on the upper Connecticut River no effective settlements were possible in the face of the French and the Indians. They had also blocked expansion around Lake George and Lake Champlain; the New York frontier extended only slightly north of Albany and in a thin line along the upper Mohawk Valley. In Pennsylvania settlers had fanned out into the Sherman and Juniata valleys, settling north on the east side of the Susquehanna River beyond John Harris' Ferry, and had penetrated down the Cumberland Valley and across the Potomac. In the early 1750s a few adventurous pioneers erected their simple cabins in southwestern Pennsylvania on the Youghiogheny River and Redstone Creek. By 1755, settlements were to be found all along the south branch of the Potomac, on the upper valley of the Tygart and Cheat rivers, as well as on the New and Holston rivers to the southwest.

Pioneers penetrated to these remote outposts partly because both the provincial and royal governments had encouraged them to settle on the western waters to create a buffer against the French. But the stratagem failed. The pioneers, too weak to resist attack during the early years of the French and Indian War, abandoned their homes and fled east. The Virginia and Pennsylvania frontiers were thrown back nearly a hundred miles. Not until 1758, when General John Forbes conquered Fort Duquesne (Fort Pitt), situated where the Allegheny and Monongahela join to form the Ohio, did the frontiersmen resume the move west, and it was not until 1768 that settlers again attempted to occupy the Holston River region.

During the war the migration of northern frontiersmen was deflected to the relatively peaceful region of the western Piedmont of the Carolinas. Although settlers had established themselves along the Hico, Eno, and Haw rivers as early as the 1740s, they did not arrive in significant numbers along the Yadkin and Catawba until the following decade. In the 1750s Anson, Rowan, and Orange were the frontier counties of North Carolina. Many of the south-bound settlers from Pennsylvania, Maryland, and Virginia continued into the back country of South Carolina to the Savannah River settling on Long Cane Creek, the Saluda and Broad rivers, and between the Tyger and Enoree.[2] At this time the Creek and Cherokee Indian confederations temporarily blocked further settlement.

The presence of powerful Indian tribes who resented the expansion of the whites as a threat to their way of life had for generations before 1763 checked or diverted the flow of migration. North of the Potomac and the Ohio rivers resided some 12,000 warriors. By the middle of the eighteenth century, New England was generally devoid of hostile Indians, but to the north were the Seven Nations of Canada and to the west in New York the remnants of the once dominant Iroquois. More than a century of conflict with rival tribes and the French had reduced the Iroquois to about 2000 braves who were divided among six tribes or "nations": the Mohawk, Oneida, Tuscarora, Onondaga, Cayuga, and 1050 Seneca. Residing on the upper Ohio was an offshoot band, the Mingo, who had joined the Delawares and Shawnee from the Susquehanna and Delaware valleys. The Delawares with 500 braves lived on the Muskingum, and the Shawnee, who had been reduced to 300 warriors, on the Scioto. To the northwest along the Sandusky River were several hundred Huron or Wyandot warriors. These tribesmen were directly in the path of the northern frontiersmen. Further removed were the Twelve Nations, or Wabash and Illinois confederacies, and around the Great Lakes resided thousands of Chippewa, Ottawa, and Huron.

The 14,000 warriors of the southern tribes were an even more formidable obstacle for the settlers. There were four main groups. The Cherokee in the valleys and mountains of Tennessee and northern Alabama counted 2800 warriors. Creek braves numbering 3600 occupied the territory from the Alabama River to the Ogeechee River as well as the Florida Peninsula. To the west of the Big Tombigbee resided some 5000 Choctaw and beyond them along the Yazoo, 500 warlike Chickasaw.

Directly in the path of the expansion of the southern frontier were the Cherokee. They had sided with the British during the early years of the French and Indian War, but had become embittered by the frauds perpetrated by English traders and incensed by encroachments by white settlers from Long Cane Creek, Little River, and the Saluda River. They rose against the British in 1759, and in the ensuing two-year struggle neither the frontiersmen nor the militia of the southern colonies could suppress them. Finally, in 1761, 1300 British troops under Lieutenant Colonel James Grant and 1200 regulars under General Archibald Montgomery invaded the Indian country and left the Cherokee towns in smoldering ruins.[3] Reduced to half their number by war and disease, the Cherokee were unable to resist effectively the westward advance of the British colonists for some years.

The test with the northern tribes came two years later following the capitulation of New France and the British occupation of the interior forts at Niagara, Pitt, Detroit, Michilimackinac, Ouiatanon, St. Joseph, Venango, and Presque Isle. Various factors contributed to the natives' dissatisfaction. The Iroquois and the tribes around the Great Lakes, feared the complete domination of the British, and the Indians who were nearest the frontier were anxious about white encroachments on their lands. A dispute between land-hungry settlers from Connecticut organized as the Susquehanna Company and the Delaware Indians over claims to the Wyoming Valley of Pennsylvania further heightened tensions. In the fall of 1762 Teedyuscung, the Delaware chief, warned off the Yankee interlopers, but an advance guard of settlers audaciously returned to the Susquehanna River the following spring and publicly threatened to kill any Indians who stood in the way. The Delaware chieftain was then mysteriously murdered, possibly at the instigation of the Susquehanna Company. The enraged tribesmen sought revenge. Both the Delawares and more distant tribes were encouraged and supplied by French traders from the Illinois country and Detroit who wanted to eliminate British competitors in the Indian trade. The contemptuous attitude of some British officers toward the natives, often referring to them as "vermin," also antagonized the Indians. At one time the British commander-in-chief advised the commandant in the Illinois country to deal "with riotous Indians as if they had been a Dublin mob. . . ."[4] The immediate cause of the outbreak in the spring of 1763 was the order by General Jeffery Amherst to abandon the French policy of subsidizing the Indians with presents.

Despite initial preparations two years earlier by the Seneca and the Great Lakes tribes for a simultaneous assault on the British posts in the interior, it was not until May 1763 that some Ottawa rose against the British garrison at Detroit and touched off Pontiac's Uprising. By surprise tactics the Indians quickly overwhelmed the small forces of between fifteen and thirty men who were garrisoning the posts around the Great Lakes. News of the successful uprising encouraged the tribes to the east. Late in May the Delawares and Mingo swept up the Monongahela, fell on the small settlements, destroyed three small posts on the communications route to Lake Erie, and invested Fort Pitt. The warriors continued to raid the settlements as far east as Fort Ligonier and Bedford in Pennsylvania. The Shawnee penetrated deep into Virginia to attack cabins at Big Levels, Muddy Creek, and Carrs Creek. Hundreds of panic-striken frontier settlers either hurriedly fled or

Pennsylvania rifles, commonly called Kentucky long rifles. (Photo by the Pennsylvania Historical and Museum Commission, Harrisburg, Pennsylvania)

sought shelter in the British posts and blockhouses. More than 2000 were killed.[5]

In the face of the concerted Indian onslaught the traditional frontier weapons and tactics of defense were of limited effectiveness. Attempts by the white settlers to retaliate were of little avail against a ruthless, mobile, and elusive enemy. The famous Kentucky or Pennsylvania long rifle was an effective hunting piece and a deadly weapon in the hands of an expert with time to aim and fire, but it had serious limitations compared to the less accurate but more rapid-firing musket. Since the slender rifles did not have standardized barrels and could not mount a bayonet, they could not be used as shock weapons. Rifle fire alone could not stop a determined assault unless the frontiersmen enjoyed overwhelming superiority in numbers or were all crack marksmen. The sharpshooting frontiersman has been portrayed in romantic folklore and often in history as the conqueror of the Indian, but in reality, although the professional hunters were proficient with the rifle, as a whole the settlers were not.[6]

The frontiersmen had not yet developed adequate tactics to defend themselves against the warriors. There was no effective defense, short

The Battle of Bushy Run, 1763. (Drawing by C. W. Jefferys, from the Imperial Oil Collection, Imperial Oil Limited, Toronto, Ontario)

of a constant twenty-four-hour watch, against raids, and every cabin was vulnerable. Moreover, log forts and blockhouses could not shelter all the settlers. The raiding Indians simply slipped around the forts, evaded patrolling rangers, and devastated the territory beyond. Successful war against the Indians required an offensive by men trained to act in co-ordinated units. Attempts by frontiersmen to fight Indian fashion, as individuals or in loosely organized bodies, often resulted in indecisive encounters or in disaster for the whites. Perceptive commanders had to learn to employ trained troops, firepower, and mobility and to bring "power to bear that the Indians were never able to match." Such a commander was the hard-bitten, outspoken Colonel Henry Bouquet. With regular troops brought from the seaboard the Swiss-born officer won a decisive battle on August 5, 1763, at Bushy Run near the Forks of the Ohio and relieved Fort Pitt. One of the most skillful professional soldiers to fight in America during the eighteenth century, Bouquet correctly analyzed Indian tactics and successfully counteracted them. He saw that the braves used three principles against an opposing force:

fight scattered; surround but give ground when hard pressed; and return to the attack when the enemy eases pressure.[7]

Despite Bouquet's victory little could be done to drive back the Indians during the remainder of 1763, but the cautious British commander-in-chief, General Thomas Gage, made plans that winter and the following spring to reoccupy the interior forts and restore peace in 1764. Bouquet was to lead one column from Fort Pitt overland into the Ohio country while Colonel John Bradstreet took another assembled at Niagara to Detroit. The British commanders had great difficulty persuading the assemblies of Virginia, Maryland, New York, and Pennsylvania to contribute men to these campaigns, even though they were aware that aggressive action was needed to chastise the warriors, halt their devastating raids on the borders, and re-establish control over the forts in the Indian country. The record of the colonies whose frontier population had suffered most was particularly deplorable as was the failure of the borderers themselves to join the expeditions.

Some Pennsylvania frontiersmen from Paxtang Township were not adverse to attacking peaceful Indians, however. A party of fifty-seven led by Lazarus Stewart cold-bloodedly murdered a peaceful band long settled at Conestoga in Lancaster County. On December 14, 1763, they again attacked the band, killing and scalping eight innocent, defenseless Indians, and in reply to a proclamation from the governor for their arrest, returned and murdered fourteen more. They then organized a march of hundreds of back-country men on Philadelphia where the remaining Indians had found refuge. Among their professed grievances was the failure of the assembly to protect the back country. These frontier worthies proved much less anxious to join the expeditions and to chastise the Indians in their own territory. After "all the noise and bustle" they had made, Bouquet expected them to volunteer, but instead they held out for bounties on Indian scalps and would serve only as packhorse and wagon drivers, employment fit for "cowards." Nor were eastern Pennsylvanians more helpful. The British commander had to haggle for months with the assembly before the parsimonious legislators agreed to raise 1000 men. Bouquet was not pleased with the prospect of marching into the Indian country with vagrants and vagabonds recruited from the streets of Philadelphia.

Neighboring Maryland whose frontiers were also being ravaged did nothing, and the cautious legislature of Virginia restricted its militia to defensive operations along its own borders. Fortunately, numbers of hardy, experienced Virginia and Maryland frontiersmen led by Thomas Rutherford, Adam Stephen, and Thomas Cresap volunteered. The Virginians earned high praise from Bouquet in contrast to the Pennsylvanians. Out of the 900 men raised from the Quaker colony, 200 deserted with arms and horses before the expedition had started. Bradstreet made similar complaints about the Yankee militia assembled in New York for the expedition along Lake Erie.[8]

Even before the motley forces under Bouquet and Bradstreet were under way the Indians were ready for peace. No pitched battle was necessary in 1764, but the gullible Bradstreet foolishly allowed himself to be drawn into negotiations with the tribes on Lake Erie while the Shawnee and Delawares were still raiding the borders. He continued on to Detroit and after conferring with the western tribes early in September, he generously granted them a peace. Bouquet was not so easily misled. With 1500 men he marched overland from Fort Pitt against the hostile villages on the Muskingum, Tuscarawas, and Scioto rivers. Confronted by this show of force, the Ohio tribes renounced their claims to the lands east of the Ohio River, agreed to make restitution for their depredations, restored their white captives, and promised to use their influence with the Wabash and Illinois tribes to get them to accept British occupation.

English officials achieved a general pacification of the northern and western tribes the next year. After preliminary negotiations by George Croghan, deputy Indian agent, Captain Thomas Sterling with a company of the 42d Regiment traveled down the Ohio from Fort Pitt in the fall and took possession of Fort de Chartres in the Illinois country. Since the beginning of the century this region had been thinly settled by the French, a few hundred traders and farmers living at Cahokia, Kaskaskia, and some minor villages. Two months later a detachment of the 34th Regiment under Major Robert Farmar came up the Mississippi from Mobile to complete the tenuous British occupation of the Illinois country. That same year at Oswego, Croghan and Sir William Johnson, superintendent of Indian affairs for the northern district, concluded agreements with the northern and western tribesmen.[9]

By the close of 1765 the British had ended the great uprising but by threats and negotiations rather than by defeating the warriors in pitched battle. Pontiac's war dramatically confirmed the hard lesson learned during the conflict with the French: if peace was to be maintained, the royal government must control frontier policy by providing for defense, regulating the Indian trade, and channeling expansion.

The French and Indian War in North America during which the French and their Indian allies had ravaged the back country and threatened to confine the British colonists to the region east of the mountains vividly demonstrated the inadequacy of control of the frontier by individual colonies. In the last years of the war with the French, British royal officials in North America formulated a program to win over the Indians and secure peace. This policy was incorporated into the royal

Proclamation of October 7, 1763, that temporarily prohibited white settlement beyond the heads of rivers flowing into the Atlantic until a more exact boundary reflecting the claims of both the white settlers and the Indians could be ascertained. Royal officials would then be able to purchase lands from the tribes, and thus eliminate Indian resentment caused by illegal encroachment or purchase by private individuals. The Proclamation also established new governments for the territories in North America acquired under the treaty of 1763. The former French colony of Canada, now known as Quebec, was limited on the west and southwest to the sources of the streams flowing into the Ottawa River. In the South the former French and Spanish possessions were grouped into two new colonies, East and West Florida.[10] British garrisons were stationed in these three new provinces and in the Indian country.

The royal government also laid down general policy for the conduct of the Indian trade and appointed two superintendents to negotiate political questions with the tribesmen. Sir William Johnson, an Irish immigrant to the Mohawk Valley, had charge in the northern district, and John Stuart, a South Carolina veteran of the Great Cherokee War, served as superintendent in the south. Underlying the need to supervise Indian relations was the great dissatisfaction of the Indians over encroachments on their land and the fraudulent trading practices of the English colonists. British traders were notorious for cheating the Indians, and attempts of individual colonial governments to regulate trading had proved ineffective. Many of the provinces made no provisions for curbing irresponsible traders, and such legislation as did exist on the statute books of one colony often conflicted with that of another. Almost all informed authorities in America—Johnson, Stuart, Governor James Wright of Georgia, and Washington—advocated reform and over-all supervision to check the excesses of those who trafficked with the Indians, "the very worst & most abandoned Set of Men," and thus stabilize the frontier.[11]

In 1764 the royal government issued a comprehensive, detailed plan to supercede trade regulations imposed by the colonies, as the chaotic state of the provincial laws was thought to be responsible for the unhappy relations with the tribes. Based on the direct experience of Indian and military officials and governors in North America this plan allowed freedom for all British subjects to trade with the natives, but only at specified locations—the Indian towns in the southern district and the garrisoned posts in the north. Individuals engaging in the trade were required to obtain licenses from the colonial governors, adhere to a set of detailed regulations designed to protect both the whites and Indians, and post bond for their good behavior. Deputies and agents appointed by the superintendents were to act as justices of the peace in the interior. The British Indian Departments also employed commissaries, gunsmiths, and interpreters. By the authority of the Proclamation of 1763 and with the cooperation of Sir William Johnson, General Thomas Gage, the commander-in-chief, put the regulations into effect in the northern district in January 1765. John Stuart instituted a comparable program for controlling trade in the southern district.[12]

A wild and abandoned lot, often as savage as the Indians with whom they trafficked, the "Crackers" or "Cracking Traders" of the southern back country refused to obey British regulations or accept the jurisdiction of the agents of the royal Indian departments. Nor was it possible for any one colony effectively to control traders operating from another. Although the legislatures of Virginia and South Carolina at times passed acts regulating the trade, their statutes did not bind the rival traders and merchants from other colonies. The competing interests of the larger merchants who had controlled or monopolized the trade before it was thrown open to all under the royal plan, the smaller, independent traders, and the host of petty storekeepers along the southern frontier who trafficked in Indian goods also made an effective solution difficult.

Chaos reigned as well in the northern district during the 1760s. The traders confined to Fort Pitt bitterly complained that settlers led by Thomas Cresap who were illegally situated on Redstone Creek and the Cheat River were selling goods below the prices set by the commissaries of the Indian departments. Many traders at the other posts—at Detroit they were called "Liberty Boys" after their counterparts in the east who also resisted royal authority—openly refused to recognize the authority of either the royal Proclamation of 1763 or the royal officials, and despite the hazards involved and without licenses, they traded directly at the Indian villages. Many of the merchants and their agents from Quebec, New York, and Pennsylvania, resenting the requirement that they trade under the surveillance of the military commanders, claimed that the system gave their French rivals of Spanish Louisiana an advantage. French traders were able to cross the Mississippi, bypass the posts, deal with impunity directly with the natives in their villages, and undersell their British competitors. The adroit French had an additional advantage because the prices offered for furs at New Orleans were higher than at the Atlantic ports. Consequently, the British merchants and traders in Canada were particularly opposed to royal regulation.

Faced with widespread opposition and the rising cost of financing the Indian departments, the British government in 1768 returned management of commercial relations with the natives to the colonies. It was hoped that having benefitted from past experience, they would justly regulate trade and prevent the Indians from venting their anger on the frontier settlements. This expectation proved groundless; and for four years the indifferent and parsimonious colonial legislatures did little. Johnson and Stuart who still had charge of political relations with the tribes retained their commissaries and deputies in the interior, but these officials had no control over the merchants and traders. The solution lay in uniform regulations that would be applicable to all traders. In 1770 New York and Virginia attempted to organize an intercolonial congress to promulgate common regulations, but the royal government, fearing that such a congress might develop into a center for organizing a revolutionary challenge to Great Britain, quashed the effort. The apathy of the majority of the other provincial legislatures also doomed the proposed congress.

For some years only the agents of the British Indian Departments and the commandants at the forts attempted to discipline and restrain the traders. At times they were able to mete out punishment, but generally their efforts were fruitless. The undisciplined traders "look upon His Majesty[']s Proclamation to be of no consequence," complained David Taitt, a commissary among the Creeks. With the failure of both over-all royal control and separate provincial regulation, the British government in 1774 finally turned over jurisdiction in the northern district to the government of Quebec, the colony that appeared able to deal adequately with the situation. All British subjects were still free to engage in the Indian trade, but they now had to obtain a license from the governor of Canada.[13]

For the British in the 1760s the question of regulating the Indian trade was closely related to the problem of defending the frontier and garrisoning the posts in the Indian country. The British army was assigned the task of administering and protecting the extensive region extending from the St. Lawrence to the Gulf of Mexico and from the Allegheny Mountains to the Mississippi River.[14] Forts Stanwix, Hunter, Brewerton, and Ontario protected the New York frontier. West along the Pennsylvania frontier beginning with Fort Augusta at the Forks of the Susquehanna stretched another line of fortifications: Ligonier, Loudoun, Bedford, Lyttleton, and Fort Pitt at the Forks of the Ohio. Guarding the Maryland back country was Fort Cumberland on Wills Creek, a tributary of the Potomac. Two posts, both named Loudoun— one at Winchester in the Shenandoah Valley, the other on the Holston River to the southwest—and Fort Chiswell, on a portage between the Holston and the New rivers, protected the Virginia frontier. Fort Prince George on the Keowee and Fort Charlotte on the upper Savannah stood between the South Carolina and Georgia frontiers and the Indian towns.

The British army also garrisoned the French and Spanish posts in Canada, the interior, and the Floridas; Forts Erie, Detroit, LeBoeuf,

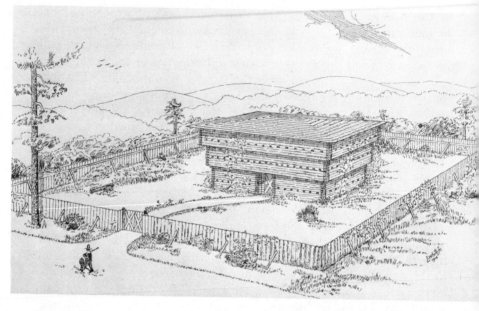

Fort Dobbs, a North Carolina fort of the mid-eighteenth century. (North Carolina State Department of Archives and History, Raleigh)

Venango, Michilimackinac, and de Chartres were in the north, and Fort Natchez (Panmure), Fort Charlotte (Conde), Fort Tombigbee, Fort Toulouse, Apalachie, Pensacola, and St. Augustine were situated on the lower Mississippi and the rivers flowing into the Gulf of Mexico.

These remote, exposed posts were difficult to maintain and expensive to supply. After 1760 the provincial legislatures drastically reduced or eliminated entirely their appropriations for the garrisons. When the British army was forced by economy measures—the colonials having refused to pay stamp duties and other British taxes—to evacuate some fortifications following Pontiac's Uprising, the Pennsylvania assembly in 1765 refused to appropriate money for the maintenance of Forts Loudoun, Cumberland, Ligonier, and Augusta. Despite a series of raids by hostile Cherokee and Creeks the assemblies of Georgia and South Carolina failed to provide adequately for the independent ranger companies or the royal garrisons on the southern frontier and the posts on the upper Savannah and its headwaters. The need to control the revolutionary centers in the East and to reduce expenses in the military and Indian departments led General Thomas Gage to withdraw troops from some posts and decrease the strength of others. Forts Edward (on Lake Champlain), Bute, Panmure, Prince George, Charlotte, and Augusta were evacuated between 1768 and 1770, and Fort de Chartres in the Illinois country and its supply base, Fort Pitt, were vacated in 1772. Both Governor James Wright of Georgia and the settlers on the Pennsylvania frontier protested these moves, but in view of the refusal of the provincial legislatures to vote men and money, Gage felt he had no alternative. The Pennsylvania frontiersmen petitioned in vain for the Quaker assembly to station a provincial garrison at the Forks of the Ohio. By the outbreak of the American Revolution, British forces were left only at Niagara, Detroit, and Michilimackinac, and a mere company of fifty men remained at Kaskaskia in the Illinois country until 1776. The British attempt to control the interior and the frontier by military force was ended.

During the decade or more that British military forces were occupying the frontier, they attempted to maintain peace by enforcing a boundary line dividing the white settlements and the Indian lands. Past experience had taught that transgressions on Indian lands, more than any other factor, led the natives to attack the settlements. To maintain peace on the borders, British military officials guaranteed the Indians their rights to the soil and temporarily prohibited settlements west of the mountains. The home government confirmed this pledge in response to complaints from the powerful Six Nations and emphatically instructed the colonial governors not to allow settlement on lands claimed by the Indians. This prohibition caused much concern, particularly among Virginians who had settled west of the mountains along the Monongahela, Greenbrier, and New rivers but had been forced by the French and the Indian raids to evacuate. Moreover, land speculating companies in the Old Dominion, as Virginia was known, had prewar claims in the west. Nonetheless, the royal government upheld the commitment made to the tribes by the military, arguing that regardless of the propriety of the previous policy of encouraging western expansion or the validity of claims by settlers and land companies, settlement west of the mountains would only provoke Indian hostilities on the frontier. The Proclamation of October 7, 1763, formally established this ban although under its provisions discharged officers and soldiers were to be granted bounty lands in the territory already cleared of Indian title east of the mountains. The Proclamation prohibited purchase of Indian lands by private individuals; only the Indian superintendents were to deal with the natives for land purchases. An optimistic spokesman for the royal government thought that nothing could more effectively pacify the Indians and bring peace to the frontier than "restraining all unjust Settlement, and fraudulent Purchase of Their Lands."[15]

Since the temporary boundary line set by the Proclamation of 1763 did not accurately reflect either the claims of the Indians or the furthest extent of white settlement and did not allow for future expansion, John

Stuart and Sir William Johnson, on behalf of the colonies and the royal government, had to negotiate a more accurate and definitive boundary. In the years following the issuance of the Proclamation both superintendents, cooperating closely with the provincial governors, negotiated with the Indians for land cessions. In November 1763 Stuart, Governor Wright, Thomas Boone of South Carolina, Arthur Dobbs of North Carolina, and Francis Fauquier of Virginia met with delegates of the Cherokee and Creeks at Augusta to settle tentative boundaries for the southern provinces. Both tribes were incensed at the illegal intrusion of whites on their lands. In a treaty signed on November 10, however, the Creeks transferred to Georgia a tract of almost 2,500,000 acres lying southwest of the Little River between the Savannah and Ogeechee, but they refused to allow the South Carolinians to settle west of Long Cane Creek. The Cherokee, speaking through Attakullakulla, the Little Carpenter, agreed to recognize the Virginia settlements as far west as the Kanawha River and as far south as the Holston. This preliminary agreement at Augusta became the basis for later, definitive negotiations with the tribes of the southern district. Two years later, Stuart, Governor James Grant of East Florida, and Governor George Johnston of West Florida concluded an agreement at Mobile with the Creeks, Choctaw, and Chickasaw.[16]

Later negotiations for definitive boundaries with the Creeks and Cherokee were begun by Stuart in cooperation with governors Wright of Georgia, Bull of South Carolina, and William Tryon of North Carolina and proceeded fairly smoothly in 1766–1767. The difficulty lay in extending the line demarcating the Virginia frontiers. The Cherokee wanted the boundary to extend in a straight line from Tryon's Mountain to Chiswell's Mine on a lower branch of the Kanawha River and then to proceed directly to the confluence of the Kanawha and the Ohio. But such a boundary would run contrary to the interests of the Virginians. Indeed, some pioneers from the Old Dominion had already claimed lands west of the New River on the basis of grants made before the French and Indian War. Some alteration of the proposed boundary might have been made for these settlers—indeed, Stuart offered to obtain a cession of land as far west as the Kentucky River—except that Lieutenant Governor Fauquier, representing the interests of land speculators, for years refused even to inform the superintendent of Virginia's position concerning the boundary. It would be to the advantage of ambitious speculators, who hoped to exploit western lands, that the boundary proposed by Stuart and the Cherokee not be accepted. On October 17, 1768, Stuart, unable to obtain an answer to his repeated requests about the line from Virginia, concluded with the Indians at Hard Labor Creek, South Carolina, an agreement for the boundary as previously specified.

By the terms of the Treaty of Hard Labor the line between the southern colonies and the Creeks and Cherokee ran from the Savannah River just north of the mouth of Rock Creek to Dewitt's Corner to the Reedy River, Tryon's Mountain, and Chiswell's Mines and then to the confluence of the Kanawha and Ohio rivers where it joined the line currently being negotiated for the northern provinces by Sir William Johnson. The Virginians refused to accept the boundary north of Chiswell's Mines, however, and by concluding an agreement at the Treaty of Fort Stanwix with Johnson and certain land speculators from Pennsylvania, they were able to force a revision of the Hard Labor agreement.

The modification of the Indian boundary line in the northern district resulted from two developments: pressure from speculators, and illegal settlements made by squatters from Virginia, Maryland, and Pennsylvania along Redstone Creek and the Cheat River, tributaries of the Monongahela. These encroachments threatened to bring on a war with the Delawares and Shawnee. Led by Thomas and Michael Cresap, the obstinate squatters defied every effort by the governments of Virginia, Maryland, and Pennsylvania, as well as attempts by the British garrison at Fort Pitt, to evacuate them even after 1768 when Pennsylvania imposed the death penalty for illegal settlements. The only practical solution to appease the natives was to purchase the lands. As early as 1765 Sir William Johnson had agreed with the Six Nations of New York on a boundary running from Owegy on the east branch of the Susquehanna across the mountains to Kittanning on the Allegheny River and then along the Ohio to the mouth of the Kanawha.

Speculators such as George Croghan, who was anxious to receive confirmation for a 200,000-acre tract of land near Fort Pitt that the Six Nations had sold to him before the war, also exerted pressure for a revision of the boundary. A syndicate of Philadelphia merchants and Indian traders led by Samuel Wharton, of the firm of Baynton, Wharton and Morgan, and William Trent bombarded Johnson and the home government with requests for a revision of the line. By this means they hoped to prevail on the superintendent to obtain for them a tract of land, later known as "Indiana," between the southern boundary of Pennsylvania, the Laurel Hill (a ridge of the Alleghenies), the Ohio, and Little Kanawha River as compensation for the alleged losses suffered by Indian traders during Pontiac's Uprising. Other interests were influencing the superintendent. The proprietary government of Pennsylvania, dissatisfied with the preliminary line negotiated in 1765, put pressure on Johnson to obtain a boundary that would include the Forks of the Susquehanna. A group of speculators in New Jersey and some New York magnates were eager to exploit the region between the Mohawk and the headwaters of the Susquehanna and Delaware rivers. To satisfy the speculators—Johnson was one himself—the susceptible superintendent departed from his initial instructions, and at the Treaty of Fort Stanwix in November 1768 he allowed the Iroquois to cede "Indiana" to the "suffering traders" of Pennsylvania. The boundary of the cession by the Six Nations was extended south along the Ohio from the Kanawka to the Tennessee and north from Owegy to Wood Creek on the Mohawk. The southern extension apparently was to serve as compensation to the Virginians who would acquiesce in the title given to the Philadelphia group for the land on the upper Ohio claimed under the Virginia charter.[17]

The cession by the Six Nations of the region between the Kanawha and the Tennessee rivers gave the Virginians a pretext for undoing the negotiation concluded by Stuart with the Cherokee. Moreover, the example set by the "suffering traders" in obtaining a private land grant from the Iroquois spurred such southern speculators as David Ross, Richard Paris, and Jacob Hite to follow suit. Stuart was able to prevent these agents employed by a group of speculators, the "Land Jobbers" of Virginia, from obtaining private land grants from the Cherokee, but he was unable to prevent Governor James Wright and the merchants and traders of Georgia from extorting from one tribe lands claimed by another. For some years Wright had been eager to open all the territory east of the Oconee River. Between 1770 and 1773 he astutely played off the Creeks against the Cherokee under the guise of canceling debts owed by the Indians to the traders. By the Treaty of Augusta, August 3, 1773, Wright obtained over 2,100,000 acres in the "New Purchase" of Georgia. The episode left the Cherokee and Creeks bitter and resentful.

Virginia land speculators aided by Lord Boutetort, their compliable new governor, were even more quick to take advantage of the negotiations at Fort Stanwix. Although the Virginians contended for a boundary extending west to the Mississippi, Stuart won a compromise by the Treaty of Lochaber, October 22, 1770. The southern boundary of Virginia was extended due west to within six miles of Long Island in the Holston River and then in a straight line to the confluence of the Kanawha and Ohio. When marking this line in the spring of 1771, a survey party led by Colonel John Donelson modified the boundary in order to accommodate squatters in the Powell and Clinch valleys. Donelson departed from the specified line and struck cross-country over the Cumberland Mountains to the headwaters of the Louisa (Kentucky) River and by that stream to the Ohio. This line became the official boundary between Virginia and the Cherokee.[18]

Thus was concluded the last major boundary negotiation with the Indians during the British regime. Despite the policy of preserving the peace of the frontier by restricting and channeling expansion, through these negotiations the royal government obtained millions of acres of land on the frontier in the pre-Revolutionary decade. In Georgia alone 6,695,429 acres were acquired. These acquisitions were necessary to meet the pressure of an increasing population within the North American colonies and the continuing tide of immigrants from Europe and the British Isles.

◁ **2** ▷

Pressures for Expansion

D*uring* the decade preceding the American Revolution a variety of motives induced pioneers to move to the frontier: religious friction in some colonies, material aspirations, blandishments of promoters, conflicts between tenant and landlord, and most pervasive of all, the pressure of an increasing population that had to depend on crude agricultural techniques to till a limited area of land. The expanding population resulted not only from a phenomenal birthrate in the colonies but also from the great numbers of immigrants who came to America following the French and Indian War. Whether they settled directly on the frontiers, or in the older regions nearer the coast and competed for land there, the peoples of the Old World contributed to the expansion of the frontier in the New. Germany and Ulster continued to send people, and in addition, Italy, Minorca, Greece, the West Indies, and especially Scotland and England helped populate North America.

Despite the brutal hardships and overcrowded conditions on the immigrant ships crossing the Atlantic where hundreds died of malnutrition and disease, thousands between 1763 and 1775 annually undertook the hazardous passage. Western Europe experienced a sudden increase in population in the second half of the eighteenth century. Moreover, the years 1769–1774 witnessed a series of calamitous crop failures there.[1] Despite the absence of official or reliable information, it is clear that the overwhelming majority of immigrants, not only from Germany, but also from the British Isles—Ireland, England, and Scotland—left their mother country due to adverse economic and social conditions: the high cost of living, increases in land rents, enclosures, and unemployment. Scotland, the native land of many immigrants, experienced a disruption of the clan system and a shift from feudal to capitalist tenure in agriculture. Along with Ireland, it also underwent a ruinous slump in the linen industry. Many, if not most, of the immigrants from the British Isles were either indentured servants or redemptioners. The former, unable to pay their passage, before embarking signed negotiable contracts to work for a period of years in return for passage. Redemptioners, or "free-willers," sailed without a written indenture on the condition that the shipmaster could sell their services to the highest bidder to defray the cost of transporting them if, after their arrival in the colonies, they were unable to find some friend or relative to pay their expenses.

But there was a future in the provinces for these immigrants. Most often the Scots-Irish and German redemptioners came first to Philadelphia and the Delaware River ports and then worked their way to the back country of the colonies to the south since it was on the frontiers in these provinces that most opportunity was to be found. The authorities of Pennsylvania, Virginia, the Carolinas, and Georgia, eager to get lands in the hands of the settlers, encouraged expansion and granted lands on easy terms. Immigrants to Georgia, after an indenture of three years, received land, livestock, utensils, and food from the provincial government. The pioneer then enjoyed ownership of his farm free from taxes for five years. The authorities of South Carolina also subsidized poor immigrants in an effort to build up the back country. Other settlers could benefit from the generous terms offered by landlords in New York who often competed with one another for tenants. Generally, New York received fewer immigrants than the other colonies because of the hold the great magnates had on the land, but it had a larger proportion of the free men among the most recent arrivals in the decade before the Revolution.[2]

Not all of the immigrants were destitute, however, for the emigration from the British Isles, particularly from Scotland, included ambitious and resourceful officers, middling men, and farmers with some property who had pooled their resources and sent agents to America to purchase land in the back settlements for the entire group. When these settlers arrived in America together, they had tracts waiting for them. They came particularly to Vermont, New York, and North Carolina. Emigration from the British Isles was often organized by persuasive entrepreneurs such as James Hogg of North Carolina who had land in the colonies to dispose of and agents located in England, Scotland, and Ireland to induce prospective buyers or tenants to migrate. Landed magnates such as Sir William and his son Sir John Johnson of the Mohawk Valley supplied over six hundred Highlanders with food, cattle, and agricultural implements worth more than £2,000 for two years and granted them tracts of land. Canny Scottish farmers formed their own companies to finance and organize their move to America. Perhaps the majority of those who invested in cooperative schemes for migration and settlement were small farmers. The cooperatives offered financial aid to the destitute, organized local forms of government, and sent out agents to obtain townships or tracts for the entire community. One of these communities was founded at Ryegate, Vermont. Often Scottish officers such as Colonel John Reid and Major Philip Skene, who served in America with the British army during the French and Indian War, obtained their discharges in the provinces, received substantial land grants by the terms of the Proclamation of 1763, and founded townships or manors in New York and Vermont. They induced Scottish tenants to migrate and supplied them with seeds, tools, land, and livestock.[3]

More numerous than the Scots who came to the colonies in the pre-Revolutionary decade were the Scots-Irish from Ulster. The decade following the French and Indian War saw a renewal in greater numbers than before the war of emigration from northern Ireland. The Scots-Irish constituted by far the largest immigrant group in the years immediately preceding the Revolution. They came singly or in families and settled for the most part in Pennsylvania and the southern colonies; some became tenants of Sir William Johnson, John Harpur, and other magnates in the Mohawk valley and around Lake George in New York.

England provided a significant number of new settlers in the pre-Revolutionary decade. A few went to the Floridas, the West Indies, and New England; more settled in New York, Georgia, Nova Scotia, and the Carolinas, and the largest proportion went initially to Maryland and then perhaps moved on to Virginia and Pennsylvania. Many were farming families from Yorkshire and Lincolnshire who migrated to the back country as a result of the efforts of such promoters as Lord Adam Gordon, the Duke of Athol, and the Duke of Rutland who organized migration to settle lands they had received in America.[4]

These immigrants from Europe contributed directly to the expansion of the American frontier when they settled in the back country and indirectly when they established themselves in the East, thereby further reducing the land available in the coastal region for an expanding colonial population. The pressure of the increasing population coupled with primitive agricultural technology created a constant and increasing demand for new land. Early marriage was the rule; and the birthrate among women of child-bearing age was exceptionally high in colonial America. In many colonies the population doubled every generation. Since climatic conditions during the decade after 1763 were generally good and agricultural prices were consistently high,[5] large-scale migration to new lands offered a practical solution to the problem.

The crude agricultural practices of colonial farmers precluded maximum or intensive use of land in the East and stimulated migration west, north, and southwest in search of new fields. Moreover, some land in the eastern and central portions of many colonies was covered with pine barrens, sand hills, and swamps and was not suitable for cultivation with the limited methods known to colonial farmers. Since the settlers were neither financially nor technologically equipped to improve the land, they simply followed the rivers inland to more suitable ground that could be cultivated with a minimum of time, effort, and expense. Wasteful use of good land also increased the need for new fields and stimulated migration. Although the Germans in Pennsylvania and elsewhere with their superior European farming techniques were less guilty, colonial farmers generally, the English and Scots-Irish in particular, wasted the soil through poor agricultural practices. After having devoted almost their entire resources to acquiring more land than they could actually cultivate, few farmers were able to afford the additional outlay in capital necessary for improved farming. Even those farmers who operated within their means were not efficient. Knowing there was an abundance of land in the interior, they spent little time in making the most of what they had on hand. As the anonymous author of *American Husbandry*, published in 1775, noted: "they depend on this plenty of land as a substitute for all good industry and management. . . ."[6]

Other factors, some related to agriculture and land holding, prompted the movement of peoples to the frontier. Settlers who had originally purchased three or four hundred acres of land could divide their farms and endow their sons with sufficient property to enable them to vote and to achieve some social standing in the community, but the process of subdivision could not be carried on indefinitely. Some members of the third and fourth generations often had to migrate. Disputed land titles in Maine, New York, and western Massachusetts also stimulated movement to newer areas, particularly to the territory west of the upper Connecticut River. After the close of the French and Indian War when the General Court of Massachusetts exerted pressure on squatters and auctioned off lands for delinquent taxes many settlers moved to that region. Pioneers from the Bay colony established new settlements in towns such as Manchester, Danby, Dorset, Panton, and Poultney in the Vermont Grants. They were joined by settlers who left the older New England colonies over religious friction. In Connecticut a bitter controversy raged for years between two Congregational factions, the Old Lights and the New Lights. Some New Lighters left to settle Bennington in Vermont. The initial founders of Arlington seem to have been Anglicans from the Yankee colony. During another controversy in Massachusetts more than a few Baptists went to the region west of the upper Connecticut to escape taxes levied for the support of the Congregational churches. The towns of Shaftsbury, Pownall, Gilford, and Dummerton seem to have contained such religious groups.[7]

In the South an economic transformation in agriculture, one with great social implications, offered a further stimulus for many to migrate west. In the eighteenth century, tenancy increased, particularly among lesser planters who raised small crops of inferior tobacco and could not compete with their larger neighbors. Moreover, by the middle of the century the Chesapeake region had reached its peak economically; by 1765 the Tidewater faced bankruptcy. The newer regions in the Piedmont were prosperous, but within a decade the value of land there and in the valley of Virginia had risen so high that an ordinary tract sold for thirty shillings an acre, and choice lots went for as much as fifty shillings an acre. In South Carolina the extension of rice and indigo production and the general increase in agricultural prices encouraged eastern planters to improve more land. Since each of these staples was better suited to a large, rather than a small, farm economy, the plantation system with slave labor expanded at the expense of the smaller units. For the smaller farmer, only the back country remained.[8]

An equally important element in opening new regions were families of means, such as the Shelbys of Maryland and the Seviers, Callaways, Campbells, Christians, and Lewises of Virginia, who continuously moved west and south to improve their social and economic position.

Another dynamic factor spurring western expansion was land speculation, the practice of acquiring virgin tracts at little or no cost and reselling or leasing them to settlers for a profit. Speculation was endemic. Almost everyone would have agreed with the comment of the shrewd Yankee, Silas Deane: "The best branch of business in America, next to [law] . . . is that of adventuring in lands, and procuring inhabitants to settle them."[9] Speculators were able to obtain substantial amounts of land under the varied and complex systems of granting acreage in the colonies. Up until the middle of the eighteenth century the four New England colonies generally followed a procedure whereby the government granted townships to groups who at various intervals systematically subdivided the soil. In principle, collective responsibility prevailed, although the New England provinces were beginning to sell townships to individuals and to groups as a means of raising money. The other provinces generally transferred the soil by bargain or sale. Two procedures were common: direct sale or outright gift to individuals for immediate occupancy and use in family-sized units; and sale at low rates in excessively large blocks to jobbers and speculators for resale later to actual farmers. All land sold was held in free socage, the freest and easiest of the English tenures, whereby a person paid a small annual quitrent and was relieved of all services. Quitrents, due to the difficulty in collecting them, were not a serious hindrance; actually, the only real limitation to acquiring soil was the financial resources of the individual.[10] But due to the desire of the royal and the various colonial governments to establish a bulwark of settlers in the back country, by the middle of the eighteenth century even those with very limited means could legally obtain tracts. To be sure, there were "squatters"—men who occupied land initially without a legal title—in Pennsylvania, Virginia, Tennessee, and Kentucky. They marked their claims on trees with tomahawks, erected crude shelters, cleared a few acres, and planted corn crops, but those who held "tomahawk" or "corn" claims most often did so where land offices were not available, in regions not legally open for settlement or where jurisdiction was not clear due to conflicting boundary claims of adjoining provinces. Usually the rights of squatters were recognized when governmental authority was established.

The royal and some provincial governments granted acreage to individuals depending on their ability to improve and cultivate the soil. In the most recently founded or less populated colonies, under the family-right system the governors could grant 100 acres to every head of a household and fifty acres for every additional member of the family— adult or child, white or black slave—up to 1000 acres, provided the family appeared to be able to cultivate its holdings. In addition, by the terms of the Proclamation of 1763 officers and men of the British army discharged in America were allowed varying amounts of land depending on their rank. Some provincial officers of Virginia and Pennsylvania also claimed tracts under the royal order. This general British policy in conjunction with local procedures for disposing of the soil remained in force until shortly before the outbreak of the Revolution when gross irregularities, particularly in New York and Virginia, led the home government to rationalize the system. An order-in-council of February 1774 and additional instructions to the royal governors ended the policy of free grants and set up new procedures. In the future, unappropriated tracts were to be surveyed into numbered lots of between 100 and 1000 acres, and after six-months notice, to be sold at public auction at a minimum price of six pence an acre with an annual quitrent of one halfpenny per acre. In some instances royal governors such as Lord Dunmore of Virginia either postponed or neglected to implement the new policy, a plan ironically comparable in most respects to the program later adopted by the Continental Congress in the Land Ordinance of 1785. In any case, the beginning of the Revolution in 1775 put an end to the attempt by Britain to regulate the disposal of land.[11]

During the pre-Revolutionary decade land in various regions could generally be acquired fairly easily by either individuals or groups. By the middle of the century New Hampshire and Massachusetts adopted the practice of selling to groups of people who bought shares in the townships of Maine and Vermont, the major areas of frontier expansion for New England after the French and Indian War. Although New York claimed jurisdiction over Vermont, most of the earlier settlers in the region obtained title to lands through the township charters issued by Governor Benning Wentworth of New Hampshire to his friends and others for a cash consideration. So extensive were his grants that any group of New Englanders with acumen and a little influence could organize as proprietors and obtain a plot six miles square. Since a single individual at times acquired ownership of a town, land jobbery was prevalent. Among the most notorious jobbers were the unscrupulous Allen brothers of Connecticut—Ethan, Heman, Levi, and Ira—who, along with Remember Baker, organized the Onion River Company and claimed 300,000 acres around Lake Champlain. In Vermont, or the New Hampshire Grants, settlers at times "squatted," or "pitched," on land that suited them regardless of the claims of New York and New Hampshire, or the rights of the town proprietors.[12]

In New York a few astute politicians and manipulators of the governor's favors were able to engross huge tracts. These speculators and landlords found it easy to circumvent the royal regulation limiting grants to 1000 acres to an individual by listing "dummy" associates in the patents who would turn over their 1000 acres to the jobber. Rather than sell to settlers, the great proprietors tended to favor a tenant system similar to that of England and advertised their holdings for rent. However, the terms by which tenants held their land differed widely even when title was derived from the same landlord. According to one back-country magnate, Philip Schuyler, the landlords made their money by charging as much as one-fourth of the value of a farm on every transfer of the property from one tenant to another.[13]

The situation in New York was exceptional for it was much less difficult for the individual settler to acquire property in the colonies to the south. In Pennsylvania all unappropriated land was in the hands of the proprietary Penn family who, by a policy of moderate prices and credits, favored the small farmer rather than the wealthy speculator. Since Indian resistance during the second third of the eighteenth century made it impractical to clear territory of native title and legally dispose of it to white settlers, squatting on unoccupied lands in the interior became commonly accepted among the Scots-Irish and German pioneers. To be sure, there were some professional squatters who made it a business of selling their "improvements" to bona fide farmers and then moving on to repeat the process, but these itinerants were relatively few. By the middle of the century the proprietary government recognized the claims of those who intended to remain, and "settlement rights" became the basis of a new type of land title. If a man had cleared his farm and was living on it, the law protected his rights. Although he was expected to pay for his land, the proprietors granted liberal credit. In practice they devised a pre-emption system. After the Treaty of Fort Stanwix in 1768 by which most of the western portion of the province was purchased from the Iroquois, the land office in 1769 put up tracts for sale in the "New Purchase" and gave squatters pre-emption on their farms. A maximum of 300 acres could be bought for £5, which was to be paid in fifteen years without interest.[14]

The land grant policies in the southern colonies were even more liberal for the prospective frontier settler although by 1763 far-sighted speculators in Virginia had already pre-empted the best lands as far west as the valley. The headright system, whereby fifty acres of land were allotted for every individual brought into the colony, was no longer used extensively there; instead, many persons received tracts for prior military service or by purchasing warrants from the provincial treasury. Headrights were still employed in the royal colonies further south. In North Carolina, however, less than half the lands in the province lay directly under the British government. The remainder belonged to members of the aristocratic Granville family in England, descendants of one of the original proprietors. No land office was open in the Granville District after 1766. In the royal portion the headright and family-right system was used.

This was also the case in South Carolina, as well as in Georgia and the Floridas, where royal officials granted families free land, subject only to small fees for surveying and patenting and a small annual quitrent that went into effect some years after the settler had established himself on the property. Certainly few in the southern back country could complain that land was difficult to acquire once it had been located. As a result, in the decade following the end of the Great Cherokee War and the Peace of Paris, thousands of settlers poured into the western Piedmont of the south.

Leading the expansion of the last British frontier were the astute land speculators and their occasional associates, the ubiquitous Indian traders and the picturesque "long hunters," hardy men who spent twelve to eighteen months in the remote wilderness in pursuit of the skins and furs of the forest animals. While the speculators provided the initial motivation for exploration and expansion, the hunters and traders spied out the routes to virgin territory and broke down Indian resistance to the advance of the white frontier; at times, some undertook initial negotiations with the natives for lands coveted by the great magnates who organized and induced the later migration of settlers. Often it was difficult to distinguish between the roles of speculator and hunter or trader. Lachlan McGilvry, John Rea, and George Galphin of Georgia, and George Morgan and George Croghan of Pennsylvania, among others, made the easy transition from trade in Indian goods to traffic in land. Daniel Boone and John Finley while hunting in the wilderness served as agents for speculators who sought to engross much of Kentucky and Tennessee.

In these two regions beyond the southwestern frontier the long hunters made their contribution in the decade, 1760–1770. At the end of the Great Cherokee War in 1761 hunters from the back country of Virginia and North Carolina banded together for sustained hunts and explorations beyond the mountains. Under the hardy backwoods leaders, Elisha Walden and Henry Scraggs of Pittsylvania and Rockcastle counties, Virginia, a score of hunters in 1761, and again in 1763, explored the Powell, Clinch, and Cumberland rivers. Also operating in Tennessee and Kentucky was a party sent out from the Illinois country by young George Morgan of the Philadelphia trading firm of Baynton, Wharton and Morgan. Led by the Philadelphian Joseph Hollingshead, it included men who were later both famous and infamous among the Ohio borderers—the youthful Simon Girty, James Harrod, and Michael Stoner. Of more immediate significance was the interest taken by the speculators of Orange County, North Carolina—Richard Henderson, John Williams, and Thomas Hart—who outfitted the hunting expeditions of Daniel Boone, Henry Skaggs, and John Finley. In 1765 Henderson sent Skaggs to the lower Cumberland and four years later dispatched Boone with four companions under the guidance of Finley for a two-year reconnaissance of Kentucky. Boone sounded out the Cherokee for the lease or sale of western lands. During the next four years other bands of ten, twenty, and forty hunters followed their path. Among them were James Knox and Valentine Harmon. During these travels many of the hunters marked out the paths for future pioneers; they later returned with their own families and became leaders in the earliest Kentucky and Tennessee settlements.[15]

More pervasive than the colorful long hunters whose activities were confined primarily to Kentucky and Tennessee were the Indian traders who undermined the resistance of the natives to white civilization. After more than a century of indirect contact with the white man, the Indian had become almost entirely dependent on his goods: guns, bullets, molds, powder, lead, and flints for hunting and war; ladles, hatchets, knives, and kettles for cooking; awls, cloth, and blankets for clothing; and mirrors, broaches, paint, and beads for decoration. In return the natives offered the white trader the skins of the animals they hunted and trapped. In the north furs, particularly beaver, predominated in the traffic, and in the south the trade was mainly in deer hides.

The Indian trade was a complex, hazardous, and far-flung business based entirely on credit and extending from the great London merchant houses to the Indian villages and towns.[16] At the apex of this trans-Atlantic traffic were such great London firms as Robert Hunter, Watson and Rasleigh, Dyer, and Allen and Company which shipped goods to America and in return received hides and furs that often found their way to distant European capitals. The London firms sent merchandise to their leading counterparts in the major colonial ports—Isaac Todd, James McGill, Benjamin and Joseph Frobisher, and Simon McTavish of Montreal; Rutherford and Livingston and Jacob Lansing of Albany; Simon and Barnard Gratz and Baynton, Wharton and Morgan of Philadelphia. At Charleston, Savannah, St. Augustine, and Pensacola were the prominent firms of Moore and Panton, William Struthers, Robert Crooke, Lachlan McGilvry, and George Galphin. At times it was difficult to distinguish between the merchants in the coastal cities and those whom they supplied in the interior.

From the coastal ports goods were transported into the back country. In the north the major means of transportation was by canoe, batteau, or ship on the rivers and Great Lakes, and in Pennsylvania and the regions to the south, strings of packhorses were used on the overland trails. At the interior posts and towns such as Detroit, Lancaster, Sunbury, or Augusta, the goods were divided into smaller cargoes and consigned to a frontier trader or merchant who entrusted them to his employees, sometimes half-breeds, or indentured servants; they then traveled to the Indian towns or the British posts to bargain for furs and hides which were shipped back to the East and across the Atlantic. The entire system, characterized by a myriad of fluctuating partnerships and fierce competition, was based entirely on credit.[17]

Relatively few men on the frontier made a success of the traffic. George Croghan—a hard worker as well as a hard drinker—who accumulated frontier capital, horses, trading posts, servants, and credit, was an exception. So fierce was the competition, not only among the traders, but also with the settlers on the frontiers—on Redstone Creek and the Cheat River, according to Croghan, "every Farmer is a Sutler"—that most of them were eliminated. The trade did "not suit a man that is dead upon his feet," observed the Detroit merchant, James Sterling.[18] After 1760 the trade along the upper Ohio was characterized by cutthroat competition, and the absence of ethics and sound business practices ruined many traders and merchants. Competition with the Canadians, who were already beginning to organize, made the situation worse in the region south of the Great Lakes where the trade was diminishing. The Canadians enjoyed a distinct advantage over their rivals to the south: they had almost direct access to the interior by the St. Lawrence River and the Great Lakes.

With the British conquest of Canada in 1760 some merchants from the older British provinces transferred their operations north while several new groups entered the trade. From the older English colonies came Alexander Henry of New Jersey, Peter Pond of Connecticut, and Gerrit Roseboom, Abraham Lansing, and Teunis Visscher of New York. They operated from Albany, Montreal, and Quebec in the trade to Detroit and its western dependencies. Jews such as Chapman Abram and Ezekiel Soloman also were involved in the northwest Indian trade. Many officers of the British and provincial forces engaged in the traffic, often forming partnerships with merchants and traders. The Scots, some having held commissions in the British forces, followed in the path of the army and soon began to establish their domination over the trade around the Great Lakes. By 1775 there were thirty Scots, fifteen Scots-Irish, and two English merchants and traders at Detroit; although they were outnumbered by the native French, the greater part of the trade was already in their hands.[19]

After the British army occupied the Floridas in 1763, traders from Georgia and South Carolina extended their activities among the southern tribes. Although most of the traffic in deer hides continued to pass through Sunbury and Augusta, a few merchants of Savannah and Charleston began operations in St. Augustine and Pensacola. By 1765 there were five traders with stores in East Florida. The best-known was William Panton of Charleston and Savannah who had moved to St. Augustine to join in the Indian trade with Thomas Forbes. By the outbreak of the Revolution Roger Kelsall and James Spaulding, who had started business in 1763 at Sunbury, had five trading posts operating in East Florida and Georgia. In the latter colony the leading trader was George Galphin, also a large dealer in land and cattle. Among the early merchants of West Florida were William Struthers and Robert Crooke.[20]

In Pennsylvania, where ties of blood and marriage often united the men engaged in the Indian trade, the Philadelphia firm of Baynton, Wharton and Morgan competed with Simon and Barnard Gratz, recent Jewish immigrants from Silesia. The Quaker house of Baynton and Wharton had been reorganized in 1763 with the aid of new capital contributed by the young George Morgan and the assistance of the London firm of Richard Neave. During the next twenty years the London house was to contribute more than £30,000 to finance its New World activities.

The boldest venture of the Philadelphia firm was an attempt to exploit the Illinois country. Success seemed assured when the partners received the contract for supplying goods to the British Indian Department and provisions for the British military garrison there. Moreover, in return for 5 percent of its proceeds the commandant of the garrison agreed to suppress all unlawful trade, namely, their rivals. With the prospects thus promising, the company in 1766 undertook operations using twenty wagons to haul goods from Philadelphia and 600 pack horses for the journey over the mountains to Fort Pitt where four ships carpenters with the aid of a dozen sawyers and carpenters constructed batteaux suitable for lightering goods down the Ohio to the Mississippi. That summer they sent down sixty-five boatloads of merchandise worth nearly £20,000. Three hundred and fifteen men manned these early forerunners of the later river packets. The oblong, flat-bottomed boats were some forty feet long with a beam of twelve feet and a depth of four and one-half feet. The development of this transportation system and the continuous outlay for goods—£75,000 in two years—drained the company of its cash and brought it into the hands of its creditors. Moreover, the venture in the Illinois country failed due to the decline of the fur trade there, competition from French and Spanish rivals who dealt directly with the natives, and the loss of the contracts for supplying the garrison and Indian department to the rival Gratz brothers.[21]

To recoup their fortunes, Baynton, Wharton and Morgan turned, as so many were doing, to the time-tested method of making money in colonial America, land speculation. The ownership of large estates not only brought wealth but increased social prestige and added weight in provincial affairs, and gave some assurance of an inheritance to one's descendants.

Land speculation was endemic in colonial America; it was practiced by resident and absentee owners alike, by those of great and those of moderate means. The cheap acquisition of tracts for sale rather than for development was rife throughout the colonies from the upper Connecticut to the Gulf of Mexico although it was not too feasible in South Carolina and Georgia during the pre-Revolutionary decade since under the family-right system settlers could obtain plots for almost nothing from provincial and royal governments eager to populate the back country.

With the transfer of vast new territories by the Peace of Paris, speculation after 1763 became almost a mania. Lawyers, manufacturers, merchants, gentry, army officers, and even a college president entertained the wildest schemes for settlements and new colonies as far west as the Mississippi. In April 1763 Lieutenant Thomas Webb of the 48th Regiment organized a harebrained speculative venture and advertised in the *Pennsylvania Gazette* for the sale of land in a proposed colony, New Wales, to be located west of Pennsylvania. General Jeffery Amherst promptly suppressed the plan for fear it would antagonize the Ohio tribes already resentful over white intrusions on their lands. Other officers in the royal and provincial forces such as Philip Schuyler of New York and Phineas Lyman of Connecticut contemplated settlements in upper New York and on the lower Mississippi. Some forty provincial and royal officers under Major Thomas Mant, who had participated in Bradstreet's expedition in 1764, sought to establish an English colony at Detroit. Most of these schemes had little chance of success for their promoters lacked the necessary contacts and resources.

Successful speculation on a large scale required several favorable conditions. Settlers were needed; if they were not available locally, entrepreneurs such as the Johnsons and Coldens of New York and the Washingtons and Masons of Virginia sought to induce immigrants to come to the colonies and to take up their land. Speculators had to acquire large tracts at little or no cost, and to do so influence with the provincial governments was essential. Finally, western connections—surveyors, frontier leaders, and Indian agents—were necessary. Invariably these men were found among the Indian traders and militia officers of the back country, and a close alliance often existed between them and the speculators. The relationship was particularly close in Virginia, Pennsylvania, and New York. In the latter province many of the prominent families worked with Sir William Johnson, superintendent for Indian affairs and a major speculator in the development of the very territory he helped to secure from the natives. The rapid extension of the frontier in New York during the late 1760s was accelerated by the fact that nearly every patent issued to jobbers included thousands of acres of land.[22]

Speculators sought to dispose of their land in a variety of ways. The ubiquitous George Croghan sold his Pittsburgh lands at £10 per 100 acres, and he also tried to emulate Sir William Johnson by establishing an enormous baronial estate of 250,000 acres around Lake Otsego in New York. He engaged Dublin farmers, artisans, and laborers as well as Connecticut settlers and tenants. However, in attempting to build his estate on credit, Croghan was forced to liquidate his holdings to satisfy his creditors. Richard Peters and the Gratz brothers then disposed of his New York lands in smaller lots. The Colden family acquired some Croghan property and other tracts that they sold directly to settlers, 550 acres for every five families.

In the 1760s the New York magnates were repeating the successful practices begun thirty years before by Virginia speculators. By the middle of the eighteenth century speculators in the Old Dominion were not only operating as individuals, but organizing into companies to engross hundreds of thousands, even millions, of acres. The competition for lands on the western waters led to a sectional split in Virginia, not a division between east and west but one between the large planter families on the Tidewater with their filial connections on the central Piedmont, the Robinsons, Randolphs, and Nelsons, and the family groups from the Northern Neck between the Potomac and Rappahannock and the northern Piedmont, the Lees, Corbins, Masons, Mercers, Fitzhughs, and Washingtons.[23]

Two closely related land organizations formed in 1749 were the Loyal Company and the Greenbrier Company. The latter, organized by John Robinson, Thomas Nelson, and the Lewis family, secured a conditional grant for 100,000 acres along the Greenbrier River. More extensive was the grant for 800,000 acres, contingent upon establishing settlers, received between 1749 and 1752 by the Loyal Company, an organization including John Lewis, Doctor Thomas Walker, Peter Jefferson, John Harvie, Thomas Meriwether, and Edmund Pendleton, the latter a protégé of the Robinson family. Lewis represented the interests of the valley. Basically a coterie from Albermarle County, the members of the Loyal Company developed extensive connections with prominent westerners, including such militia officers and surveyors as William Preston, Andrew Lewis, John Donelson, and Daniel Smith.

The chief rival of the Loyal Company for western lands was the Ohio Company, organized in 1747 by Thomas Lee. This company petitioned the following year for 200,000 acres near the Forks of the Ohio, but frustrated by the Randolph-Robinson group, the Ohio associates turned to the royal government in London. In 1752 they received an additional 300,000 acres conditional on settling 200 families. But no specific boundary was fixed; and their claims conflicted with those of the Loyal Company.[24] At the end of the French and Indian War some members of the Ohio Company, the Lees, Washingtons, and a few Marylanders, expanded their activities by forming the Mississippi Company. Its agents in London, initially Thomas Cumming and later Arthur Lee, sought a grant from the royal government for 2,500,000 acres near the confluence of the Ohio and Mississippi rivers. They later shifted their site to a location west of the Allegheny Mountains between the 38th and the 42d degrees north latitude. For over five years George Mercer, Cumming, and Lee were unable to make any headway in London due to the prohibition by the royal government against settlement on western lands until they were cleared of Indian title. As a result of propaganda and the lobbying efforts of Pennsylvania land speculators, however, the British ministry was persuaded to negotiate with the tribes for a westward revision of the boundary lines. This was achieved by the treaties of Fort Stanwix and Hard Labor in 1768.

The leading figures among the Pennsylvania speculators were Samuel Wharton of the Philadelphia trading firm and George Croghan. Operating with Croghan was Colonel Thomas Cresap of western Maryland who had privately purchased lands on the tributaries of the Ohio from the Iroquois. Associated with both Wharton and Croghan were Governor William Franklin of New Jersey and several prominent Pennsylvania politicians. They hoped to secure lands, supposedly as restitution for losses incurred during Pontiac's Uprising of 1763 by Pennsylvania merchants and traders engaged in the Indian traffic. Under the leadership of Samuel Wharton and William Trent, a syndicate was organized to control the shares for the £86,000 presumably lost in 1763 by the "suffering traders."[25]

The speculators made a concerted effort to secure the aid of Sir William Johnson in obtaining a grant of land from the Indians as compensation and to convince the British ministry that some revision in the boundary line was necessary for the security of the frontier. Unless the ministry revised the boundary line, a land grant from the Indians would be worthless. The lobbyists for the land speculators in London were successful, and when Johnson received authorization to negotiate a new line for the northern district, William Trent, Samuel Wharton, and George Croghan laid the preliminary groundwork with the superintendent and the chiefs of the Six Nations who confirmed the grant made to Croghan nineteen years before and gave to the "suffering traders"— actually the Pennsylvania–New Jersey syndicate—an area known as "Indiana." This tract was bounded by the Little Kanawha, the Laurel Hill, the parallel of the southern boundary of Pennsylvania, whose western terminus was still not surveyed, and the Ohio River; it contained some 2863 square miles or approximately 1,800,000 acres. The Treaty of Fort Stanwix negotiated by Johnson made the general cession to the Crown conditional; the Indians would only cede the lands if the royal government accepted the "Indiana" grant. The speculators sought to force the British government to recognize the grants made them if it was to receive the larger cession.

In London, however, the Secretary of State, the Earl of Hillsborough, suspected that the arrangement made at Fort Stanwix was a piece of jobbery. To overcome his objection, Wharton and Trent, who had by then traveled to the British capital, shrewdly brought in various Britons including the prominent banker, Thomas Walpole, and certain politicians, as well as Benjamin Franklin and his friends, as partners in the American land venture, and in 1769 they organized the Walpole Associates. Only Samuel Wharton represented the original American syndicate.

Hillsborough refused the bid made by the associates to purchase "Indiana" for the sum paid by the Crown for the entire cession at Fort Stanwix, £10,000. Instead, he suggested that they apply for an area ten times as large, enough for a separate colony, expecting that the British treasury would raise the purchase price proportionately to a figure the speculators could not afford to pay. By offering shares to various politicians and members of the treasury, however, the Walpole Associates were able to conclude an agreement for only the original price, £10,000.

The boundaries of the proposed colony, later called "Vandalia," followed a line running from a point opposite the mouth of the Scioto River south to the Cumberland Gap, by the Cumberland and Allegheny mountains to the western boundary of Maryland and the southern boundary of Pennsylvania to the Ohio, and down this stream to the mouth of the Scioto. So delineated, the new province threatened to overlap a sizable portion of Pennsylvania, whose western boundary had not yet been surveyed, and to block the Virginians from expanding into Kentucky. Consequently, the proprietors of the Quaker colony and Arthur Lee and George Mercer, agents for the Mississippi and Ohio companies, bitterly contested a patent for the new colony. The opposition of the Penns and Lee proved immaterial, but the Walpole Associates did conclude an agreement with Mercer. Fearing the greater political influence in London of the larger syndicate and having for years received no instructions from the Ohio Company, Mercer merged the interests of his group, as well as those of the Virginia officers claiming lands in the west by military grants, with the Walpole Associates. Thus was formed the Grand Ohio Company. But the Virginia officers and the Ohio Company, apprehensive over the dominance of the larger Anglo-Pennsylvania syndicate, refused to accept Mercer's commitment and continued to oppose the grant for Vandalia.

In London the Walpole Associates pressed the issue with the home government. Wharton sent bogus petitions to his back country cohorts, Cresap and Croghan, to be signed by "frontiersmen" and returned to England to be used by the associates on the Privy Council to undermine the objections raised by Hillsborough. They finally prevailed in August

1772 when the Privy Council overruled the Secretary of State and approved the establishment of a new proprietary colony in the interior. The new province was extended to the Kentucky River to include the territory acquired from the Cherokee when John Donelson ran the boundary line agreed upon by Stuart and the Indians at Lochaber in October 1770. However, three years later the Vandalia proprietors were still frustrated by the obstinate refusal of the Crown law officers to pass the patent. The officers particularly objected to Franklin, now *persona non grata* to the British administration, receiving any "favors" from the Crown. The charter for the new colony had not yet been issued when the onset of the Revolution forced the American speculators to turn to the Continental Congress and their own resources.

Following the return of William Trent to America in the summer of 1775 the original "suffering traders" of Pennsylvania met at Pittsburgh and decided to sell their "Indiana" lands, offering 400 acres for fifty Spanish dollars and guaranteeing title to squatters who had occupied the land before May 1, 1776. They were strongly opposed, however, by both the governments of Pennsylvania and Virginia who claimed jurisdiction over the upper Ohio. In fact, following the evacuation of the British garrison from Fort Pitt, open hostilities had broken out in 1774 between partisans of both colonies.

In addition, Virginia was being challenged by private speculators who sought to purchase and settle large tracts of land both north and south of the Ohio in regions claimed by the Old Dominion under a seventeenth-century charter. Initially, three private land companies were involved: the Illinois Company, the Wabash Company, and the Louisa or Transylvania Company. In 1773 William Murray, a long-time agent for the Franks and Gratz firms in the Illinois country, organized a speculating venture, the Illinois Company, that included his employers and many Pennsylvania merchants and traders. Employing a spurious opinion originally issued in 1757 by the law officers to the Crown on the purchase of lands by the East India Company in India[26] Murray purchased two tracts of land along the Mississippi and Illinois rivers from local Indians. The following year he expanded the company to include Lord Dunmore, the land–jobbing governor of Virginia, and eight speculators from Maryland. In addition, in 1775 Murray helped form another land venture, the Wabash Company, for which he purchased Wea lands along the Wabash River from a Piankashaw chief, Old Tobacco. These two groups merged their interests during the Revolution to form the United Illinois and Wabash Land Company and contested with Virginia for control of the region north of the Ohio.

Of more pressing concern for the Virginians were the activities of another set of speculators. A coterie from back-country Orange

Daniel Boone, painted from life by Chester Harding. (The Filson Club, Louisville, Kentucky)

County in North Carolina, Judge Richard Henderson, William Johnston, John Luttrell, Jr., John Williams, and the brothers Thomas and Nathaniel Hart in 1774 formed the Louisa Company. In January 1775 David Hart, Henley Bullock, and James Hogg, the Scottish-born entrepreneur, also joined. Henderson and his associates issued a call for settlers for a proposed new proprietary colony, Transylvania, and between March 14 and 17 he met with more than one thousand Cherokee Indians at Sycamore Shoals on the Watauga River to purchase a great tract. On the second day of the conference the Indians offered to sell the rights to the soil above the Louisa (Kentucky) River or a tract between the Kentucky and the Kanawha rivers. Since Virginia already claimed this region on the basis of the cession made by the Cherokee at Lochaber in 1770, Henderson refused the offer and threatened to depart with his goods if he did not get all the land between the Kentucky River and the highlands south of the Cumberland together with the "Path" or right of way between the Holston River and the Cumberland Mountains. Employing the technique used by other speculators, Henderson sought to purchase from the Cherokee a region claimed by other tribes. Occonostota later accused him of misleading the prospective settlers. "You, Carolina Dick, have deceived your people. Why are you always telling lies? We told you that those lands were not ours[,] that our claim extended not beyond the Cumberland Mountains, and that all land beyond Cumberland River belongs to our brothers[,] the Chickasaw." The young war chief, Dragging Canoe, also warned him that Kentucky, claimed by the Shawnee, was "bloody ground and would be dark and difficult to settle. . . ."[27]

Despite these warnings, Henderson persisted, and with the lure of trading goods that he claimed were worth £10,000—which he never fully paid—he prevailed on some of the older, infirm chiefs to sell the Kentucky and Cumberland basins. Almost immediately he dispatched Boone and a company of axmen to blaze the Wilderness Path from the Holston settlements through the Cumberland Gap. Early in the spring of 1775 Henderson himself led the first party to settle Boonesborough in Kentucky.

The prediction of Dragging Canoe proved correct, for Henderson encountered strong opposition to his colony not only from the Shawnee but from the government of Virginia, which denied both the legality of his Indian title and his proprietary government. Faced with opposition by the Old Dominion, Henderson, like the members of the Illinois and Wabash companies, contested the jurisdiction of Virginia and appealed directly to the authority of the Continental Congress. The prolonged, heated conflict in Congress among speculators of Virginia and other states was to set the background for the creation of the federal domain and the land policy of the infant republic. Yet by the outbreak of the Revolution, the land speculators had led the advance of the frontier up to, and in some cases beyond, the Appalachian Mountains.

◁ **3** ▷

Expansion in the North,
1763-1775

*A*lthough settlers often moved singly into the hinterland, generally
the expansion of the frontier during the Revolutionary era was accom-
plished through a variety of corporate or cooperative organizations.

The most natural type of joint venture for migration and settlement
was by groups of families, the fundamental social units. Even the Scottish immigrants adopted this technique. David Allen and James Whitelaw, in their search for suitable lands throughout the North American
back country, represented a corporate body of 200 families from the
environs of Glasgow who eventually migrated and settled together in
Vermont. In the winter of 1773–1774 Rufus Putnam and Phyneas Lyman
of Connecticut led more than 400 Yankee families to West Florida.
Nearly every town along the lower Connecticut River contributed families to the enterprise. In migrating to Vermont, the Yankees used the
same technique. William Bradley of New Haven, who had seen service
on the frontier during the French and Indian War, brought his wife
and four sons into the country in 1762; his brother Jesse, his cousin
Elisha, and their relative Jabez and his brother and father-in-law fol-

lowed with their families and settled nearby. Often neighbors from some Connecticut town would decide to move together, they obtained a grant in Vermont, located their lands as a group, and elected their own officials.[1]

Family migrations were also common on the middle and southern frontiers. The Shelbys of Frederick County, Maryland, migrated as a unit to the lower Holston in 1772, as did the Robertson brothers, James, Charles, and Mark, with their families. In eastern Tennessee, William Bean erected a solitary cabin, but the nucleus of the pioneers who soon settled around him was made up of his friends and relatives from Pittsylvania and adjoining Virginia counties. Three generations of adventurous Boones moved as a family unit from Bucks County, Pennsylvania, to the Shenandoah, to the Yadkin country of western North Carolina, and finally to Kentucky, where they helped found Boonesborough. Nearby Harrodsburg was founded by the Harrod brothers and their families from the Monongahela country. Six miles below their settlement on the Salt River was another station established by the five McAfee brothers from Botetourt County, Virginia. Few of the first pioneers in Kentucky were new to this type of family movement, and in many instances they represented the second or third generation of the westward migration. The same pattern was to be found on the upper Ohio, at Redstone Creek, Graves Creek, and Wheeling Creek, where the Zanes and related families from the south branch of the Potomac in Hampshire County, Virginia, established themselves. Their friends, David Shephard, John Wetzel, and the McCulloch brothers, joined them with their families.[2]

At times provincial governments encouraged joint ventures by offering townships with free land, tax exemptions, subsidies, agricultural implements, and supplies. By such means Georgia and South Carolina helped groups of Germans, French Huguenots, and Quakers found such back-country townships as New Bordeaux, New Rochelle, Wrightsborough, Hillsborough, and Queensborough.[3] Townships for the collective settlement of the frontier were also granted in New York. Ryegate, established by Scottish immigrants on the upper Connecticut was one example; Argyle founded in 1764 on the upper Hudson by second-generation Highlanders under the Campbells was another.

Some frontier townships grew out of the efforts of entrepreneurs who attracted settlers and subsidized them, thus helping to build up the back country. After the French and Indian War the proprietors of the Kennebec Company divided their Maine lands into townships and offered tracts to those who would bring in settlers. Many single entrepreneurs acquired land in the back country and induced humbler folk to follow. Captain Jonathan Willard of Colchester, Connecticut, obtained a grant in Vermont for a town, acquired the rights to most of the land, and with the help of hired men, established Pawlet. He then persuaded settlers from Colchester and Canterbury to migrate. Individual entrepreneurs, both civilian and military, were prominent in the recently established Floridas. Nicholas Turnbull and Dennis Rolle acquired tracts large enough for townships and imported hundreds of settlers from southern Europe and the Mediterranean for their manorial communities, Rollestown and New Smyrna.

Many who held back-country tracts they hoped to develop were British officers who had been awarded land under the Proclamation of 1763. An enterprising officer with influence in a provincial council or at Whitehall Palace in London could acquire even more acreage. Operating either singly or in groups, these officers attracted tenants for their estates and communities. Lieutenant Colonel Turlbutt Francis and a group of officers received more than nineteen thousand acres in three tracts in Pennsylvania: on the west branch of the Susquehanna, in Buffalo Valley, and on Bald Eagle Creek. They divided and leased the land for a term of years to tenants. Lieutenant Colonel John Reid established tenants at Otter Creek Falls near present New Haven, Vermont. Many British officers who had served in the North American campaigns against the French were Scottish tackmen, landholders who ranked below the laird or lord but above the humble cottager. Feeling the squeeze as capitalist agriculture replaced the medieval system in the Highlands, they took advantage of the offer of land to establish their own estates and persuade their countrymen to migrate. The activities of these Scottish officers contributed greatly to the expansion of the frontier along the Mohawk and around Lake George and Lake Champlain. Traditionally a colony of large estates, New York was a favorite target of immigrant tackmen officers such as Philip Skene who had served on the New York frontier. By 1760 he had induced thirty families to go to his estate near Lake George and had hired many indentured servants. After the war he brought discharged soldiers from the British army of conquest in Cuba to the New York frontier, and in 1765 he obtained a patent embracing some twenty-nine thousand acres where he established Skenesborough. In addition to opening several roads, he built a sawmill, a general store, a forge, a post office, and houses for his settlers.[4]

Some provincial officers attempted to emulate their English and Scottish colleagues. In 1773–1774 Washington tried to secure English and Irish immigrants to settle on his estates. Employing gangs of contract and convict labor under supervisors, he had his lands cleared and a cabin erected on each tract. He hoped to sell or rent these "improvements," which were located along the Youghiogheny, Monongahela and other tributaries of the upper Ohio. But Washington encountered fierce resistance from such rival speculators as George Croghan and Michael Cresap. The son of a frontier leader of western Maryland, Cresap engaged six or seven young men at the wage of £2-10s a month and began erecting cabins and renting land, often on the very same Ohio bottoms claimed by the Virginian. At times officers with military warrants sold their rights to entrepreneurs who then founded back-country communities. William Gilliland, an Irish-born merchant of New York, in 1765 bought up various military rights and established a 20,000-acre estate between Crown Point and the Bouquet River. In the following years he employed laborers and mechanics to open a road, clear part of the land, build two gristmills and two sawmills, and erect twenty-eight buildings. He then leased part of his estate on terms reasonable enough to attract tenants.[5]

At an early time tenancy was woven into the frontier pattern. It logically followed from a situation in which it was easy for men of wealth and influence to engross large tracts of virgin land, but difficult for the ordinary farmer or rural laborer to secure plots cheaply. Moreover, there were many indigent immigrants without capital for seeds, tools, and livestock. Such was the case in New York and to a lesser degree elsewhere. In order to profit from their holdings, the great landed proprietors including Sir William Johnson disposed of lots and farms to both tenants and installment buyers and often supplied them with credit and other necessities for beginning a new community. However, landlords such as William Smith, Jr., James Duane, the Johnsons, and the Coldens did not always have it their own way; they often had to compete with one another for tenants by offering advantageous terms to prospective buyers and leaseholders. Johnson advertised in the *New York Journal* and even had to recruit tenants in England and Scotland. While developing Johnstown he constructed roads, mills, and other improvements, including a church and a school, and imported a teacher and a physician. In 1773 he obtained several hundred tenants and for two years supplied them with food, shelter, and implements at a cost of £2000 while instructing them in growing maize and other crops unfamiliar to new immigrants. Although Highlanders, next to Germans, were the most numerous of his tenants, Johnson's rent rolls included some English as well as Anglicans from Connecticut. The latter had come to the Mohawk Valley with a minister who had been fined for preaching in the Nutmeg colony with only a license from the Bishop of London, an authority the provincial government did not recognize. By the outbreak of the Revolution some six hundred tenants had settled on Johnson's Mohawk lands. The Johnsons, like Philip Skene and James Duane,[6] were capitalist entrepreneurs in New York. Here as elsewhere they furthered the expansion and population of the back country by providing the economic wherewithal and services for prospective settlers who lacked means to establish themselves on the frontier.

The romantic stereotype of the humble yeoman farmer single-handedly settling the frontier does not do justice to the complexity of the westward movement in the eighteenth century. The speculative entrepreneurs and commercial developers who individually or in companies laid the groundwork for settlements by providing land, credit, and community services also were important.

Geography, climate, and cultural ties influenced the pattern of settlement. People moving from Europe to America or from one section of the colonies to another sought whenever possible to settle on land resembling the soil they had left and with which they were familiar. This was particularly true of the Germans and Irish. The preferences of both national groups resulted in a pattern of settlement in which the Irish and the Germans established separate, distinct communities. They rarely mixed to form a frontier melting pot. Differences in religion, culture, and language led to antagonism between the two most prominent national groups on the frontier and kept them apart. Most Germans held a low opinion of "the dumb Irish" who, for their part, heartily reciprocated. The Highlanders from Scotland also preferred to form distinctive communities. Like the Germans they were a group apart, much less amenable to assimilation with the English than were the Scots-Irish. Each national group tended strongly toward those regions where they would be among friends in a familiar cultural setting. Once settled, the Highlanders and Germans tended to remain fixed.

In marked contrast were the restless Scots-Irish. While some remained sedentary, thousands seemed to feel almost a compulsion to move repeatedly. Long before the fertile areas in the Susquehanna and Cumberland valleys of Pennsylvania were taken up, many Ulstermen for various reasons, or indeed for no discernible reason, moved down the Great Valley of the Appalachians into Virginia and then into the Carolina Piedmont. Soil was being freely granted in the Carolinas and Georgia; this contrast to the cost of land in Pennsylvania and Virginia and the unprecedented Virginia land tax, not repealed until 1768, also drew the Scots-Irish into the southern back country.[7]

Settlers were attracted not only by cultural ties and the availability of land, but also by the most feasible routes. The ports of entry for the Scots-Irish and Germans were usually the Delaware River ports of Philadelphia, Chester, and New Castle; about three-fourths of the immigrants went on from these towns to the western and southern frontiers. A hundred miles west of Philadelphia the Great Valley of the

Appalachians cut southwest across the Potomac, through Virginia and by the Roanoke Gap, providing access to the southern Piedmont. By the middle of the eighteenth century the path was well marked for the immigrant settlers. Beginning at the Schuylkill River ferry opposite Philadelphia the "Great Wagon Road" ran west through Lancaster to Harris' Ferry on the Susquehanna and then through York and Gettysburg down the Cumberland Valley and across the Monocacy River in Maryland to Williams Ferry (Williamsport) on the Potomac. Across the river in Virginia it passed through Winchester, Stephensburgh, Strasburgh, and Staunton. Connecting the lower Shenandoah Valley with Alexandria, Colchester, Fredericksburgh, and Falmouth were four main wagon roads that followed the gaps in the Blue Ridge. At the end of the valley at Roanoke the Great Wagon Road turned east through the Staunton River Gap, crossed the Blackwater, Pigg, Irvine, and Dan rivers to its original terminus at Wachovia, on a branch of the Yadkin, 435 miles from Philadelphia. By 1760 the road had reached Salisbury, and after the South Carolina Piedmont was opened, it passed through the Catawba Valley to Pine Tree (Camden) where another road from Charleston joined it as it turned west and then south, forking beyond Congaree for the Ninety-Six District and Augusta on the Savannah River, 735 miles from the Pennsylvania capital.

Sections of the Great Wagon Road as well as other back-country thoroughfares were developed from much older Indian trails. The Great Warriors Path from Roanoke, later known as the Cumberland Road, extended from the valley of Virginia down the middle fork of the Holston River to Long Island, presently Kingsport, Tennessee. Leaving the Holston Valley at Moccasin Gap in Clinch Mountain, it wound for a hundred miles through the Clinch and Powell river valleys and through the Cumberland Gap where it forked, the right branch leading to the Kentucky River and the left to the Falls of the Ohio. Other Indian trails to the north were later used by the pioneers through western Pennsylvania. The Shamokin Path and the Kittanning, or Frankstown, Path, also known as the Allegheny Path, with their various branches led west from Philadelphia through such back-country centers as Carlisle, Lancáster, Bedford, and Fort Ligonier to the Ohio and its tributaries.

Many pioneer families traveled on roads built by the British and provincial armies during and immediately after the French and Indian War. Troops of the 31st Regiment cut a road from Mobile in West Florida, and the forces under General Jeffery Amherst built the Crown Point Road from Lake Champlain through the Green Mountains to the upper Connecticut River. A Virginia regiment in 1761 opened a road that traversed the Holston River from Fort Chiswell to Long Island.

Later known as the Great Road, or the Island Road, it was an open invitation to settlers. Braddock's troops cut one of the earliest of the military paths from Fort Cumberland at Wills Creek on the Potomac across the Allegheny Mountains to the Youghiogheny River and then to the Monongahela. Soldiers under General John Forbes opened another military road to the Forks of the Ohio. Following the Indian "Trading Path," it began at Bedford, passed through Raystown, and extended west to Ligonier and Pittsburgh. Like the Roman legions had done in Europe 2000 years before, the British regiments, in expelling the French in North America, helped advance civilization.

The fall of New France in 1760 inaugurated an unparalleled outpouring of people from the lower New England colonies. Insufficient land for an expanding agricultural population, religious discontent, social tensions, and the hope of a better life induced thousands to migrate. With the last of the unappropriated and forfeited tracts in western Massachusetts and Connecticut taken up and the frontier free of the French and the Indian menace, population flowed to the Susquehanna, to the lower Mississippi, and to northern New England and Nova Scotia.

Migration to the far northeast reached significant proportions in the four years following the capture of Montreal and then continued more slowly until the early 1770s. Although the new settlers to Nova Scotia included Pennsylvanians, Marylanders, and Ulstermen, two-thirds of them were New Englanders. The district of Maine also experienced a great growth. With the Bay colony supplying the bulk of the new population, between 1759 and 1776 ninety-four towns were founded, and the territory between the Penobscot and the St. Croix rivers—long disputed with the Indians—was opened. Here, too, speculators were active. When the General Court of Massachusetts in 1763 reverted to the earlier practice of granting land for previous military service, speculators ordinarily bought the claims of officers and soldiers and sold them to settlers or proprietors. That same year the General Court granted thirteen townships in the district east of the Penobscot to thirteen sets of proprietors with the provision that they settle sixty families in each. County divisions were also established. By 1772 thirty towns on the Penobscot and nine on the Kennebec were founded; they had a total of 250 families, an average of six for each town.[8]

The major region for the expanding New England frontier, the New Hampshire Grants, stretched west of the upper Connecticut river to Lake Champlain. Although new settlements were made on both sides of the river—eighteen were established on the east bank in New Hampshire—the bulk of the pioneers settled west in present-day Vermont, where immigrants from four New England colonies, particularly Connecticut, mingled with a scattering of English and Scottish settlers. Both New Hampshire and New York had long contested for jurisdiction over the area, but it was not until the end of the French and Indian War that effective settlement of Vermont began. In 1760 Governor Benning Wentworth of New Hampshire went into the business of granting townships. By 1764 he had covered the more desirable portions of the region with tiers of townships, and only the central, mountainous portions and the heavily forested region to the north remained clear. Three tiers were laid out on the west side of the Connecticut for some sixty miles; another three tiers were on a line from twenty miles east of the Hudson to as far north as Poulteny; and three tiers stretched north along the eastern shore of Lake Champlain to Highgate. Aside from granting town charters, New Hampshire did not establish larger units of government nor exercise governmental jursidiction for the territory west of the Connecticut.

The town charter for Windsor was typical of those granted by Wentworth. It was a printed form with blank spaces for information such as the number of shares, boundaries, dates for town meetings, and the names of the town officials to be elected. The tracts were more than six miles square and contained 23,500 acres divided into sixty-eight shares; two shares, or 500 acres, were reserved for the governor, one for the Society for the Propagation of the Gospel in Foreign Parts, one for the first settled minister, one for the glebe of the Church of England, and one for the support of public schools. These provisions were all based on royal instructions to the governors of New Hampshire.

After 1760 a constant stream of settlers flowed into Vermont, formerly a wilderness broken only by a few isolated military posts such as Fort Dummer (Brattleboro) on the Connecticut River. Many New England soldiers had served in the area, and more than one veteran became an advance agent for future settlers on returning to his Massachusetts or Connecticut home. Following the war Captain Samuel Robinson of Hardwick, Massachusetts, gathered a company of twenty-two people, organized more than thirty families from Connecticut and Massachusetts, and in 1762 founded Bennington. The charter of another town, Windsor, was obtained in 1761 through the efforts of Colonel Josiah Willard, a noted speculator. Willard was a proprietor in at least eighteen Vermont and New Hampshire towns, and his brother Oliver secured five townships from Governor Wentworth. There is little evidence that the original proprietors of Windsor had any desire to develop the settlement; they were merely interested in holding and then selling the lands for a profit. During the early years of settlement, the shares were concentrated in the hands of a few men who controlled the land and its government and disposed of their holdings to settlers who came later. Willard made a profit of 300 percent on his investment when he sold out to Israel Curtins.[9] Settlers like Curtins developed the town.

While the early proprietors were interested in speculation, many of the earliest pioneers in Vermont seemed in many cases to have moved for religious considerations or because of the legal and social disabilities under which they had suffered in the orthodox Congregational towns of the older New England colonies. "Come-outers" from three separatist churches in Hardwick, Sunderland, and Westfield, Massachusetts, later joined by others from Norwich, Connecticut, in 1762 established a separatist church organization in Bennington. This simultaneous migration beyond the jurisdiction of Massachusetts and Connecticut of the four congregations and their meeting at Bennington was not mere coincidence. Religion was not the only motive for moving to the Vermont frontier; pressing debts, the scarcity of land, and the opportunity for economic and social advancement also stimulated settlers.

In 1762 only about seventy families had settled in a dozen towns east of the Green Mountains, and about fifty families were to be found in the region to the southwest near Bennington. Within nine years, however, their numbers increased to 4669; and by 1776 approximately 20,000 people lived in the Grants. Most had pushed up the Connecticut River to the good lands along its western tributaries, the West, Williams, Black, White, and Wells rivers. So extensive was the flow from the Nutmeg colony that the region was frequently called "New Connecticut." The migration from the "Land of Steady Habits" was in two simultaneous streams. Settlers from Tolland and Windham counties, especially from the upland regions of Lebanon, Hebron, Mansfield, and Coventry, settled on both sides of the upper Connecticut in western New Hampshire and eastern Vermont. Many of them were old friends and neighbors, and they tended to be conservative and law-abiding in the Grants. Ironically, the region from which they migrated was a hotbed of radicalism and extremism during the pre-Revolutionary years. Among the new settlers were a few college graduates and men of wealth. For the most part orthodox Calvinists and adherents to the standing order, they established in eastern Vermont nineteen of the twenty-one Congregational churches in the Grants. Less conservative were the settlers beyond the Green Mountains who came from the western portion of Connecticut, Canaan, Salisbury, Cornwall, Goshen, Milford, and the other hill towns of Litchfield County. They included sectarians and religious skeptics, deists and freethinkers, and some Anglicans and Baptists who objected to paying taxes for the support of the churches. All responded to the lure of cheap, supposedly fertile land. So did the clusters of pioneer families from Rhode Island and New Hampshire. There was also a colony of New Yorkers from Dutchess County as well as settlers from

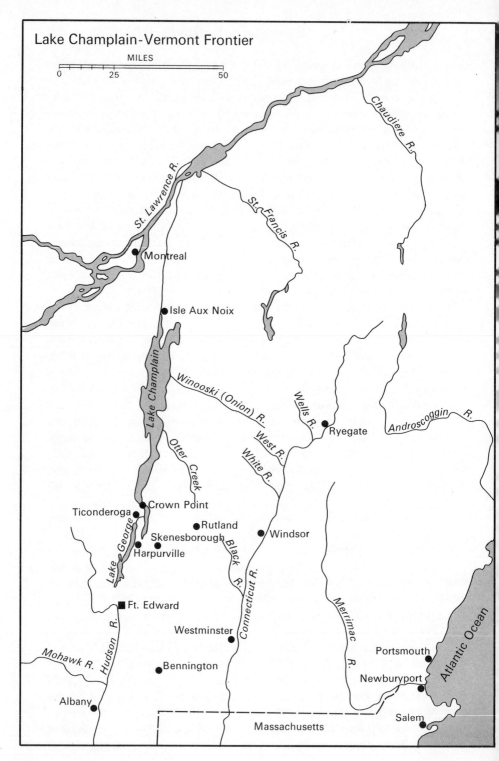

Lake Champlain-Vermont Frontier

MILES
0   25   50

Montreal

Isle Aux Noix

St. Lawrence R.

Chaudiere R.

St. Francis R.

Lake Champlain

Winooski (Onion) R.

Wells R.

Androscoggin R.

Ryegate

West R.

White R.

Otter Creek

Ticonderoga

Crown Point

Rutland

Windsor

Skenesborough

Harpurville

Lake George

Black R.

Connecticut R.

Ft. Edward

Merrimac R.

Westminster

Portsmouth

Mohawk R.

Hudson R.

Bennington

Newburyport

Atlantic Ocean

Albany

Salem

Massachusetts

48

western and central Massachusetts. Groups of Scots occupied Ryegate and Barnet on the upper Connecticut.[10]

From the outset the settlers found themselves embroiled in disputes over land titles, a source of controversy in Vermont for years. When Benning Wentworth of New Hampshire issued over 129 charters for Vermont, he was perhaps consciously exceeding his authority in a region claimed by New York, but he was adding to his own wealth in the form of fees and about 100,000 acres of land. Those to whom he granted townships included not only his relatives and associates but speculators from New Hampshire and other New England provinces. In effect, Wentworth went into the business of land granting. Much of the territory west of the Connecticut was initially taken up by opportunistic entrepreneurs rather than by farmers who actually intended to settle. The speculative nature of their operations was indicated by the large number of plural grants. Dummy names were used to conceal excessively large holdings by one individual, and often several members of a family received grants that were turned over to a speculating relative. By 1765 although some tracts in many towns had been settled, almost none were occupied by the original grantees. Even as late as 1769 less than half of the townships west of the Connecticut had any settlers.

Jobbers and entrepreneurs from New York opposed the Yankees. Although New York authorities had claimed the region for some years, up to 1764 they had issued only a few patents. But with officers, soldiers, and speculators applying for land, New York pressed the issue with the royal government and received an order-in-council, dated July 20, 1764, granting it jurisdiction as far east as the Connecticut River. New York declared the charters issued by the governor of New Hampshire void and ordered the survey and sale of lands held by settlers who had already paid for their holdings under New Hampshire title. Claimants who had settled before May 23, 1765, were given an opportunity to appear at Albany within a specified time with their deeds and other evidence of ownership. Town charters issued by Governor Wentworth were not accepted, however. New York created two new counties: Cumberland in the south in 1766 and Gloucester in the north in 1770. In 1772 Albany County, which up to that time had covered the entire New York frontier, was divided, and the region north of the Batten Kill and west of the Green Mountains was included in Charlotte County. Sheriffs and judges were appointed under New York authority for these counties.

Public and private land speculation was as widespread in New York as in New England. It was Lieutenant Governor Caldwallader Colden who in the late 1760s issued the majority of the really large patents from New York. In less than one year he granted some 174,000 acres;

over the next few years approximately a million acres including the Princeton patent of 1765 went to James Duane and some of his friends. The crusty New York executive also granted Socialborough, a large tract comprising the Wentworth town of Rutland.

In retaliation, some of the settlers and speculators claiming lands under New Hampshire title, sent an agent, Samuel Robinson, to London to arouse the fears of the influential Anglican missionary organization, the Society for the Propagation of the Gospel in Foreign Parts. Robinson's argument that New York, in contrast to New Hampshire, did not set aside lands for the use of the Society's missionaries apparently was effective. A royal order-in-council of July 24, 1767, required the authorities of New York to suspend granting lands in the disputed region. Boldly disregarding this order, successive governors and councilors of New York continued to issue patents for millions of acres to speculators. Even a great proportion of the military patents soon came into the hands of jobbers.[11]

Settlers on each side of the Green Mountains reacted differently to the establishment of New York jurisdiction and the granting of lands to New York interests. Those east of the mountains generally submitted to New York authority and between 1766 and 1770 bought confirmatory charters. West of the mountains where the bulk of the New York grants applied, the situation was different. Probably the greatest mistake made by the New York magnates was to bring ejectment suits in 1770 at Albany against the settlers to force them to accept New York jurisdiction. Had the authorities of New York made a clear distinction between the interests of the settlers and those of the absentee speculators with New Hampshire titles and recognized the rights of the former without demanding considerable fees, they might have won their support. Although Governor Henry Moore in November 1768 was willing to uphold the rights of persons who had actually settled on and improved land, the fees charged by New York to confirm titles were set at too high a rate and were not reduced by a later governor, William Tryon, until 1772. By that time many settlers were already alienated. Significantly the towns that did procure New York grants were largely those in the Connecticut Valley, the most populous region. Only pioneers in the towns in the southwest where the speculators with New Hampshire titles were most active resisted the authority of New York. The jobbers, including the Allen brothers of Salisbury, Connecticut, who were attempting to operate on a very large scale with very little capital, could not afford to pay the fees for a New York patent on thousands of acres. Neither did the speculators on either side accept the solution proposed by the British government in 1773: grants made by both New York and New Hampshire after 1749 would be valid, and in the case of overlapping claims, waste (unimproved) lands would be awarded to the later patentees as compensation. The remaining soil in the district was to be granted at £5 per hundred acres.

Violence broke out in the Grants with the winning of ejectment suits at Albany in 1770 by the New York magnates and the entrance on the scene of the ambitious Allen brothers, Ethan, Heman, Heber, Levi, Zimir, and Ira. Along with their cousins, Remember Baker and Seth Warner, and a few associates such as Jonas and Stephen Fay and Thomas Crittenden, they were to constitute the leadership in the movement against New York and eventually to strive for an independent Vermont. Absentee proprietors from Salisbury who had New Hampshire titles had selected Ethan Allen to manage their cause in the ejectment suits at Albany. The New York landlords attempted to win over Allen, but rejecting their offer and an attempt to establish peace and harmony in the Grants with the cryptic statement, "The Gods of the hills are not with the Gods of the valleys," Allen proceeded to Bennington with the disturbing news of the decision of the court at Albany. The Bennington settlers then resolved to resort to force; they formed a military association, electing Allen colonel commandant with Baker, Warner, Robert Cochrane, and Gideon Warren as his lieutenants.

The Green Mountain Boys began a reign of terror against settlers who submitted to New York jurisdiction. These farmers were forcibly dispossessed, threatened, and beaten, and their homes were burned. For two years the Green Mountain Boys hounded New York officials, harrying out of the region anyone offering resistance. The Allens sought to intimidate New York authorities into making the substantial concession of confirming their titles. Moreover, they sought to convince the settlers that New York was exploiting them with debt collections, expropriation of their land, and a denial of their fundamental rights.

In an effort to placate the settlers the government of New York in 1772 offered some concessions. In May Governor Tryon proposed a compromise, but while the Fays were negotiating with Tryon, the Allens were terrorizing and ejecting Colonel John Reid's Scottish settlers on Otter Creek. Intent on acquiring this region, the Allens in conjunction with Thomas Chittenden and Abidad Pratt of Salisbury established the Onion (Winooski) River Land Company in the winter of 1772–1773 and began advertising sales in New England newspapers. With the Fays defending the action of the Allens at Otter Creek there was no chance for compromise. Since the commander-in-chief of the British army in America, General Thomas Gage, would not send troops to interfere, rioting continued and finally culminated in the famous Westminister "massacre" in 1774. When a hundred settlers who were attempting to stop an action for debt collection seized possession of the Cumberland

County court, the sheriff and a posse of fifty men surrounded the building. In the ensuing riot, two men were killed and eight injured. This enraged the settlers from the nearby towns and a few of the Allen followers from west of the mountains. Yet the Green Mountain Boys, for their part, had been guilty of "far more man-handling and property damage to New York adherents than can be traced to any enforcement activity by the New York authorities."[12]

The settlers themselves were divided in sentiment; most were willing to remain under New York jurisdiction provided their lands were confirmed to them at low prices; some in the towns on the Connecticut River wished to be annexed to New Hampshire; and a few favored separate political status. Viewed realistically, however, the struggle in the Grants during the early years of settlement was basically between two groups of speculators. The conflict set the stage for the civil war between Loyalists and Patriots during the Revolution and for a potential separatist movement to join with the British in Canada. Moreover, the Vermont dispute was to help shape partisan politics in the Continental Congress after 1775.

Utilizing the confusion of overlapping colonial boundaries, land speculators fomented disorder to establish their land titles elsewhere on the northern frontier. But the violence marking the early settlement in Vermont and the Pennsylvania back country was lacking on the New York frontier where the jurisdiction of the Empire colony was exclusive and complete, and the landed magnates had clear and almost absolute pre-emption of the best land. Under their aegis the long dormant New York frontier was expanded.

By the middle of the eighteenth century the back settlements had not extended much above Albany on the Hudson and the lower Mohawk and its tributary, Schoharie Creek. For years the French and the hostile Indians to the north and the powerful Iroquois immediately to the west had prevented further expansion. However, the great landed families had already covered the central portion of the colony with patents and awaited only the removal of the French and Indian menace. With the capture of Quebec and Ticonderoga in 1759 soldiers and officers rushed to the lands around Lake George and Fort Edward, and approximately forty thousand acres near the southern end of Lake Champlain were granted to Robert Harpur to accommodate nearly one hundred Protestant families from Ireland. William Gilliland, Philip Skene, and William Beekman also received substantial grants for settlers. The removal of the French stimulated expansion west along the Mohawk and its tributaries to the headwaters of the Susquehanna and Delaware rivers.

The greatest boon, however, was the success of Sir William Johnson and the speculators associated with him in negotiating the boundary at Fort Stanwix in 1768 that cleared the area between the Mohawk and the Pennsylvania line of Iroquois title. In the following months speculators took out patents for lands along the upper Susquehanna and Delaware rivers and the Tianaherha, or Unadilla, River on the west. Lake Otsego with Cherry Valley just to the south lay roughly in the center of this region. In developing the area the speculators surveyed, subdivided, and sold the lands to different proprietors. Very few lots were conveyed by the original patentees to actual settlers. Johnson himself set up several hundred Highlanders as tenants on his own estate at Johnstown. John Harper, an "honest Yorkshireman," and a distant relative of John Wetherhead, Johnson's business agent, came with his family and in 1771 founded Harpersfield.

When Albany County was divided in 1772, Tryon County with Johnson's estate as the seat of government was created to administer the western frontier region. About ten thousand whites resided within its boundaries by the outbreak of the Revolution. The Germans in the Mohawk and Schoharie valleys and the Scots-Irish on the upper Susquehanna and upper Delaware were predominant among the frontier settlers in central New York.[13] When the extension of the Indian boundary in 1768 opened new areas for legal settlement, some frontier families along the Mohawk migrated south and west to the expanding frontier of Pennsylvania where land could be obtained on better terms from the proprietary government than in New York.

The Pennsylvania frontier had begun to receive an overflow of settlers from the northern provinces even before the boundary negotiations of 1768 had cleared the way. Immediately after the French and Indian War the Susquehanna Company of Connecticut sent pioneers to the Wyoming Valley, a region contested with the Yankees by both Pennsylvania and the Delaware Indians. Following a massacre during Pontiac's Uprising of 1763 the valley lay unoccupied until the Treaty of Fort Stanwix cleared the Forks of the Susquehanna of Indian title, and the Susquehanna Company undertook a massive migration. Money was appropriated for supplies, and provision was made for five towns to be laid out, each five miles square, along the banks of the north branch of the Susquehanna. These "gratuity towns" were to be awarded to the initial 240 settlers sent out in the spring of 1769. Following the New England tradition, three lots in each town were reserved for schools and ministers.

The decision of the Susquehanna Company to occupy the disputed land touched off a frontier war between the Yankees and Pennites. Both sides relied on outside support: Pennsylvania brought in Amos Ogden, John Jennings, Charles Stewart, and their followers from nearby New Jersey; the Yankees enlisted the aid of Lazarus Stewart and the "Paxton

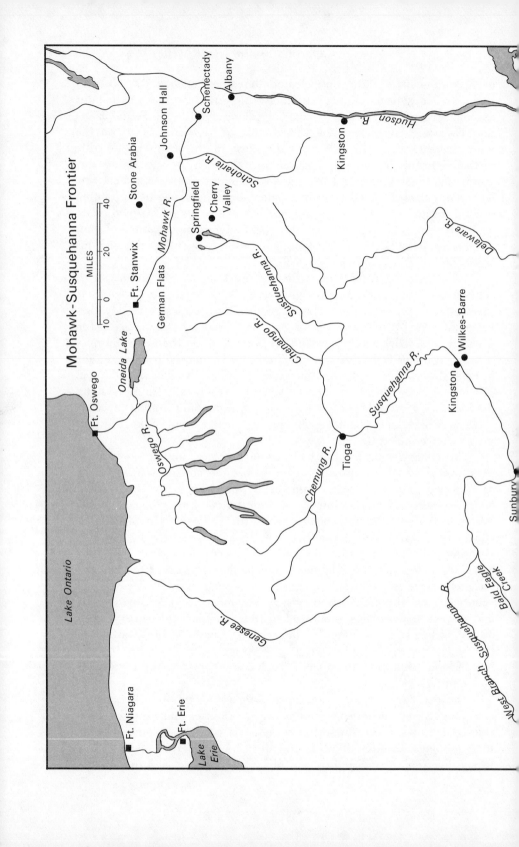

Mohawk-Susquehanna Frontier

MILES

10   0   20   40

Boys," a band of back-country ruffians supposedly dissatisfied with the proprietary government, the underrepresentation of the back-country counties, and the failure of the assembly to offer protection against the Indians.[14] In exchange for a township under the authority of Connecticut, two score Paxton Boys in February 1770 took possession of Fort Durkee in Wyoming. Intermittent fighting continued until the summer of 1771 when a large force of Connecticut settlers permanently reoccupied the district. Organized initially under Colonel Zebulon Butler in blockhouse settlements against the hostile Pennites, the Yankees had established towns on both branches of the Susquehanna by 1772. Settlement rights to newcomers from New England were sold for forty to sixty dollars.

The bases of the Connecticut settlements in Pennsylvania were such townships as Wilkes-Barre, Pittston, the Forty Township or Kingston, Plymouth, and Nanticoke (later, Hanover). To the northeast in southern New York were the Yankee townships of Lackaway and Bozrah settled in 1774, and on the west bank of the Susquehanna were the settlements of Charleston, Judea, and Muncy. In population, traditions, and institutions these rustic villages were merely Connecticut towns transplanted to the Pennsylvania frontier and subsidized by the parent company at Hartford. The Susquehanna Associates appropriated funds for roads, mills, tools, and provisions; and in distributing the land—including house, farm, meadow, and mountain lots—they used the customary New England system. Under this system, a town was organized, surveyed, and divided into lots by the settlers even before they left Connecticut. The arrangement for government was determined beforehand between the company and the settlers. In 1769 settlers' committees, appointed by the company but with members also chosen by the pioneers, constituted the administration of the infant settlements. Five years later, however, the government of the Nutmeg colony extended its jurisdiction over the Susquehanna villages. The company continued to use the committee system to locate and survey towns, admit shareholders, and decide controversies over land, but in January 1774 the General Assembly of Connecticut annexed the Wyoming settlements—now called the Westmoreland District—to Litchfield County. Zebulon Butler and Nathan Denison were appointed justices of the peace, and four deputies were sent to the general court at Hartford to represent the 2000 Yankee settlers in Pennsylvania.[15]

Although the Yankees were well established on the Susquehanna by 1774, neither the Pennsylvania settlers nor the proprietors of the colony accepted the situation. Violence again erupted and continued into the Revolution. Many Pennsylvania partisans, displaced by the Yankees, later joined the Tory rangers under John and Walter Butler.

While the Yankees were occupying the north branch of the Susquehanna and the Wyoming Valley, the Scots-Irish and Germans were extending the Pennsylvania frontier further west toward the Forks of the Ohio. There earlier pioneers had been forced to withdraw before the French threat, but in the wake of the British army under General John Forbes that captured Fort Duquesne in 1758, they again went west taking up their old settlements in Sherman's Valley, on both sides of the Juniata River, and west of the Tuscarora Mountains. The Juniata Valley was not re-occupied until 1766, but within ten years the more desirable portions of this mountainous district had a considerable body of settlers.

The great rush west of the Susquehanna did not come until the revision of the Indian boundary line in 1768 and the opening of the New Purchase in the following spring. Land was sold at £5 per hundred acres with one penny quitrent and payment a year after application. Terms for credit were generous—the settler did not have to pay until he received his patent, and payment was often delayed indefinitely. Improvement rights of squatters were recognized against all other claims, even those of the proprietors. Nor did the colony make much of an effort to compel squatters to protect their titles. On April 3, 1769, the opening day of the land office, 2790 applications were filed. In the next four months over a million acres, including the choicest tracts, were sold with a restriction of 300 acres for each application. Although speculators bought military claims and applied them to the New Purchase, land jobbing was not as rampant in the late 1760s and early 1770s as it was to be after the Revolution.

There was some difficulty with squatters on the west branch of the Susquehanna. The conveyance of the land from the Iroquois had fixed the boundary with the Indians at Tiahaghton Creek, identified by the Penns as Pine Creek but by the Indians as Lycoming Creek fifteen miles to the east. Rather than antagonize the Indians, the Penns temporarily banned settlement in the disputed area, but to no effect. Scots-Irish, German, and Dutch pioneers squatted on the land and adopted the "fair play" system to protect their holdings. All settlers were compelled to obey a tribunal of three annually elected magistrates in disputes over land boundaries. Offenders were, at times, driven off by force.[16]

The arrangement at Lycoming was exceptional, for the New Purchase provided a vast area for legal settlement. With the opening of the region in April 1769 the rush was on from Ireland and Germany. Some families tarried a year or two in the older settlements in the East to improve their position and then moved to another location further west. The Scots-Irish brought from Ireland not only the names of their old towns for their settlements—Armagh, Derry, and Donegal—but also their Presbyterian faith and their Bibles, spelling books, Latin grammars, and catechisms. With the influx of new settlers and the expansion of the frontier, new counties were quickly created. In 1771 Bedford was carved out of Cumberland, and the following year Northumberland County was created from parts of Berks, Bedford, Lancaster, Cumberland, and Northampton. By 1772 the pioneers beyond Laurel Hill, located over one hundred miles west of Bedford, were petitioning for their own county. The Pennsylvania assembly responded in March 1773 by creating Westmoreland County to cover the region west of the Alleghenies.

The Pennsylvania migration across the mountains after 1769 met on the tributaries of the upper Ohio an earlier migration from Virginia and Maryland, a movement that had started even before the French and Indian War. French and Indian incursions had driven back the first pioneers, but with the advance of the British army to the Forks of the Ohio, the settlers in 1758 once more moved into the Monongahela country. Traders opened stores at Pittsburgh; the army cleared the old Braddock Road from the Potomac; and Colonel James Burd opened an extension to the mouth of Redstone Creek. Settlers with military permits established themselves around Fort Pitt, Fort Burd (Fort Redstone, or modern Brownsville), and Fort Ligonier. As early as 1765 resourceful hunters and squatters from Virginia and Maryland began to infiltrate over the Braddock Road to the Monongahela, Redstone Creek, and the Cheat River. They were encouraged by such frontier speculators as George Croghan and Thomas Cresap of Frederick County, Maryland, who had privately purchased lands from the Iroquois and by Christopher Gist, his sons, and his son-in-law, William Cromwell who had claims under the Ohio Company of Virginia.[17]

As many frontier observers predicted, these encroachments on Indian lands, often accompanied by the murder of the natives in the vicinity, antagonized the Indians, even the Wyandot, Shawnee, and Huron as far west as Sandusky and Detroit. Despite repeated proclamations by provincial authorities and attempts by detachments of the British army stationed at Fort Pitt to evacuate them, the squatters remained. The situation was eased somewhat in 1768 when the royal government purchased the disputed region as part of the Fort Stanwix cession. The Crown had paid the lordly Six Nations of New York £10,000 for cession, but the Shawnee, Delawares, and Mingo who resided on the upper Ohio received nothing. In the years to come they were to deeply resent the settlers, particularly the Virginians who occupied the banks of the Youghiogheny, Monongahela, and Ohio which were opened for occupancy in 1768 by the royal and provincial governments.

Among the whites themselves a fierce rivalry sprang up quickly as speculators competed with one another and with squatters for the land. William Crawford, who had settled at Stewart's Crossing on the Youghiogheny, was making surveys and "improvements" in the region not only for George Mason and the Ohio Company of Virginia but for George Washington and other Virginia officers with military warrants. The agents for these speculators were also using "tomahawk" claims but were having a difficult time enforcing them against squatters. "The man that is strong and able to make others afraid of him seems to have the best chance as times go now," Crawford reported in 1772.[18] Many of the settlers were encouraged in their claims against both the Virginia speculators and the government of Pennsylvania by Croghan and Thomas and Michael Cresap who hoped to have their private land grants from the Iroquois incorporated into the proposed new colony of Vandalia. From 1771 through 1773 Croghan had surveyors running out lines to mark off tracts and was selling his land at £10 per hundred acres in addition to offering bond to make good the titles. To allay the fears of prospective buyers Croghan and his associates propagated the fiction that the western boundary of Pennsylvania did not extend beyond the Allegheny Mountains.

Facing a severe shortage of food, the settlers in the Monongahela country were ripe for the propaganda of the speculators that Pennsylvania was threatening their land titles. Many of them in the summer of 1771 agreed to associate, to drive off all law officers, and to impose a fine of £50 on any person refusing to adhere to their articles of agreement. Chaos reigned under the guise of resisting oppression. In 1772 the Redstone settlers drove off Thomas Woods, a sheriff of Bedford, and one of his deputies. Led by Abraham and William Teegarden, John Death, Andrew Gudgell, and Michael Cock, the associates stripped the officials naked and threatened to kill them if they returned to the settlements. Two hundred and twenty squatters signed a petition charging the Pennsylvania government and its local officials with oppression and injustice. George Brent, a former Maryland lawyer and a relative of the Cresaps, presented the complaint. The settlers demanded that no sheriff's process be served until a definite boundary had been run to ascertain the jurisdiction of Pennsylvania. Not until the British army evacuated Fort Pitt and Pennsylvania established Westmoreland County, did the government of the Quaker colony take steps to run its boundary with Virginia.

At this point Lord Dunmore, the governor of Virginia, intervened. In an effort to win the support of the Pennsylvania veterans of the French and Indian War to the cause of Virginia, he intimated at Pittsburgh in 1773 that he would issue patents for land surveys to all officers presenting certificates of military service. Shortly after the governor left the Forks of the Ohio, a "grand meeting" was held at Fort Redstone

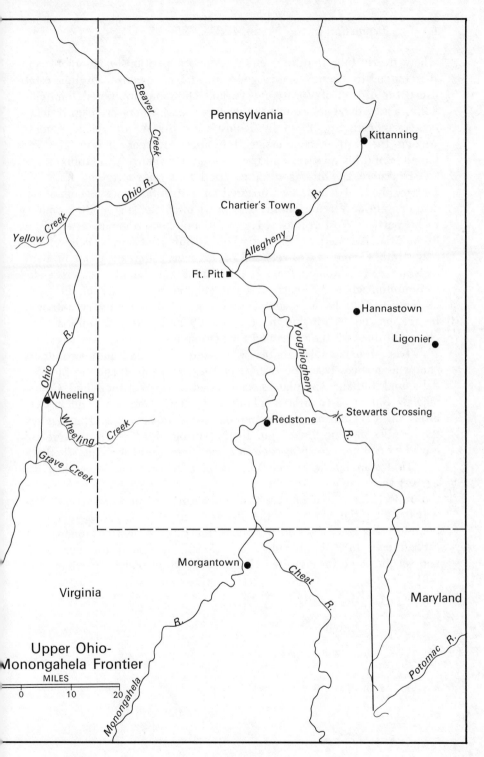

Pennsylvania

Kittanning

Chartier's Town

Ft. Pitt

Hannastown

Ligonier

Beaver Creek

Ohio R.

Yellow Creek

Allegheny R.

Youghiogheny R.

Ohio R.

Wheeling

Wheeling Creek

Grave Creek

Redstone

Stewarts Crossing

Morgantown

Cheat R.

Virginia

Maryland

Monongahela R.

Potomac R.

Upper Ohio-Monongahela Frontier

MILES

0   10   20

where nearly four hundred settlers signed a petition to Dunmore complaining of the Pennsylvania government. In response Virginia established the district of West Augusta, and Dunmore appointed John Connolly, a rascally back-country adventurer, and others as magistrates to contest officials appointed by Pennsylvania in Westmoreland County. Among the justices commissioned by the governor of Virginia were Croghan and his relatives and friends who had interests in "Indiana."

Dunmore and his agents then tried to seize control by force. On January 1, 1774, Connolly appeared in Pittsburgh with a commission as a captain of Virginia militia and proclaimed the surrounding country to be part of West Augusta. He called on the settlers to assemble as his militia. Arrested on the order of Arthur St. Clair, a Pennsylvania magistrate, Connolly was released on his own cognizance, but in a few days he collected men from the Redstone settlement and proceeded to Staunton where he received a commission as a justice of the peace of Augusta County. Now armed with both civil and military authority, he reappeared at Pittsburgh on March 8 and with his "militia" took charge of the post, then renamed Fort Dunmore.

The Monongahela frontier was sharply divided into two armed camps as justices from the district of West Augusta, including the Vandalia and Indiana speculators, contended with Westmoreland County officials. Simon Girty of later infamy was among Connolly's ruffians who broke up a session of the Westmoreland County court at Hannastown, thirty miles east of Pittsburgh. In the spring of 1774 arrests were followed by counter-arrests as each side sought to establish its jurisdiction.[19]

That summer, when the Virginians were preoccupied with a war against the Shawnee brought on by their own aggressive expansion on the upper Ohio, the conflict with Pennsylvania temporarily abated. Notwithstanding the efforts of the Pennsylvanians to settle a temporary boundary between the two provinces, the dispute on the Monongahela carried over into the Revolution, seriously hampered the war effort, and set the stage for civil strife between Tory and Patriot partisans.

◁ 4 ▷

Expansion in the South,
1763-1775

*T*he boundary dispute at the Forks of the Ohio with the ensuing chaos and the confusion over land titles induced many frontiersmen to leave the Monongahela country and move down the Ohio to the lower Mississippi where they joined a larger migration from almost all of the Atlantic provinces to the Floridas—the most recent, and the most distant, frontier in British North America.

Although the Spanish population and many of the French left the Gulf coast after the Peace of Paris in 1763, a vigorous boom in Florida real estate began almost immediately. English and American speculators started to plan investments in the new provinces. Since both royal and provincial officials were eager to settle the Floridas and create a buffer region, land was easy to acquire on generous terms there, as well as in Georgia and South Carolina. Generally, the government awarded land to all—speculator, entrepreneur, and small settler—who could develop it and made a point of encouraging, and even subsidizing, foreign Protestant settlers. Grants to individual families were common. Although many large tracts were alloted, most were later forfeited

61

due to the failure of the proprietors to settle the requisite number of families.

West Florida developed more quickly than its eastern neighbor, the peninsula. First officers and soldiers of the British army arrived, and then in 1764 after news of the new province had been carried to London and the older British colonies, settlers and planters came out. Initially the lands immediately surrounding Pensacola and Mobile were taken up. During the next twelve years settlers arrived either by ocean vessel or overland by the valleys and rivers of the Appalachian system and the Mississippi River. Most of the earliest holders were civil and military officials, but men of the 35th Regiment joined the growing population of West Florida and petitioned for land along the Escambia, Middle, and Chester rivers. By 1768 two new movements in settlement began, one into the upper valleys of the Tombigbee and Alabama rivers, the other up the Mississippi. The latter reached boom proportions within the next five years. Settlers soon formed communities between Manchac and Baton Rouge in the Natchez country and in the region drained by the Bayou Sara, the Homochitto, and the Bayou Pierre.

By the summer of 1770 the movement to West Florida from the older colonies had assumed substantial proportions. Daniel Huay and John McIntire led an advance guard to Natchez made up of eighty pioneers from the Redstone Creek settlements who had come by way of the Ohio and Mississippi rivers. Other families from the back country of North Carolina and Virginia were reported ready to follow this initial contingent. The following autumn more than two hundred families from the Holston River area commissioned John Clark to represent their intention to settle in West Florida, provided they could obtain provisions for six months. The provincial council extended aid as it had with the Huay and McIntire group.[1] After his unsuccessful involvement in the Wyoming Valley dispute, Captain Amos Ogden obtained 25,000 acres near Natchez and in 1772 brought out settlers from New Jersey. The following spring additional New Jersey families arrived by way of the Ohio and Mississippi rivers as did settlers from the Pennsylvania back country. In June a sloop from North Carolina arrived with thirty-three passengers who formed a settlement on the Mississippi.

The largest single contribution to the population of West Florida resulted from the migration of 400 families from Connecticut during 1773-1774. This Yankee settlement on the Mississippi stemmed from the efforts of the Company of Military Adventurers, a forerunner of the Ohio Company of New England formed after the Revolutionary War. As early as 1759 General Phineas Lyman, who had commanded a Yankee regiment during the French and Indian War, had become interested in frontier settlements about Lake George and Lake Cham-

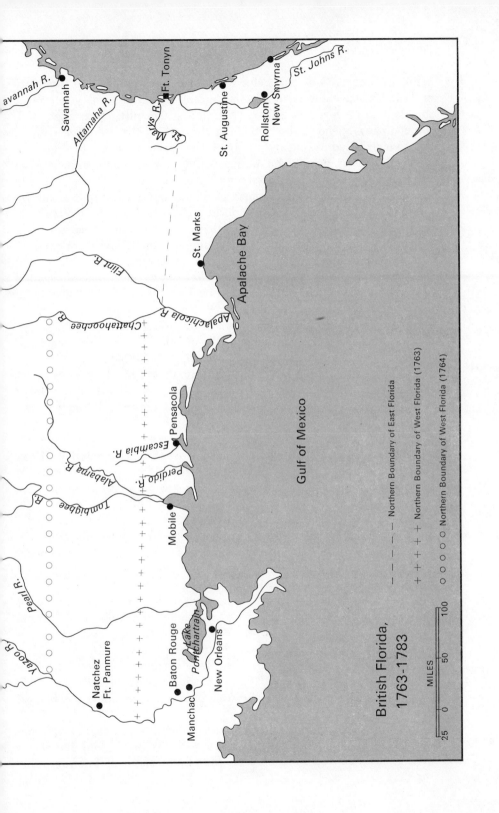

British Florida,
1763-1783

MILES

25   0   50   100

– – – – Northern Boundary of East Florida
+ + + + Northern Boundary of West Florida (1763)
○ ○ ○ ○ Northern Boundary of West Florida (1764)

Gulf of Mexico

Apalache Bay

St. Marks

Savannah R.

Savannah

Altamaha R.

St. Marks R.

Ft. Tonyn

St. Augustine

Rollston   New Smyrna

St. Johns R.

Flint R.

Chattahoochee R.

Apalachicola R.

Pensacola

Escambia R.

Perdido R.

Alabama R.

Tombigbee R.

Mobile

Pearl R.

Yazoo R.

Natchez
Ft. Panmure

Baton Rouge

Manchac

Lake
Pontchartrain

New Orleans

plain. In June 1763 he had helped organize veterans into the Company of Military Adventurers to obtain a grant from the royal government sufficient to erect a new colony. A standing committee was appointed; the company opened subscriptions at the rate of three dollars a share; and Lyman sailed to England to obtain the approval of the royal government. For years he lobbied unsuccessfully for a colony anywhere in the interior—along the Mississippi or the Ohio or at Detroit. As late as 1770 the British Commissioners of Trade refused to approve his request for 150,000 acres in West Florida. Disgusted, the resourceful Lyman threatened to bring out his settlers even without official sanction. Apparently he did just that. In the summer of 1772 he returned to Connecticut claiming to have obtained a grant between the Yazoo and the Mississippi, although he could not offer proof. The Yankees accepted his word, however, and dispatched an exploratory party to West Florida. Governor Peter Chester and his council, eager to populate the province, granted them lands on the Yazoo for five townships. Following the return of this advance group, the main body of 400 families from the Connecticut River towns migrated together during 1773–1774.[2]

As a result of this last influx the population of West Florida increased to 2500 whites and 600 slaves. They were settled on the lower east bank of the Mississippi, particularly at Manchac and Natchez, and on the Gulf coast around Pensacola and Mobile.

Although the British and provincial governments granted lands on the same terms in East Florida, settlement in the peninsula did not assume the same proportions or characteristics as in the region along the Mississippi. The barren, sandy soil, as compared to the more fertile regions of the Georgia and South Carolina back country, restricted settlement to the small northeastern corner of the province along the St. John's River and the eastern shore south of St. Augustine. Entrepreneurs and planters from England, Georgia, and South Carolina dominated the region. The first application for land came from Dennis Rolle, an English member of Parliament, who arrived in 1764 with a score of indentured servants from the streets of London to develop a plantation, Rollston, on the St. John's River. When these servants and others imported later deserted, Rolle brought in Negro slaves. Other planters followed Rolle's example. One of the larger operators was the Scottish merchant and slaver, Richard Oswald, who arrived in 1766 and with 110 slaves settled on a 20,000-acre tract between Halifax and the Timoka River.

Planters also arrived from Georgia and South Carolina; among them was Doctor John Moultrie who moved with his family and 100 slaves from Charleston and took up land four miles south of St. Augustine.

Here he founded an estate, Bella Vista, and constructed a large stone mansion and thirty other buildings, laid out parks and gardens, planted thousands of fruit trees, and lived in "imposing style." Doctor Andrew Turnbull, who first arrived with his family in 1766, undertook perhaps the most ambitious project. Turnbull received two tracts of 20,000 acres each near Mosquito Inlet (now Ponce de Leon); he established a cotton plantation on his lands and had cattle driven down from Georgia and South Carolina. Fourteen hundred indentured servants were imported from southern Europe—Greeks from the Peloponnesus, Italians, and Minorcans. The project failed. Some servants attempted to flee, and by 1773 almost 900 had died of scurvy and other diseases. In the summer of 1777 the colony, New Smyrna, was broken up and the tenants encouraged by Governor Patrick Tonyn to desert.

Despite the efforts of British and colonial officials and entrepreneurs to build up East Florida, by 1774 the population numbered only 3000, what it had been during the Spanish regime. It was not until the influx of Loyalist refugees from the coastal cities and the back country of Georgia and South Carolina during the American Revolution that the population at St. Augustine and the settlements near the mouth of the St. John's River increased. However, the restoration of the Floridas to Spain by the Peace of 1783 put an end to this migration, and Loyalist refugees and old settlers alike evacuated with the British army.[3]

In part, the settlement of East Florida was an extension of the settlement of the coastal region south of the Savannah River by wealthy planters from Virginia, the Carolinas, and Georgia. The pattern of expansion in Georgia up the Savannah River to the back country of the Piedmont differed greatly. From 1763 to 1775 a tremendous area, over six million acres, was cleared of Indian title and opened for settlement. Until 1763 the frontier on the Georgia side of the Savannah had not progressed much beyond Augusta, but at that time the government encouraged migration from the provinces to the north and from Europe. In addition, the provincial assembly freely granted land to families, provided townships, waived taxes for some years, and even had roads to the back country constructed.

Immigrants soon flocked to the Georgia backlands to join the thousands who moved down from the north. In 1768 Quakers found Wrightsborough on the Little River, and by 1771 the district held over 260 families. Scots-Irish from Ulster settled in 1768 between Lamberts Creek and the Ogeechee, about 120 miles from the coast. Within three years the town of Queensborough held some seventy families; 200 more lived in the environs, and 200 additional families arrived the following year. More land—1,600,000 acres between the Savannah and Oconee rivers and 500,000 acres between the Ogeechee and Altamaha rivers—was obtained in 1773 from the Indians. These lands were sold to settlers rather than granted freely by family rights. Despite the opposition of the natives and occasional skirmishes between the races that ensued in 1774, the whites rushed into the "New Purchase." Peace was impossible, for the settlers were determined to possess the rich lands as far as the Oconee.

Except for the presence of a considerable rough, lawless element, the migration to the Georgia back country was almost entirely a movement of pioneers from outside the province—settlers from the Long Cane region of South Carolina, North Carolinians, Pennsylvanians, and even West Indians. Only thirteen of those applying for land held more than one slave.[4]

The flight of hundreds of frontier families, among them debtors, criminals, and some settlers simply escaping chaotic conditions in the interior of the Carolinas, reflected the disturbances accompanying the expansion and development of the southern Piedmont. The sources of the difficulties in North and South Carolina differed greatly; in the latter colony they were directly related to the social, economic, and political dislocations caused by the Great Cherokee War of 1759–1761.

The settlement of the South Carolina back country was delayed for two decades until the defeat of the Cherokee. However, after 1761 the population of the province located above the fall line (the line running through the points in rivers where no further navigation is possible due to rapids) doubled to 10,000 within four years and continued to increase at a phenomenal rate in the next decade. By the outbreak of the Revolution the back country boasted 50 percent of the total, and 79 percent of the white population of the colony. This remarkable growth resulted from the efforts of the government of South Carolina to rehabilitate and settle the interior by granting bounties to subsidize foreign immigrants, waiving taxes for new settlers, and liberally awarding lands under family patents. Yet the majority of the new settlers were not bounty immigrants but Scots-Irish and Germans, a part of the great movement of peoples flowing south from western Pennsylvania and Virginia. Free land in the southern Piedmont and social and economic dislocation northward induced many to move.

Discontented back settlers from the provinces to the north and new arrivals from the British Isles and Europe, as well as those from the seaboard of South Carolina, came as groups, families, and individuals to form distinctive communities. The Germans, including the Swiss, settled chiefly at Orangeburg, in the fork between the Broad and Saluda rivers, at Saxe Gotha south of the lower Saluda, on the upper Congaree, and in the Ninety-Six District. Welsh immigrants from Pennsylvania

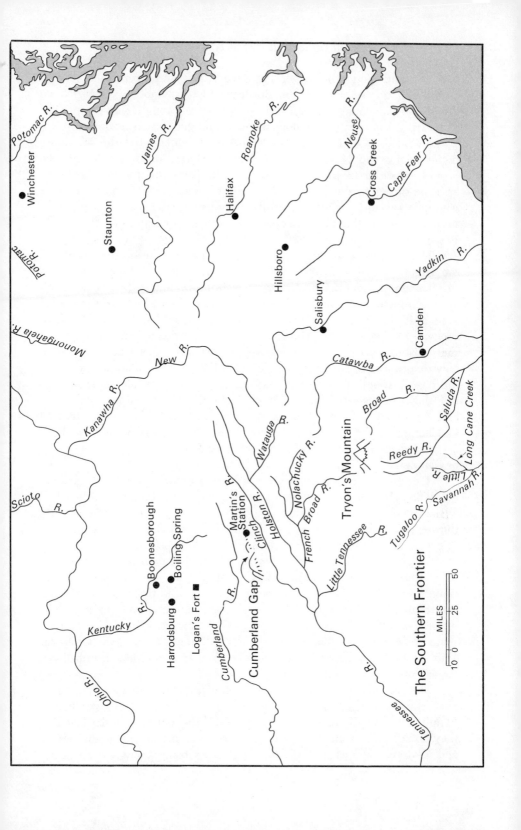

The Southern Frontier

MILES

10 0   25   50

took up land along the upper Pee Dee River, and French Huguenots established themselves at New Bordeaux in the Ninety-Six District, on the upper Savannah River, and in the Hillsborough Township. The Scots-Irish, a majority of whom were second-generation colonists, penetrated nearly every part of the Piedmont but dominated the Waxhaws region along the North Carolina border. Both the Germans and the Scots-Irish either worked their way south from the northern colonies or came directly from Europe to Charleston and then to the upcountry. Although the interior was generally a land of small farmers, there were some slaves—in the 1760s between six and seven hundred, or roughly 10 percent of the population.[5]

The settlers were filling in a region suffering from the legacy of the Great Cherokee War—lawlessness, dissolution, and economic and social maladjustment. Governmental institutions and authority were almost completely lacking. In South Carolina the parishes were the local units of ecclesiastical and civil authority, but those that were established, such as St. David's, St. Mark's, and Prince William, extended only a short distance to the northwest. As the western areas were populated, only theoretical, unsurveyed lines divided the parishes. The back country did have justices of the peace and constables to carry out their rulings, but these magistrates possessed jurisdiction only in minor civil cases and no jurisdiction in criminal matters. To reach the courts located in Charleston, 100 to 250 miles away, a week's journey by horseback or two weeks by wagon was necessary from such centers as Ninety-Six or Camden.

A criminal element from the north soon entered this legal vacuum. By 1766 outlaws had banded together, dominated communities, and formed connections with other gangs in South Carolina and with horse thieves in nearby colonies. They initiated a campaign of rape, murder, thievery, and destruction. So extensive was their power, so impregnable were their strongholds, and so weak were the agencies for law and order that many settlers and officials, out of fear, duress, or greed, became their secret allies. Others cowered under the threats of force and extortion. The summer of 1767 saw an orgy of crime and violence. The terrorized settlers from Ninety-Six and the Congaree, Saluda, and Broad rivers looked first to Charleston for aid. Although Lieutenant Governor William Bull and Chief Justice Charles Skinner sympathized with them, the assembly did not offer help.

The respectable element in the back country then decided to "regulate" the frontier communities by taking the law into its own hands. Families and neighbors associated to resist the outlaw bands. Initially, they acted only to meet force with force. Well-organized in the Santee and Wateree regions in 1767, the Regulators rode through the country burning the houses of those reputed to be in league with the criminal element. Among their leaders were Gideon Gibson and Morris Murphy in the Pee Dee District, Moses Kirkland on the lower Saluda, Thomas Woodward and Edward McGowan in the region between the Broad and the Catawba rivers, Henry Hunter and the Anglican missionary, Charles Woodmason, from Camden, James Mayson, a magistrate and militia officer of Ninety–Six, and Robert Cunningham, a popular militia officer on the Sandy River. The Regulators also attempted to spur the colonial authorities to action. To placate them the provincial government appointed some of their leaders as officers of two ranger companies that were to patrol the back country and named leading Regulators as magistrates to replace those accused of conspiring with the outlaws. But no adequate provision was made for county and circuit courts. Moreover, the provincial authorities had several leaders of the vigilantes arrested and tried.

At this point the Regulators went into open rebellion against the government—capturing officials and refusing to pay taxes. By 1768 the movement had taken a new course. The Regulators had broken the criminal element in the back country and forced many of the outlaws to move into North Carolina; yet they continued to "regulate" the countryside. They flogged men, forced vagrants to work, stripped and ducked women whom they thought were morally lacking, and generally attempted to impose their own concepts on their neighbors. The provincial authorities could not ignore these excesses, particularly when victims of Regulator violence instituted suits in the Charleston courts. By 1769 resentment against them had built up and led to the formation of a counter-organization, the Moderates, who found a champion in the hard-bitten mercenary, Joseph Coffel (or Schofel). An armed clash between the two groups was narrowly averted in March 1769. Some measure of stability was finally restored when the provincial authorities repudiated Coffel, and the assembly passed a court bill to redress the grievances of the Regulators. Six new judicial and administrative districts, four of them in the back country—Cheraws, Camden, Orangeburg, and Ninety-Six—were established with a circuit court for each. Lieutenant Governor Bull offered rewards for criminals and during 1770 and 1771 pardoned a large number of Regulators then under indictment. Others were restored to their offices and commissioned as militia officers and magistrates.

Ill-feeling in the back country continued between the former Regulators and Moderates and was later to influence the loyalties of men during the Revolution. Moreover, the concession and reforms made by the coastal politicians in the assembly did not redress all of the grievances of the back settlers who considered their treatment under the future Patriot leaders much more objectionable than under the British government. Many former Regulators, as well as Coffelites, were to become Tory partisans.[6]

The back country of North Carolina, settled somewhat before that of South Carolina, was also troubled by a Regulator movement, but one differing in origin, character, and aims. Basically, the disturbances in North Carolina were a reaction to the abuses of local government in a rural society that was still in a relatively primitive stage of economic development.

The expansion of the North Carolina back country in the 1750s and 1760s created the problem of erecting new counties and integrating the leaders of the frontier communities into the political structure of the colony. West of the fall line, Granville County was established in 1746, Anson in 1749, Orange in 1752, and Rowan in 1753. Mecklenburg was created later. By 1771, however, despite the real and relative increase of population in the back country, seven western districts returned only seventeen members to the provincial assembly, while the remaining counties elected sixty-one. Not only were the westerners under-represented in the provincial legislature, but they had little control over local officials. The magistrates of the county courts, appointed by the governor, named the sheriffs, constables, and almost all other local officers. Multiple officeholding by eastern favorites of the provincial regime was widespread. Prominent westerners with aspirations of their own who resented the domination of these outsiders, may have played on the dissatisfaction of the settlers. Much of the subsequent violence was to be directed against Edmund Fanning, a Connecticut-born favorite of Governor William Tryon, and his clique in Orange County.

The back settlers resented threats to their land titles, excessive rents, the payment of taxes in a region short of specie, and the malpractices of county officials and lawyers, particularly the charging of excessive fees. Rioting broke out in 1759 during a session of the Halifax court at Enfield and again in Mecklenburg in 1765 when farmers led by Thomas Polk manhandled a group of surveyors. Dissatisfaction spread in 1766 to Brunswick, Cumberland, and other counties where many small farmers refused to pay taxes. These developments were overshadowed by the more sensational events in Orange and adjacent counties that attracted attention during 1768 and brought on the War of the Regulation.

Early that year settlers of Orange County met to protest the method of collecting fees used by the sheriff, Tyree Harris. Borrowing the name of the movement then underway in South Carolina, they agreed to meet periodically to obtain justice from the local county officials. A dispute broke out over the seizure for nonpayment of taxes of a horse, a saddle, and a bridle belonging to one of the Regulators. On April 8, 1768, a band of sixty to seventy Regulators led by William Butler, Peter Craven, and Ninian Bell Hamilton rode into Hillsboro, took over the court, mistreated several inhabitants, and fired on Fanning's house. In retaliation Fanning with twenty-seven armed men, mostly officeholders, arrested Butler and Herman Husband, charging them with inciting rebellion. At the instigation of Fanning and John Gray, lieutenant of the militia, the governor issued a proclamation against the rioters and called out the militia. With wild rumors circulating throughout the back country, the movement quickly spread to adjoining counties. That summer Tryon with more than 1000 militiamen toured the back country to prevent a repetition of the violence at the Hillsboro court. Although noting that there appeared to be no "gentlemen" among the insurgents, the governor admitted that there was some justification in the charges of the Regulators that Fanning was guilty of demanding excessive fees. Consequently, he wisely pardoned three of the accused rioters.

Dissatisfaction continued in the back country, however. The more rowdy elements were active as vigilante groups, and the more judicious sought redress by legal means. In the elections for the assembly, Herman Husband, John Pryor, Thomas Person, and Howell Lewis, men who either belonged to, or sympathized with, the Regulator movement, were elected in Orange, Granville, and Rowan counties. Petitions from these districts asking for vote by ballot, property rather than poll taxes, payment of taxes by commodities rather than specie, reforms in land tenure and quitrents, and restrictions on fees, as well as freedom in ecclesiastical marriages, were presented to the assembly during the fall of 1769. This short-lived assembly did nothing, and the session called in March 1770 was prorogued before it met.

Violence broke out again during the summer of 1770, this time directed against Judge Richard Henderson at the superior court in Hillsboro. During September 24 and 25, armed Regulators forcibly took over the court, selected their own jurors, and brutally clubbed sheriff Thomas Hart, John Williams, the attorney of the court, and Fanning. Other rioters openly plundered Fanning's home, broke the windows of most of the houses in the village, and terrorized the inhabitants. Henderson, Tyree Harris, and Francis Nash, the objects of their wrath, fled.

While the provincial government sought to remove the immediate cause of discontent by regulating the fees charged by local officials and lawyers, it also took direct action against the rioters. Samuel Johnston introduced a bill, condemned by the Regulators as the "Bloody Johnston Act," for curbing riots. Early in May 1771 General Hugh Wadell was sent to organize the loyal militia of Anson, Mecklenburg, and Tryon counties. The Regulators also began to collect men; however, when passing through the Moravian settlements at Wachovia to oppose the Loyalist militia many of the insurgents admitted that they were "forced to do so by their neighbors." Indeed, the Moravian settlers in the Piedmont charged that the entire Regulator movement was a "contrivance of certain rebellious heads," and that many of the back settlers did not know what they wanted.[7]

Thwarted from making a stand on the Haw River by the quick march of Tryon with a superior force of militia, the regulators were cornered at the Alamance River on May 16, 1771. After a short battle the ill-prepared insurgents were quickly dispersed and disarmed. While Waddell pacified Mecklenburg and Rowan counties, Tryon tried the ringleaders of the Regulator movement. Although six were hanged after a trial at Hillsboro, the others were treated leniently and pardoned. Husband and William Butler were among those who fled. A tenuous peace returned to the back country much to the relief of many of the settlers. As one put it, no longer would persons and property be endangered by "Club law."[8]

Not all of the Regulators accepted the defeat, and for those who remained, there was some hope. William Tryon was transferred to New York, and the royal governor who replaced him soon began to court the discontented settlers in an attempt to gain support against the eastern political leaders who had led the anti-Regulator movement and now resisted the government of Great Britain. Before the outbreak of the Revolution, other Regulators had left their homes in despair and sought new frontiers in the Georgia back country across the Savannah, on the lower Mississippi, and in the Watauga and Holston river settlements. On the headwaters of the Tennessee River they met the vanguard of Virginia pioneers who were expanding the southern frontier across the mountains. The East Tennessee country fell within the charter limits of North Carolina, but since the boundary line between the Tarheel colony, as North Carolina was called, and the Old Dominion had not been extended west, the region was thought to belong to Virginia. Her pioneers led the advance and predominated during the initial years of settlement.

The Virginia frontiersmen pushing northwest to the upper Ohio, southwest down the valley to the Holston and the headwaters of the Cumberland and Tennessee rivers, and by 1774 into the Kentucky Basin, generally did not suffer from the disabilities under which the back settlers of the Carolinas lived. Economic ties between east and west were close, and the German Reformed congregations, the Lutherans, and the Scots-Irish Presbyterians were able to operate within the established

Anglican church. Only the Baptists, a small minority in the Piedmont east of the Blue Ridge, had serious cause for complaint; without licenses their ministers could not preach, teach, or perform weddings. Moreover, the leading families in the valley who led the migration across the Alleghenies were closely allied by political and family ties with prominent easterners. Unequal representation for the population of the western counties, later a burning question, was not an issue in the pre-revolutionary decade since the westerners generally accepted eastern political leadership, and the legislature, dominated by the Tidewater and Piedmont interests, created new administrative districts to keep pace with the increase and expansion of the western settlers. In 1763 Augusta County included the valley and the trans-Allegheny region. It was divided in 1769 with the establishment of Botetourt County. Three years later in response to petitions from settlers on the Holston, the portion west of the Kanawha River became the county of Fincastle. This area was divided three years later into Kentucky, Washington, and Montgomery counties. The district of West Augusta was set up for the pioneers to the northwest on the tributaries of the Ohio between the heads of the Potomac, Cheat, and Greenbriar rivers and in 1776 divided into Ohio, Yohogania and Monongalia counties.[9]

The discord that marred the expansion of Virginia after 1763 sprang from the competing claims for choice lands of rival speculators and settlers from Virginia and the other colonies, particularly North Carolina and Pennsylvania.

The early Virginia advance across the mountains had been turned back in the 1750s by the hostile French and Indians. However, with the renewal of migration, by 1768 settlers had reached the southern extremity of the valley of Virginia and the long parallel valleys west of the Alleghenices; to the northwest squatters had established themselves on Redstone Creek and other tributaries of the Monongahela and the Ohio. Land speculators such as Thomas Walker of the Loyal Company, Patrick Henry, and William Fleming were already contemplating exploitation of the region watered by the Mississippi.

It was not until the negotiations for new boundary lines with the Indians began in 1768, that the rush to the western region gathered force. Requests from individuals and groups for 1000-acre land grants in the newly opened regions poured into the Virginia Council. The first settlements made after the Treaty of Fort Stanwix in the district of West Augusta were grouped in a circular belt on the middle New and Greenbrier rivers, on the Kanawha, on the Monongahela, and on Wheeling and Graves creeks. Among the earliest settlers in the Monongahela region were John and Samuel Pringle, deserters from the garrison at Fort Pitt, who induced families from the South Branch Valley to join them. Zackwell Morgan established a settlement at Morgantown, and Ebenezer Zane and his brothers set up another on Wheeling Creek. At the same time Thomas Reich, John Stuart, Robert McClannahan, and William Morgan were founding settlements on the Kanawha River. These pioneers took their land by "tomahawk" rights, for not until 1773 did the government of Virginia recognize the squatters' claims. Until 1779 Virginia did not issue a single patent to the settlers for the territory south and west of the Kanawha. In the southwest the soil was claimed by the Loyal Company on the basis of a conditional grant made before the French and Indian War and was not completely cleared of Indian title until 1772.

A number of influential men settled on the lower valley and Holston frontiers at an early date. About 1769–1770 Arthur and John Campbell moved to Wolf Hills (Abington); many of their friends and other neighbors from the Staunton region also migrated. Captain William Russell, who was the son of a well-known lawyer and had been educated at the College of William and Mary, founded "Castle's Woods" in the valley of the Clinch west of the Holston. William Preston moved from Staunton in 1773, established himself at the Old Draper's Meadows site, and founded an estate, "Smithfield." From Frederick County in western Maryland came Evan Shelby who settled on the Holston in 1771. He advised his sons Issac and John to purchase military rights and join him, hoping that other former officers would come to the new region. If they did, the Holston would be settled by "a much Better sort [of] People" than would ordinarily be the case.[10] These early leaders on the Holston–New River frontier were related by marriage with almost all of the other inhabitants of the region who attained any prominence. Often educated and holding good positions, they had important connections with influencial eastern leaders in provincial politics.

Within a few years of the beginning of the American Revolution, population reached Long Island of the Holston, presently Kingsport, Tennessee, and extended to the headwaters of the Tennessee in a region then believed to fall within Virginia's jurisdiction. By the early 1770s there were several distinct settlements: two north of the Holston, one in Carter's Valley, and the other near Long Island; and two south of the Holston, one at Sycamore Shoals on the Watauga River and another on the Nolichucky. In 1769 Captain William Bean of Pittsylvania County, Virginia, had built a cabin on the Watauga, a source of the Tennessee. The next year James Robertson who had been born in Brunswick County, Virginia, but was living in Wake County, North Carolina, joined him as did several other families from the Wolf Hills settlement and the Yadkin country of North Carolina. In 1771 John Carter opened a trading store in the valley which bears his name, and the following year John Brown of South Carolina opened another store on the Nolichucky and brought in several North Carolina families. Between 1771 and 1774 about four hundred families arrived. Since these settlements were beyond the Indian boundary line, in 1772 the pioneers obtained from the elderly Cherokee chief, Attakullakulla, or the Little Carpenter, an eight-year lease for £2000. After having rented the soil, the settlers would not concede the Indians any rights and sought to obtain permanent title when Richard Henderson and his associates in the Louisa Company concluded the Treaty of Sycamore Shoals in March 1775 with one faction of the Cherokee. Dragging Canoe, the militant leader of the younger Cherokee, claimed that Henderson and the Wataugans had purchased the land from elderly, infirm chiefs who were too old to hunt or fight and were without authority. Repudiating the sale, the younger warriors threatened the settlers. Disputes over land titles broke out shortly, even among the frontiersmen themselves.

The controversies over land titles, particularly the settlers' suspicion that the Watauga and Nolichucky settlements lay outside Virginia, led to the adoption of the famous Watauga Compact, whereby the pioneers formed an association and elected five commissioners or tryers, a majority of whom were to decide disputes among the inhabitants. From the wording of a petition written by John Sevier and sent by the settlers to the North Carolina convention in the summer of 1776, it is clear that the Watauga Compact dealt with disputes over property and land rights and was not concerned with government as such. Since the settlers were outside Virginia and without constituted government, they feared the influx of fugitive debtors and wanted to record wills and deeds and protect land titles. Therefore, they simply adopted familiar Virginia laws. This arrangement, extant until 1776, provided no innovation attributable to a frontier setting. Threatened with possible Loyalist and Indian pressure at the onset of the Revolution, some of the Wataugans asked to be incorporated into North Carolina. After the provincial congress at Halifax recognized the settlements, the pioneers sent six delegates, including Charles Robertson, John Carter, John Haile, and John Sevier, to represent the Washington District in the North Carolina convention.[11]

Beyond the settlements on the headwaters of the Tennessee system and Powell's Valley—a long reach of fertile land on the eastern side of the Cumberland Mountains—and through the Cumberland Gap lay the Kentucky Basin. The early settlement of Kentucky was the result of several diverse lines of expansion involving speculators from North Carolina and Virginia and the movement of people from those states and the Monongahela country. The dynamic elements in the early settlement of Kentucky were the landed magnates of Virginia, and to a lesser extent, the speculators from North Carolina who stimulated expansion and fastened their claims to the best lands long before the common settlers arrived in appreciable numbers. Many Virginia speculators were particularly interested in this exceptionally fertile region, one that was claimed by several Indian groups although apparently occupied by none. Early in 1774 William Byrd, John Page, Patrick Henry, and William Christian agreed to purchase lands from the Cherokee and sent William Kennedy to sound out the Indians. The more aggressive North Carolina speculators from Hillsboro were the first to act, however.

Richard Henderson and his associates, even before purchasing lands, published a broadside advertising for settlers on Christmas Day 1774: they would sell plots of 100 acres for twenty shillings. The following month they sent Joseph Martin to take possession of Powell's Valley In a conference held in March 1775 at Sycamore Shoals Henderson offered the Indians merchandise purported to be worth £10,000, but which one observer described as only ten wagons loaded with "cheap goods, such as coarse woollens, trinkets, some firearms, and spirituous liquors," for an estimated twenty million acres. Initially, the associates had coveted the region between the Kanawha and the Kentucky rivers, but this area had been pre-empted by both the Vandalia Associates and by the Lochaber boundary line run by John Donelson in 1771. Consequently, Henderson accepted the Kentucky River as the northern and eastern limits of the purchase and the Cumberland watershed on the south and west. This vast country was conveyed by the "Great Grant"; the "path Deed" ceded a corridor from the Holston River through Powell's Valley and the Cumberland Gap. The circumstances surrounding these transactions are mysterious; for instance, Henderson had not as yet obtained the questionable "Yorke-Camden" opinion dated in 1772 that purportedly sanctioned land titles based on private purchases from the North American aborigines. This document was an edited and abridged version of an original opinion issued in 1757 by two English lawyers regarding the rights of the British East India Company to acquire title to soil in the subcontinent of India. Both the British and the later American governments were to deny its application to North America. Moreover, in regard to Henderson's purchase at Sycamore Shoals in 1775, the Cherokee later informed Indian superintendent John Stuart, that they were unfamiliar with the papers they were prevailed upon to sign, having been told by the speculators that they were "talks" to the colonial governors relating to trade.[12] Whatever the case, many of the younger warriors strongly resented the action of the older chiefs and refused to acknowledge the cession; so did the governors of Virginia and North Carolina who issued proclamations against Henderson. Yet it was the settlers themselves who were to suffer most from the ensuing confusion in Kentucky.

Henderson, despite his dubious title, proceeded with his plans to settle Kentucky. On March 30, 1775, he dispatched Daniel Boone with thirty axmen to cut a trail from Long Island of the Holston through the Cumberland Gap to the Kentucky River. Ten days later Henderson himself with a party of settlers set out, arriving on April 20 at "Fort Boone," or Boonesborough, at the mouth of Otter Creek, 150 miles from the Ohio.

But other settlers and speculators, rivals from Virginia and the Monongahela country, had preceded the Henderson group. Foremost among them were surveyors in the employ of provincial officers with military bounties and land speculators from Virginia. The most active were Captain William Bullitt and Captain James Wood representing the Virginia officers and Captain William Thompson representing the Pennsylvania veterans. In the Bullitt and Thompson parties descending the Ohio from the Kanawha in 1774 were two young men who were to be important in the history of the border, George Rogers Clark and James Harrod. Inasmuch as Bullitt was operating only under a commission as surveyor from the College of William and Mary and never had been commissioned by Colonel William Preston, the chief surveyor of Fincastle County, the studies he made were later disputed. Preston stubbornly refused to recognize the validity of the Bullitt surveys and had his own deputy, John Floyd, resurvey the land. Working with the Floyd party were Isaac and Abraham Hite and the McAfee brothers from Botetourt County. Early in 1775 the McAfees returned to their surveys on the Salt River, but fearing Indian raids, they withdrew to the Cumberland Gap where they met Henderson. "Carolina Dick" prevailed upon them to join his group, but once at Boonesborough they decided to move to their first location on the Salt River.

Still another contender in the Bluegrass region was the Ohio Company of Virginia. It still had not located the grant made before the French and Indian War for 500,000 acres. As early as 1770 its leading members turned their attention to Kentucky and in 1773 appointed William Crawford as official surveyor with Hancock Lee as his assistant. Lee, who had served as a deputy surveyor for Fincastle County, and his assistants, including George Rogers Clark, in 1775 made extensive surveys in Kentucky for the company. The young Clark was hired for £80 a year plus all the land he could secure in the region of the North Elkhorn and Licking valleys. Although the surveys for the Ohio Company were supposed to include only 200,000 acres, in reality they totaled four times that amount.[13]

Benjamin Logan. Charcoal drawing made by an unknown artist from contemporary descriptions. (The Filson Club, Louisville, Kentucky)

The Virginia and North Carolina speculators were to meet opposition from squatters who founded settlements at the same time the magnates were attempting to lay claim to the more choice areas of Kentucky for the Bluegrass basin was a great center of interest. "What a Buzzel is amongst People about Kentuck? to hear people speak of it one Would think it was a new found Paradise," wrote one Virginian, the Reverend John Brown.[14] In May 1775 John Floyd and thirty others founded St. Asaph's on the Dick's River. The settlers at St. Asaph's, also known as Logan's Fort, included two lawyers, John Todd and Alexander Spottswood Dandridge, Benjamin Logan, and according to Henderson, several other gentlemen of good family. More humble folk, squatters from the Monongahela, also arrived. With a party of forty-one men James Harrod began laying the foundation of Harrodsburg on the Salt River in 1774.

Evidently they hoped to obtain 400-acre settlement rights. After Harrod's men had erected crude shelters to qualify as improvements, they drew lots for these "lottery cabins." The Harrods and the McAfees had chosen, unknown to each other, almost identical locations for their settlements before they had to return to their respective homes during an Indian crisis in 1774. The following spring Harrod gathered his men on the Monongahela to go back to the site of the settlement on the Salt River chosen the year before, but on arrival, he found that the McAfee brothers had returned with Henderson, Colonel Thomas Slaughter, and other pioneers from Virginia and North Carolina. The Harrods then founded a new settlement, Boiling Spring, six miles to the south, and the McAfees and Slaughter remained at Old Harrodsburg. In addition to the four larger settlements in Kentucky founded in 1775, individuals and small groups of fourteen and fifteen men established smaller stations such as McClellan's, Hinkstons, and Martins. The pioneers expected to patent their 400 acres later as settlement rights.

The population of Kentucky during the first year fluctuated considerably from 50 to 300 persons. Some settlers who were apprehensive over the Indian danger left; indeed, many of the first venturers came out temporarily to locate land and then returned to the East.

Difficulties among the settlers over land led to the establishment of the first rudimentary government in Kentucky. Rivalry over well-watered land with good springs was particularly keen. Thomas Slaughter's men at Harrodsburg complained to the Boonesborough settlers that Harrod's followers at Boiling Spring were riding throughout the countryside marking every piece of land that caught their fancy and building cabins, or rather "hog pens," to publicize their claims. In this manner they were able to pre-empt every good spring within 800 square miles. Henderson, who claimed the proprietorship by right of purchase from the Cherokee, feared to rule in favor of the Harrodsburg settlers. Simply by refusing to comply with his judgment, Harrod's men would make a mockery of his authority. To escape the dilemma, Henderson issued a call for a convention of delegates from the four principal stations, Boonesborough, St. Asaph's, Harrodsburg, and Boiling Spring. The men of each community were free to elect delegates after first consenting to bind themselves by the decision of the convention to obey the laws that the representatives would pass and a majority of the proprietors— Henderson and his associates—would approve.

The setting was rustic, but the procedures followed by the eighteen delegates who met at Boonesborough under the Great Elm Tree on May 23 were reminiscent of the proceedings of the Virginia House of Burgesses or any other colonial assembly in its relations with the provincial governors; addresses were made and received, officials chosen, and bills given successive readings and then passed. On the last day of the session Henderson presented a plan of government by which the settlers annually elected delegates, and the proprietors appointed civil and military officers as well as judges. The latter were answerable to the people. The legislative authority was to consist of the delegates, a council of twelve, and the proprietors.[15]

For several reasons friction soon developed to disrupt the infant colony. The pioneers had come to Kentucky from various provinces— North Carolinians predominated at Boonesborough; Monongahela men had settled Boiling Spring; and Virginians made up the great majority at Harrodsburg and St. Asaph. Moreover, the Henderson Associates were selling lands that might be obtained freely under settlers' rights if Virginia jurisdiction could be established. Dissatisfaction was particularly evident at Harrodsburg where eighty-two settlers led by James Harrod, Abraham and Isaac Hite, and the McAfees sent a petition drafted by Peter Hogg, a lawyer from Augusta County, to the Virginia legislature. They complained of the increase in the price of land imposed by Henderson and asked Virginia to assume jurisdiction. Moreover, new settlers arriving from Virginia refused to recognize Henderson's Cherokee deed. Among those who broke with the North Carolinian was the influential Benjamin Logan of St. Asaph. In the spring of 1776 George Rogers Clark, an ambitious and not altogether scrupulous young man, also arrived at Harrodsburg.

Shortly after the appearance of Clark, the resentment against the Henderson regime came to a head at Harrodsburg with the new settlers protesting the increase in land prices and demanding to pay the same rate as the original settlers. Hoping to benefit from the repudiation of the Transylvania claim to the soil, land speculators from Virginia also contributed to the dissatisfaction. At Clark's instigation a convention was called at Harrodsburg on June 6, and the settlers decided to appoint Clark and Gabriel Jones, a land jobber and lawyer from the valley, as delegates to the revolutionary convention at Virginia to ask for the overthrow of the Transylvania jurisdiction. Initially Clark seemed to prefer independence for Kentucky, but after he and Jones had traveled east across the mountains and negotiated with the Patriot leaders of the Old Dominion, Virginia assumed jurisdiction over the disputed area and incorporated the pioneer settlements as the county of Kentucky. The Transylvania proprietors did not accept this action. Meeting at Boonesborough in September they boldly declared recognition for an independent colony and appealed to a rival political authority for recognition. Henderson and John Williams were selected as their delegates to the Continental Congress at Philadelphia.[16] The controversy in Congress between Virginia and the speculating companies with Indian titles to the land waxed throughout the Revolution and was to influence the policy governing the West the revolutionary government later adopted.

During the twelve years following the French and Indian War the southern frontier had expanded and developed to an advanced stage. In the Carolinas the Piedmont had been occupied and filled in, and the overflow of population had crossed the Savannah River into the Georgia back country north of Augusta. In these regions the pioneering period had been reached. But on the outer frontiers, in East Tennessee and the Kentucky Basin, the frontiersmen had but a tenuous and precarious hold. They were particularly exposed in regard to the hostile Indians who had viewed with ever-increasing apprehension and resentment the westward march of the pioneers and the friction and violence between the races that accompanied the surge of the frontiersmen.

◁ 5 ▷

The Struggle with the Indian Tribes, 1773-1776

*T*he outbreak of the American Revolution in 1775 interrupted the expansion of the frontier for almost a decade; in the back country there was waged not only a struggle for American independence from Great Britain, but a civil war between Whigs and Tories and a savage conflict between Indians and whites. Although the white protagonists on each side initially attempted to keep the warriors neutral, the racial antagonisms that had accompanied more than a century and a half of expansion predisposed the natives to side with the British against what they considered a proven enemy. So brutal had been the relations between the races that it was difficult at times to tell who had been the more savage. Both the Indians and the frontiersmen had resorted to indiscriminate murders and retaliation in the decade preceding the Revolution.

The greatest menace to the stability of the frontier was often the aggressive, undisciplined settler himself. He regarded the Indian as an animal to be exterminated without fear of punishment from law officials. According to one Indian agent, the magistrates of the Virginia and Pennsylvania frontier counties who ought to have preserved the peace "rather encourage[d]" the murder of natives.[1] It fell to the governors to take effective action, but often the provincial executives professed themselves at a loss. Francis Fauquier of Virginia explained that the frontier inhabitants, those most exposed to retaliation by the tribesmen for violence committed on the Indians, were the very people who protected callous murderers from justice. Such actions were inevitably to bring on an Indian war. "Government is set at open Defiance, not having Strength in her hands to enforce Obediance to the Laws of the Community," Fauquier remonstrated. His analysis was repeatedly confirmed throughout the following decade, and his prediction tragically fulfilled in 1774–1775.

The problem was prevalent throughout the frontier from the Susquehanna to the Savannah but was particularly acute in the Georgia–South Carolina back country and along the borders of Virginia and Pennsylvania. In 1773 Thomas Fee, a cowardly Augusta blacksmith, treacherously killed an Oakfuskie chief, Mad Turkey. Imprisoned in the jail at Ninety-Six in South Carolina, Fee was soon released by a group of sympathetic settlers. It was almost impossible to bring anyone to justice on the frontier for the murder of an Indian. The frontiersmen themselves regarded such a deed as a "meritorious action. . . ." In Cumberland County, Pennsylvania, a Mohawk returning from the south was murdered and scalped. The suspect, Samuel Jacobs, escaped to the Virginia back country.[2] A particularly brutal slaying occurred in Pennsylvania early in 1768, just five years after the butchering of the Christian Delawares by the Paxton Boys, and at a time when tensions with the Indians were high over encroachments on their lands. On January 10, Frederick Stump, a roughneck German settler of Penn township in Cumberland County, and his eighteen-year-old servant, John Ironcutter, slaughtered six Indians, including two women, and hid their bodies under the ice in the river. Fearing that the news might be carried by other natives, the two whites went to the Indians' cabin on Middle Creek the next day and killed another squaw, two young girls, and an infant. Stump claimed to have acted in self-defense, but he had scalped his victims, a sign the Indians understood as a declaration of war. A militia officer, Captain William Patterson, apprehended Stump and Ironcutter on January 23, but a few days later a party of seventy armed men from Sherman's Valley forced the jail at Carlisle and carried off the prisoners. John Holmes, the Cumberland sheriff, led a posse to Sherman's Valley, but the frontiersmen would not give up Stump and Ironcutter unless the magistrates promised they would not be taken out of the county for trial. It was William Patterson who eventually left the county, however. Subjected to threats and fearing for his life, he prudently moved his family to Philadelphia.[3]

Much the same situation prevailed on the borders of the Old Dominion. Indeed, the Indians called any aggressive frontiersman a Virginian. Appeals of the provincial authorities were to little avail. In Augusta County, Virginia, two men who had murdered a passing Cherokee in 1765 were apprehended, but one, James Clendening, was rescued before he could be jailed, and the other, Patrick Duffy, was freed by more than one hundred men who broke into the jail. The rioters swore that they would not allow a man to be confined or brought to justice for merely killing an Indian. Warrants for the apprehension of the rioters were met by a sardonic counter-proclamation issued by the audacious "Augusta Boys" offering a reward of £1000 for the arrest of Andrew Lewis, the county lieutenant, and £500 each for William Fleming and Captain William Crown of Staunton.[4] The Augusta rioters, supported by the Paxton gang of Pennsylvania, escaped punishment simply because the government at Williamsburg felt itself powerless. The Cherokee and other tribes were resentful, particularly since the Virginians continued to murder Indians along the upper Ohio and in the Monongahela country. By 1771 the situation had deteriorated so drastically that Cornstalk, the Shawnee chief, warned Alexander McKee, a deputy Indian agent, that the time was not far off when all the Indian nations would unite and strike the whites.[5]

Encroachments on Indian lands by both speculators and squatters, as well as the dubious tactics used to clear native title to the soil, also caused dissatisfaction among the Indians and brought on early in the 1770s the danger of a general Indian war. Many of the northern warriors had disapproved of the extensive cession of land made by the Iroquois at Fort Stanwix in 1768 although they had been tempted by the presents offered by Sir William Johnson. The younger, more warlike braves were particularly concerned over the loss of their immediate hunting grounds. In the southern district, the Cherokee, Creeks, Choctaw, and Chickasaw were also uneasy.

In addition to the continuous demand for Indian land, the very method of negotiating the boundary lines produced animosity. Frontier authorities often found it expedient to bargain with one nation for lands claimed or actually occupied by another. Georgia officials used this ingenious but dangerous tactic in obtaining the 2,100,000 acre "New Purchase" north and east of the Broad River from the Upper Creeks and the Cherokee in June 1773. The disgruntled Lower Creeks soon retaliated, killing no less than fifteen whites and two Negroes on the Georgia frontier. A small band then routed a force of 100 frontier militia and 25 provincial rangers. So great was the panic that the settlers from the Saluda, Reedy, and Pacolete rivers, expecting a widespread Indian attack, precipitously withdrew.[6] A comparable case of "purchasing" Indian lands led to an even more dangerous state of affairs in the North. The Shawnee protested not only the right of the Cherokee to sell their hunting grounds in Kentucky, but with the Delawares, Cherokee, and Mingo, a western offshoot of the Seneca, they contested the sale by the lordly Iroquois of the entire left bank of the Ohio as far south and west as the mouth of the Tennessee River. In 1771 at Fort Pitt, the Delaware, Killbuck, warned that "Black Clouds begin to gather fast in this Country."[7]

In the early 1770s it was clear that pressure on the Indians was leading to a coalition of the tribes in the northern and southern districts. Indeed, a union of the two groups seemed imminent in the spring of 1774. Some Indian nations traditionally hostile to one another were on the verge of putting aside their differences and uniting against the common white enemy. Early in 1774 delegates from the Mingo and Delawares conferred on the Scioto River with emissaries of the Overhill Cherokee concerning measures to be taken against the aggressors; intertribal warfare was to cease and a united front presented to the frontiersmen. A mission of young Cherokee led by the Raven of Chote traveled northward to negotiate peace among the different tribes, and specifically, to resolve the long-standing feud with the Six Nations.[8]

The role of the Overhill Cherokee and Shawnee in these negotiations was especially significant, for both tribes were to be directly involved in two incidents that brought on an Indian war in 1774. These episodes stemmed from efforts by the whites to reach Kentucky. In the fall of 1773 William Russell of Virginia and Daniel Boone of North Carolina undertook to lead the vanguard of a movement through the Cumberland Gap. In Powell's Valley a party of Delawares who were returning from a mission to the Overhill towns with two Cherokee and two Shawnee interpreters attacked the whites. They killed six men and drove back the rest. The following spring captains Thomas Bullitt and William Thompson led a surveying expedition down the Ohio to mark out tracts in Kentucky. This open attempt to survey the Kentucky Basin alarmed the Delawares, Mingo, and particularly, the Shawnee, who were already resentful over the settlements founded there by the Zanes, Cresaps, and others and apprehensive that John Connolly's armed militia at Pittsburgh would be used against them.[9] With relations between the two races so tense, the subsequent actions of Connolly and his strong-willed patron, Lord Dunmore, seemed almost calculated to force the Indians into some hostile act.

The crisis came in April on the Ohio River when a small band of Cherokee attacked a canoe owned by a Pennsylvania trader. Using this as a pretext, Connolly issued a warning that the *Shawnee* were on the warpath and that the frontiersmen should be ready to repel any insults from the savages. Taking this as an open invitation, borderers under Michael Cresap at Wheeling attacked the Shawnee on the Ohio. They claimed to have acted under orders from Connolly at Pittsburgh. The most brutal episode, one often erroneously attributed to Michael Cresap, occurred on April 30 when a party of border ruffians led by Michael Greathouse lured a small band of Mingo across the river at Yellow Creek, plied them with liquor, and murdered all of them except for one infant—men, women and children were indiscriminately slaughtered in the butchery that wiped out the entire family of Chief Logan. Anticipating the vengeance of the Indians and expecting a general uprising on the frontier, many white settlers hastily collected in makeshift blockhouses, and hundreds of others fled east across the Allegheny Mountains. Logan and the Shawnee who had lost relatives in the attacks by Greathouse and Cresap did retaliate against a few Virginia cabins, but then declared themselves satisfied. Soon after this Cornstalk asked Alexander McKee and officials of Westmoreland County, Pennsylvania, to restrain Connolly and the Virginians from further violence.

Despite the intelligence received from the Shawnee and Delaware villages by agents of Pennsylvania and the British Indian Department that the Indians were no longer on the warpath, Connolly ignored all pleas and pushed for war. Misrepresenting the situation, he wrote Dunmore that the Shawnee had made clear their intention of warring against the whites. The governor of Virginia needed no urging; the fact that the assembly did not take any action suggested that the governor and his cohorts were fomenting a war to force the Indians to cede lands. Imputing the blame for the frontier crisis to the Indians, Dunmore then mobilized the back-country militia. The bombastic governor was confident of victory even though the southern and western tribes might unite against the Virginians. Thus began Lord Dunmore's War.[10]

The forces gathered by the Virginia governor in the summer of 1774 were hardly adequate to cope with a general Indian coalition. By stripping the frontier counties of ammunition and their best men, the governor was able to send out three columns: one of 400 men led by Major Angus McDonald advanced against the Shawnee town of Wapatomic; another 1000 under Colonel Andrew Lewis marched to the mouth of the Kanawha; and Dunmore assembled 1200 men at Pittsburgh to descend the Ohio.

While Dunmore was marshaling his forces, the Shawnee and some hostile Delawares were attempting to bring in the other tribes of the north, west, and south. But their efforts were to no avail. Personnel of the British Indian Departments, unable to foresee the outbreak of the Revolution, had acted immediately to offset Shawnee diplomacy. Guy Johnson, who had succeeded his uncle as Indian superintendent,

John Stuart, and their agents prevailed on some tribes to remain neutral and played off one group against the other.[11] The Shawnee, isolated and greatly outnumbered, were obliged to face Dunmore's forces alone.

The Virginia frontier militia, poorly equipped and hastily provisioned, soon broke down in the late summer campaign. While the militia was immobilized in three separate columns, too far apart to support one another, 300 Shawnee and a few Delawares slipped across the Ohio and on October 10 opened fire on Lewis's force at Point Pleasant. After a day of indecisive firing the Indians withdrew across the river with few losses. The Virginians had suffered 81 men killed and 140 wounded. Lewis then joined Dunmore who was already short of supplies. With many of the frontier militia already thinking of abandoning the campaign, the governor marched his combined forces overland to the Shawnee villages on the Scioto where the greatly outnumbered Indians sued for peace and agreed to remain north and west of the Ohio River. By the provisional agreement concluded at Camp Charlotte, the whites were left in possession of the left bank of the Ohio. A definitive treaty with the Ohio tribes and the Iroquois under the auspices of Guy Johnson was scheduled to be concluded the following spring.

At the beginning of the Revolution in 1775, the situation changed drastically. Ironically, the British Indian superintendents were never able to fully repair the damage wrought by their diplomacy during the summer of 1774 or to immediately call on the Indians whenever they were needed against the Whig frontiersmen. At the outset of the Revolutionary War officials of the royal government and the Continental Congress at Philadelphia initially sought to keep the Indians neutral, or at least to prevent their opponents from enlisting the warriors. But both sides misinterpreted negotiations with the Indians that were calculated to deprive the enemy of their aid as active efforts to enlist them as combatants. Consequently, each side, thinking that the other was enlisting the braves, resorted to the same tactic. Although Whig officials were able to intimidate some of the smaller, weaker tribes residing close to the frontier into joining them, for a variety of reasons the British were more successful in enlisting the natives to fight against the frontiersmen. The most important factor in determining the British-Indian alliance was the conflict between the Indians and settlers that had accompanied the expansion of the frontier in recent years. The war between the Whig frontiersmen and the Indians during the Revolution was but the culmination of the tension between the two races that had been mounting during the previous decade.

The Continental Congress, adopting the organization of the British Indian Departments, rejected the previous system of separate control of Indian affairs by different provincial governments and attempted to establish unified regulation under boards of commissioners. In 1775 it created three departments: the northern for New York and the Six Nations; the middle for Pennsylvania, Maryland, and Virginia frontiers; and the southern covering the Carolina and Georgia back country. Later in the war Colonel John Allan of Massachusetts was appointed for the eastern district, the region including the tribes of eastern Maine and Nova Scotia.[12]

Despite unfounded rumors propagated by the Whigs of New York and Massachusetts that the British, at the instigation of their commander-in-chief, General Thomas Gage, were enlisting the Indians, Congress initially decided in 1775 that pending proof of the British attempts, it would merely try to keep the warriors neutral. If the British endeavored to secure the aid of the Indians, then the Whigs would follow suit. Operating independently of Congress, the revolutionary governments of New England upset the policy of Indian neutrality. Early in 1775 Massachusetts sought the aid of the Micmac and Penobscot tribes of Maine and by April enlisted the Stockbridge for use against the British forces then beseiged in Boston. Massachusetts also sent Samuel Kirkland and other missionaries who had resided among the Oneida to gain the active support of the Six Nations. Up to this point the British had only attempted to keep the northern Indians from joining the Whigs. A contest then ensued between Guy Johnson and the Whig emissaries, who circulated rumors that the superintendent was attempting to raise the Indians against the Mohawk frontier. Johnson, threatened with capture and cut off from the supplies he needed to influence the natives, left the Mohawk Valley for Canada with a party of Loyalists and Mohawks. Having received secret instructions from Gage in Boston, Johnson held conferences with delegates from the northern tribes at Oswego and Montreal. Evidently he asked their aid in keeping open the British lines of communication against rebel attack and, if necessary, in fighting a defensive war. Guy Carleton, the governor of Canada, who at that time was facing invasion forces under Richard Montgomery and Benedict Arnold, would not allow the braves to fight outside Canada.[13] In fact, he dismissed all but the handful who were later to serve as scouts in resisting the invading Whig forces under Montgomery. Carleton soon had sole jurisdiction over the Indians, for that winter Johnson and his Mohawk secretary, Joseph Brant, sailed for England.

With the Whig forces already in possession of the British forts on Lake Champlain and threatening Canada, Gage feared further attacks against Niagara and Detroit. For the first time, in the summer of 1775, he issued orders to Carleton and John Stuart, superintendent in the southern district, to use Indians against the frontier. As justification he cited the Massachusetts Whigs as having previously used them against the British. Fortunately for the frontier settlers, Carleton and Stuart did not implement the commander-in-chief's orders during the first two years of the war.

Although Gage's successor, Sir William Howe, planned to use Indians in his northern campaign for 1776, he depended on Guy Johnson to raise the warriors. However, the superintendent did not return to America until July, and not until November was he able to send Brant in disguise through the Whig lines from New York City to the Indian country. On reaching Niagara the following month, Brant circulated messages to the Canadian, New York, and western tribes to come down and participate in indiscriminate attacks on the frontier so as to free some Mohawks held hostage by the Whigs in New York. On learning of Brant's plan, Carleton ordered the commanders at the western posts to divert the warriors from the Mohawk chief.[14] The commandant at Detroit in 1776 was the ambitious Henry Hamilton. The local Indians had requested permission to attack the Ohio frontiersmen, but since Hamilton had no orders, he deterred the warriors and cautioned the Whigs at Pittsburgh against antagonizing the Indians and bringing on a savage war. By September, however, some of the Ohio bands were sending out small parties against the settlements on the Ohio.

Not until the summer of 1777 with the invasion of the New York frontier did the British enlist the Indians in the northern district. However, more than a year before, Congress on the advice of Washington and others that the Indians would inevitably join either the British or Americans had abandoned neutrality and sought to obtain the aid of the warriors for proposed campaigns against Canada, Detroit, and the other western forts.

In the southern district a struggle developed between Congressional, South Carolina, and Georgia commissioners and the officials of the British Indian Department. Here, too, both sides initially sought to keep the tribes neutral and to supply the natives with a limited amount of ammunition to keep them from going over to the enemy. But the activities of the back-country Loyalists, hard pressed by the Whigs and cut off from support of regular British forces, complicated the situation. In September 1775 John Connolly with the support of Lord Dunmore had appeared in Boston and proposed a plan to Gage for seizing control of the Forks of the Ohio with a motley force of back-country Loyalists and Indians. The British garrisons in the interior posts were to assemble at Detroit, attack Pittsburgh, and aided by the Indians and local frontier Loyalists, move on Virginia. This harebrained plot fell through when a servant betrayed Connolly, and he was apprehended by Whig officials in western Maryland. The only result was the evacuation of the skeleton British garrison of fifty men from Kaskaskia to Detroit. By 1776 the Illinois country was a military vacuum.[15]

Thomas Brown, a Loyalist fugitive from South Carolina, offered a more practical plan involving the use of Indians to relieve the hard-pressed Tories in the southern back country. With the support of Governor Patrick Tonyn of East Florida, Brown, who had been tarred, feathered, and tortured by zealous Whigs at Augusta, proposed opening a passage from the Floridas to the Loyalists by an overland expedition of British regulars through the Creek and Cherokee towns. John Stuart, the superintendent who had been falsely accused by the Whigs of inciting the Indians and forced to flee Charleston, was strongly opposed to indiscriminate use of the warriors. Although Stuart and Sir Henry Clinton, commander of the British force destined to arrive off the southern coast, discussed a plan for British troops to march from the Floridas to the Indian villages, no such expedition was ordered when Stuart moved first to St. Augustine and then to Pensacola. Nor had Stuart ordered his deputies to enlist the Indians. Yet by the spring of 1776 there were two groups operating independently for the British in the Indian towns: Stuart's agents, and the Loyalists from the South Carolina back country. Evidently Brown had informed his followers of the plan, considered but never adopted, for British regulars to march through the Indian towns to relieve the Tories in the interior.

At first, circumstances favored Brown and the Tories since the Cherokee, especially the younger warriors, resented the fraudulent purchases of their lands from the older chiefs. In March 1776 Dragging Canoe warned John Stuart's younger brother, Henry, deputy Indian agent at Mobile, that he intended to drive off the pioneers in the Nolichucky and Watauga settlements. At the request of the younger Stuart, who accompanied Alexander Cameron to the Cherokee towns, the Indians postponed their attack for twenty days until the agent wrote the settlers, warning of the danger and suggesting that they move to West Florida where they might secure free land from the British authorities. After a noncommital reply from the Wataugans, Stuart sent another, more urgent letter. Instead of heeding this warning, the Wataugans urgently appealed to the authorities of Fincastle County, Virginia. One resourceful settler, apparently Jesse Benton, appears to have forged a letter purportedly from Stuart and Cameron stating that a British force was to land at Pensacola, march through the Creek and Cherokee country, and with the support of the Indians, attack the frontiers. Widely circulated, this letter stirred the indignation of the settlers and convinced them that the agents of the British Indian Department were inciting the Indians. Actually Cameron and Stuart were seeking to hold back the Cherokee.

At that point a delegation of Iroquois, Shawnee, and Delaware chiefs arrived at the Overhill towns on a mission to re-form the alliance broken by John Stuart and Guy Johnson two years before. The northern tribesmen were now calling for a united effort against the settlers. Their plea and the urging of some Tories among the Creeks, who might have been led by Brown to expect a British force, aroused the Indians. Once the Cherokee went on the warpath, Henry Stuart and Cameron tried to restrain them from attacking settlements beyond the boundary line. The two agents then traveled to the Creek and Choctow country and extracted promises from the natives not to join the Cherokee under Dragging Canoe but to remain quiet until they heard from John Stuart.[16]

Except for the aid of a few back-country Tories, the Cherokee fought alone in the summer of 1776. Warned of their attack, the Watagua and Nolichucky settlers broke up the assault of the braves under Dragging Canoe, Abram of Chilhowe, and the Raven of Chote. While the Overhills were harassing the eastern Tennessee and Virginia frontiers, the Middle and Valley Cherokee, joined by a few Tories, were raiding the Carolina and Georgia borders. These attacks incurred the enmity not only of the Whigs in the back country but of some who would have preferred to remain neutral in the dispute with the mother country.

Isolated and facing an aroused, overwhelmingly superior, white militia, the Cherokee had little chance. During the summer and fall, the states of Georgia, North and South Carolina, and Virginia sent over 5000 militiamen into the Cherokee country. Finally, the older chiefs agreed to cede part of their hunting grounds in order to make peace. Dragging Canoe and his followers withdrew down the Tennessee River to Chickamauga Creek where they formed a new tribe known as the Chickamaugas. These diehards continued to attract new adherents until by the end of 1778 they numbered 1000 warriors. Under Dragging Canoe, the Chickamaugas continued to raid the southern settlements.

But the bulk of the Cherokee had been crushed in the abortive war of 1776. They signed one peace with the South Carolinians at Dewitts Corner on May 20, 1777, and another with the Virginians and North Carolinians at Long Island two months later.[17] The immediate danger to the southern frontier was ended. Except for sporadic raids by the Chickamaugas under Dragging Canoe, the Cherokee were never again a serious military factor. Not until the British invasion of the South in 1779 was any attempt made to recruit the Creeks in large numbers. The British were to use the bulk of these warriors against the Spanish in West Florida. The relatively few Indians who fought the Americans provided little real assistance in the southern campaigns; in fact, their frequent visits to St. Augustine, Savannah, and Augusta later in the Revolution were more of a nuisance than a help to the British.[18]

On the northern frontier the warriors were not a threat until 1777. Even after the British employed the Indians to force the Whigs to com-

◁ 6 ▷

Whips, Tories, and Neutrals: Political Allegiances during the Revolution

*T*he war of the American Revolution in the back country was often a bitter fratricidal conflict, dividing families and cutting across lines of national origin and class standing. Landed magnates, tenants, and independent farmers were to be found on both sides. Moreover, religious affiliation did not distinguish the back country from the seaboard or groups within the back settlements. While the Presbyterian Scots-Irish of Pennsylvania tended to be Whig, those of the Carolina back country initially were Tory or neutral. The Germans of the Mohawk Valley were Patriots, but those in the South remained passive. The motivation and commitment of individuals and groups varied from total involvement to alignment for expedience and waxed or waned with the successes or failures of the contending forces. At the outset, however, the Whigs had certain advantages; they were strategically located, were armed and well-organized, and had immediately seized the initiative. These factors were decisive. Lacking over-all leadership and organization and cut off from effective aid from the British regular forces, the Tories in the back country were defeated piecemeal during 1775–1776 by the aggressive Whigs who were able to dominate both Loyalists and neutrals.

The attitude of the frontier leaders and their role in the power structure of the various colonies were also decisive in determining the position of the back country during the Revolution. Where the frontier magnates had been admitted to positions of authority, as in Virginia, the back country supported the revolutionary movement, but in those regions where the back-country elite had been excluded from power by the Whig leaders, the back settlers tended toward Loyalism, or more often, neutrality. Moreover, the strength of the Whigs and Tories was relative, dependent on an uncertain and changing military situation. Where no British force was available to offer protection and where there was no focal point about which the Tories could organize, Loyalism tended to be weak or dormant. The presence of active Crown officials, governors, or Indian superintendents was important. They attempted to bring together Tory factions initially in South Carolina, North Carolina, and New York.

In the frontier regions, especially in New York and the South, whatever issues initially divided Patriots and Loyalists were later lost in the confusion and bitterness of raids, massacres, and lawlessness as the revolutionary conflict became increasingly savage. The names "Whig" and "Tory" became almost meaningless. Moreover, the revolutionary governments tended to label as "disaffected" or Tory many who had merely grown weary of the conflict or who would not serve in the militia or pay taxes.

It is impossible to determine with any exactness the numerical strength of the two factions. Estimates based on militia lists are misleading for, as was the case in Georgia and South Carolina, men often changed sides several times or were compelled to join the forces of whichever side was in control locally. In New York, the Tryon County Committee of Safety tried to compel the Scottish settlers on the Charlotte River to enlist in the Whig militia; many of the back country Loyalists captured at King's Mountain in South Carolina joined the Patriot forces rather than be hanged or imprisoned. In western Maryland, the settlers almost to a man had apparently either joined the Whig militia or subscribed to the Continental Association. This was not the entire story, however. In 1775 when the Whigs were associating the population of Frederick County, one of their officers, James Fleming, came to an understanding with a Loyalist, Hugh Kelly, who had been organizing the Crown's supporters. Under the guise of forming a Whig association, Kelly, Fleming, and their aides in Maryland and portions of western Virginia and Pennsylvania secretly formed a Loyalist movement *within* the Whig association. More than nineteen hundred men joined. Since these secret Loyalists could do nothing without the support of British troops, they remained quiet. Consequently, the extent of the Tory movement was never revealed.[1]

The underground nature of the Tory organization may explain the apparent lack of Loyalist support on the upper Ohio at the outbreak of the Revolution. At the beginning of the war, the Whigs quickly seized the initiative and thereby gained an advantage they never lost. The frontier magnates of Virginia, Colonels William Preston, William Christian, and Arthur Campbell, dominated the meeting of the Fincastle County Committee of Safety held on January 20, 1775, at Chiswell's Mines and nominated the current militia officers to enforce the Continental articles of association. In the months that followed, the committee took action against anyone who refused to serve in the Whig militia, declared for the King, spoke disparagingly of the committee, or showed "an unfriendly disposition" to the Patriot cause. In the frontier region disputed between Virginia and Pennsylvania partisans of both colonies held separate meetings on May 16, 1775; one at Pittsburgh by a committee of Virginians in the name of the inhabitants of Augusta County west of Laurel Hill and the other thirty miles to the east at Hannastown by the committee for Westmoreland County, Pennsylvania.

The Patriots, although in firm control by the summer of 1775, did not go entirely unchallenged. There were rumors that some of the leading men in the western country were disaffected and that a few local leaders were secretly corresponding with British officials at Niagara. Reports of Tory plots in the Monongahela country persisted. Some Loyalists taken into custody by Colonel Zackwell Morgan of Monongalia County confessed that they had secretly sworn allegiance to George III and implicated some of the leading men at Pittsburgh. Among the suspects were Alexander McKee, a former Indian agent, and Simon Girty, who had been recruiting men for the Patriot forces in the Monongahela settlements. When Girty's company was ordered to Charleston, he resigned his commission. Evidently McKee had acted as a secret Tory agent for Dunmore from the outset of the Revolution, and with John Connolly he had received instructions to raise several battalions among the frontier Loyalists for the royal service. On the night of March 28, 1778, McKee, Girty, the Indian trader, Matthew Elliot, and four other men escaped from Pittsburgh across the Ohio to the Indian villages and made their way to Detroit. Girty's brothers, George and James, later joined him. In the years to follow they led Indian raids against the frontier.

The defection of McKee and Girty and the increase of Tory activity in the Monongahela country in the spring of 1778 gave rise to fears that many of the settlers in western Pennsylvania and along the upper

Ohio were in league with the British. Settlers from the Monongahela and as far east as Bedford were reported moving off to join the enemy. The next year, with a British attack rumored, Hugh Kelly and James Fleming began raising men in the Redstone and Allegheny settlements. But the ruthless Zackwell Morgan with a force of Whig militia was able to crush the conspiracy. Some settlers, among them Gideon and Jeremiah Long, then confessed that they had taken the oath to the King.[2]

The year 1779 also saw an open conflict on the southwestern Virginia frontier between Tories and the dominant Whigs. Here Toryism, or perhaps only disaffection, was initially manifested by the refusal to pledge loyalty to Virginia and serve in the state militia. Whatever the case, in the summer of 1779 Tories from the Yadkin country of North Carolina and the New River region in Virginia combined to raid the lead mines in Montgomery County. They were surpressed by the militia led by William Campbell and William Preston, who then plundered the Loyalists and compelled some to enlist in the Whig forces or to give security for good behavior. Encouraged perhaps by general war weariness and the presence of the British army in the South, disaffection continued and even spread. In 1780 an uprising of 1500 Loyalists occurred along the New, Holston, Clinch, and Nolichucky rivers. Patriot authorities defeated them at Ramseur's Mill and again imposed punitive measures. Despite severe repression, disloyalty persisted.

General war weariness also increased discontent along the upper Ohio where the failure of Pennsylvania and Virginia to satisfactorily settle their boundary dispute added to the disaffection and led some to listen to local land jobbers and demand the creation of a new state. Early in December 1780 Colonel Daniel Brodhead reported that a considerable number of settlers west of the Allegheny Mountains were waiting for a favorable moment to submit to the British. Indeed, the health of the King of England was often drunk in public company. Disloyalty and rivalry continued for the remainder of the war. As late as 1784 one observer placed the settlers of western Pennsylvania into four categories: the proponents of Pennsylvania, the advocates of Virginia, the supporters of a new state, and the enemies of all—the once formidable Tories. Each abhorred the others "as heartily as ever did Guelphs and Ghibellines" of feudal Italy.[3]

Even more strong was the animosity, indeed the hatred, between Whigs and Tories in the Mohawk Valley, the center of Loyalism for the northern frontier. Although the Catholic Highlanders made up the core of the Loyalist resistance, and the Protestant Germans tended to favor the Whig cause, the bitter clash cut across lines of family, class, religion, and national origin. Before the Revolution, the Johnsons and their connections, among them John and Walter Butler, had politically dominated the Mohawk frontier. When the Whigs led by Adam Loucks, Christopher P. Yates, Isaac Paris, John Frey, and Andrew Finck, Jr. organized in the Palatine District as early as August 1774, the Johnsons and the Butlers sought to exert counterpressure. In March 1775 they had a resolution of loyalty to the Crown passed by the grand jury at Johnstown. But at the end of May Guy Johnson, the Butlers, and their adherents left for Canada. The Whig Committee of Safety was able to seize control. Regular government in Tryon County came to an end, for only one justice was left who would freely join the Whig association. The Whigs began exerting pressure on the settlers, arresting those considered dangerous and attempting to coerce the Scots to join the Patriot militia. Sir John Johnson refused to comply. With the aid of Captain Alexander McDonald he hoped to raise a Loyalist force and hold the valley for the Crown. However, Philip Schuyler, the long-time rival of the Johnsons from neighboring Charlotte County, was able to dominate the Mohawk region with a large force of outside militia. In May Sir John and 200 of his Highlanders, mostly McDonalds from Glengarry, fled through the Adirondack Mountains to Canada. Numerous Loyalist sympathizers remained; more than 300 Tory families lived in the Caughnawaga District alone. Those who had men fighting with the British were fined; elderly men and women were deported to New England, and their property confiscated. Many women and children were left without support. Subsequent raids by the Butlers, John Johnson, and Joseph Brant were designed to rescue these families.

Western New York also served as a center for the Loyalists from the northern Pennsylvania frontier. There the Whigs had exerted pressure on disaffected persons who constituted a considerable element on the upper Susquehanna and Delaware rivers. In Sinking Valley and Bald Eagle Valley where the Tories were particularly numerous, the Whig partisans confiscated their property and even stripped their wives and children of clothing. The popularly elected magistrates showed little mercy in enforcing the confiscation laws. In Northampton County those who refused to take the loyalty oath to the revolutionary government were jailed. Many of the settlers who had opposed the Yankees in the Susquehanna dispute slipped off to join the British rangers at Niagara and Unadilla. By 1779 the Loyalist population on the upper Susquehanna frontier had entirely evacuated to the British centers in western New York and Canada.[4]

Just as numerous potential Tories on the Susquehanna took advantage of raids by the Mohawk Joseph Brant and the Butlers to show their true sentiments, hundreds of Loyalists in central and northern New York revealed themselves by joining the British forces in the summer of 1777 on their march down Lake Champlain to the Hudson. Uprisings against the Whig authorities broke out in Albany and the frontier counties of Tryon, Charlotte, Cumberland, and Glouchester—the last two in the New Hampshire Grants. At first, the population in Vermont was uncommitted, but after some hesitation, the settlers at Bennington resolved to support the revolutionary movement and gain their aims by submerging the dispute with New York in the general American cause. Nonetheless, significant Loyalist sentiment existed in the Grants, and it swelled the longer the Continental Congress delayed recognizing the independence of Vermont from New York and as the British threatened the region. In 1777 some Tories in the Otter Valley openly declared their sympathies and were making their way to Canada. Roger Stevens, a settler on Otter Creek, became a recruiting officer, and with his men he established an advanced British post at Pointe au Fer on Lake Champlain to obtain intelligence and attract recruits from the northern New York and Vermont frontiers.[5]

As the war continued, the situation in Vermont became more serious for the Whig leaders. In an effort to maintain their tenuous authority against New York and to curry favor with the settlers, they imposed no taxes but financed their government by expropriating the estates of New Yorkers. Many persons, including Loyalists, malcontents, and deserters, moved into the region to escape military service and war taxes. Moreover, there was growing sentiment that the United States could not win the war; this attitude was encouraged by British frontier scouts who promised rewards and immunity for those supporting the King. Such promises were particularly alluring since there were no Continental troops assigned to protect the Grants. Neither was there any internal unity in the face of what only later turned out to be an exaggerated British threat from Lake Champlain and Canada. To some, American independence was still foremost, but to others, loyalty to the Crown now seemed the best course.

For the Allens, the Fays, and Thomas Crittenden, there was another factor to be considered. For years the Bennington party had tried unsuccessfully to win Congressional recognition of the political integrity of Vermont and establish its land claims against New York. By 1780 members of the Allen faction, convinced that separate political status for the Grants within or without the British Empire was crucial to securing their property titles, opened secret talks with the British. But they failed to achieve their aims. Late in 1781 the extent of their negotiations was revealed for the first time to the Whig authorities in New York and Philadelphia. With the surrender of a major British army at Yorktown, the British position and, consequently, the threat posed to Vermont was weakened. Indeed, the British ceased all offensive operations, and although negotiations continued between the Vermonters and General Frederick Haldimand at Quebec, there was no longer any pressure on the Grants.[6]

Paradoxically, the strongest initial support for the Crown came not on the northern frontiers where British aid was readily available, but from the back settlements of Georgia and the Carolinas. Here the royal governors attempted to use the back-country population in an effort to hold their provinces for the Crown. Up to the beginning of the Revolution the interior settlers had not been involved in the disputes with the mother country, as had the populace of the seaboard. In fact the great majority of the German and Scots-Irish settlers had benefitted from the liberal land policy of the royal government. The issues that most concerned the upcountry had been the controversies with the eastern sections of the colonies, not with the imperial government. Moreover, the westerners as a whole had been grossly under-represented in the provincial assemblies, and the frontier gentry had not been readily admitted to positions of power and influence. At the outset of the Revolution, the majority of the back-country settlers either opposed the break with the mother country or at best were neutral. The passiveness of the Germans was particularly irritating to the eastern Whigs. Many of the Scots-Irish, second-generation settlers from the colonies to the north, were scarcely more enthusiastic. Indeed, they purportedly threatened in 1774 to send 2000 armed men to prevent the eastern Patriots from imposing an economic boycott on the mother country.

Since North Carolina lay close to Virginia, which was firmly under Whig control, South Carolina was the key to the South; and the South Carolina and Georgia back settlements formed a single cultural and geographical unit.

Both the Whigs and Tories made an early appeal to the population of the South Carolina back country. In June 1775 Lord William Campbell, the royal governor, received assurances from the leaders of the Ninety-Six and Camden districts that thousands of settlers were loyal to the King. Aware of the critical situation, the provincial Congress made a deliberate effort to win support for the revolutionary movement. It granted more representation to the recently settled interior, formed local committees to enforce the Continental Association against trade with Great Britain, raised troops to patrol the interior, and commissioned some back-country leaders as officers. Although the Germans would not take up arms against the King, they tended to be passive and consequently were much less dangerous to the Whig cause than was the militant Scots-Irish party in the Ninety–Six District formed under militia officers Thomas Fletchal, Robert and Joseph Cunningham, and Joseph Robinson. In July the western militia was mustered; three regiments representing men from the entire region from the Broad to the Savannah rivers were present. None of the 1500 assembled joined the Continental Association set up by the provincial Congress. Instead, they subscribed to a counterassociation that had evidently been initiated to appeal to a large neutral element. Some who had formerly supported the Whigs, among them Colonel Moses Kirkland, now went over to the Loyalists. Although numerically strong, the back-country Tories were short of arms and cut off from aid.

Through propaganda, coercion, and economic sanctions the eastern Whigs attempted to eliminate the Loyalist leadership and win over the Piedmont. Ezekiel Polk's company of rangers rode roughshod over the region. Early in August 1775, a band of Sons of Liberty led by Thomas Graham abducted Thomas Brown, a recent English settler from New Richmond to Augusta; they burned the soles of his feet and tarred and feathered him. An outspoken opponent of the Whigs and, according to Patriot propaganda, the son of Lord North sent over to America to "poison" the minds of the people, Brown became an active Loyalist recruiter in the back country. Yet the initiative lay with the Patriots. They would not allow anyone who did not subscribe to the Continental Association to buy or sell at any of the crossroads country stores. In addition, the Whig Council of Safety in Charleston sent William Henry Drayton and two ministers, the Presbyterian William Tennent and the Baptist Oliver Hart, to harangue the settlers. During the summer of 1775 they toured the back country addressing meetings, holding private conversations with the leading men, and inducing settlers to join the Association and the separate military units not controlled by the Loyalist militia officers.

The Whig delegation was able to divide the back country. When Drayton signed a truce with the timid Fletchal on September 16, Brown and the Cunninghams denounced the agreement and fled to East Florida to seek outside support. A large Whig force under Richard Richardson raised by the revolutionary government at Charleston dispersed the outnumbered Tories who retreated toward the Indian country. The Tories were finally defeated at Great Cane Creek on the Reedy River later in the year in the "Snow Campaign." The Whigs were now in firm control, and Loyalism as an organized force ceased to exist in the South Carolina interior.[7]

The decisive victory of the Whigs in South Carolina by the end of 1775 helped to assure the success of the Patriots in North Carolina where Governor Josiah Martin had placed his hopes of holding the province until the arrival of a British army on two groups: the former Regulators, and the recently arrived Highlanders settled along the Cape

Fear River. The Regulators had long held grievances against the very seaboard magnates who now led the revolutionary movement against the Crown. Martin, on becoming governor in 1771, had toured the back country, conciliated the Regulator leaders, and liberally granted the King's pardon. His studied policy seemed to have born fruit in the spring of 1775 when he received full assurances from the Regulator leaders in Anson, Rowen, Surrey, and Guilford counties of their devotion to the Crown and their utmost disdain of the "profligate and abandoned Republican faction. . . ." The Patriot leaders were apprehensive over the situation in the Piedmont. By what I can find," complained Samuel Johnston, "the old Regulators are all against us."[8]

The North Carolina Whigs on the seaboard employed the same tactics used so successfully by the Patriots of South Carolina. Thomas Polk and his supporters were not above using force, and the North Carolina delegates to the Continental Congress prevailed on the Presbyterian, German-Lutheran, and Calvinist ministers in Philadelphia to ask their coreligionists in the Carolina back country to join the Whig cause. Late in 1775 the Continental Congress appointed two Presbyterian ministers, Elihu Spencer and Alexander McWhorter, to win over the settlers. In addition, the country merchants at Cross Creek (modern Fayetteville) refused to sell supplies to anyone failing to subscribe to the Continental Association.

The Tories, for their part, had not been inactive, but the success of the Loyalist movement depended on proper co-ordination between a British force expected to land at Cape Fear and the poorly armed Highlanders and Regulators who would rendezvous at Cross Creek under the royal standard and march to the coast. Contrary winds delaying the arrival of the British fleet off Cape Fear doomed the Loyalist cause.

Early in 1775 Governor Martin had hoped to raise two or three thousand former Regulators for the royal cause, but the back settlers were having difficulties. Deprived of their arms after the Battle of the Alamance in 1771, many of them were now driven from their homes by roving parties of Whigs; as "outlyers" they were forced to hide in the forests. In small groups some managed to gather at Cross Creek in answer to Martin's call for the Loyalists to assemble under the King's banner, but instead of finding the British troops and weapons as they had expected, they found only a few Highlanders. Some turned back immediately; others deserted on the march to Cape Fear. In all only about five hundred of the former Regulators and Highlanders were adequately equipped for combat when over a thousand Whig militiamen under Richard Caswell—he had played a prominent role in the defeat of the insurgents at the Alamance in 1771—broke up their march at Moore's Creek near Wilmington on February 27, 1776. The Whigs then took heart. Samuel Johnston boasted that not one influential man or anyone worth more than £100 in property had joined the Loyalists. But quiet was not immediately restored. The former Regulators who had not joined the Highlanders in their march from Cross Creek formed bands on their way home and raided the farms of those who favored the Whig cause. The Patriots retaliated scouring the forests on the upper Yadkin. Many Loyalists were forced to go into hiding.[9]

The initial defeat of the Loyalists in the southern back country condemned them to the position of a persecuted minority, cut off from outside aid and constantly on the defensive before the Whigs, who instituted a program of loyalty oaths to the revolutionary governments along with terror, banishment, and confiscation to consolidate their position. In despair, some Loyalists, particularly those in the South Carolina Piedmont, fled to the British forces in East Florida led by Joseph Robinson, Thomas Brown, and Evan McLaurin. John York, Richard Paris, and Joseph Coffel of anti-Regulator fame led sizable parties during 1777 and 1778. These refugees brought word that a strong, persecuted minority in the upcountry was ready to assemble at a favorable moment.

The initial experience of the British forces invading Georgia and South Carolina in 1779–1780 seemed to confirm these reports. General Archibald Campbell reported that a considerable number of "irregulars from the upper country" under the denomination of "Crackers" had joined the British forces occupying Augusta. Fourteen hundred men swore allegiance to the King and were formed into twenty militia companies. But with every turn in the tide of war, the back settlers changed sides. Expediency and the need for survival, rather than principle or conviction, motivated most of them in the bloody partisan warfare that raged in the back country during the next two years. The British were never able to organize a dependable militia in the interior, and their own regular forces were too small to hold the vast area and at the same time cope with the Continental field army. By the end of 1781 they had begun to withdraw from the South. Many of the Loyalist militia in Georgia and South Carolina deserted to return home and protect their property, and on the way, enlisted in the Whig volunteers. Yet hundreds preferred to leave with the British army. Following the evacuation of Savannah, Governor Patrick Tonyn of East Florida reported that about fifteen hundred white refugees and one thousand slaves had joined the British. Although there were a few respectable families among them, according to Tonyn, they were chiefly "backwoodsmen." With the return of the Floridas to Spain by the terms of the peace treaty of 1783, some Loyalist refugees went to the West Indies, others to their former homes, and perhaps as many as four thousand melted away into the wilderness of the southwest, some going as far as the lower Mississippi.[10]

Although Kentucky was subject to raids and eastern Tennessee quickly came under the control of the Whigs at the start of the war, throughout the conflict the infant settlements across the mountains were a refuge for those who wished to escape the turmoil of the Revolution. Brown's settlement on the Nolichucky River contained some Tories, but bands of mounted rangers from the Holston and Watauga settlements hunted down Loyalists and those suspected of harboring them. More than seventy suspects were captured and forced to take an oath to be true to the rights and liberties of America, and others were forced into the Continental army and had their lands confiscated by the court of Washington County. After 1778 many who were not in sympathy with the Revolution, fled the Watauga settlements for the lower Mississippi and Kentucky river areas.

Since few questions were asked in the Kentucky settlements, refugees who sought to escape the troubles in the East went there. Attempting to win over these frontiersmen, British authorities offered them 200 acres of land, humane treatment, and protection from the Indians. Despite the efforts of the Whig leaders along the Ohio frontier, some settlers did desert, and individuals and groups who had been captured often accepted the British offer. A few later returned to the Patriot side. The entire population of Martin's and Ruddle's stations who surrendered in 1780 to a British force took up lands about Detroit and Niagara.[11] As did many others, they simply made the best of a difficult situation, one not of their own choosing.

Few in the back settlements had a real choice during the Revolution. Most, perhaps, would have preferred to be neutral. But those who did take sides did so for a variety of reasons that cannot be explained entirely by class, religion, or any other factor extending to groups. In many instances the choice was an intensely personal one.

◁ 7 ▷

The Initial Years of the War, 1776-1779

*P*rimitive supply and transportation facilities as well as the great distances to be traversed in the West during the Revolution precluded the movement of large groups of men against major objectives and the effective occupation of territory. With few exceptions the conflict in the back country was largely a defensive struggle waged mainly between the frontier militia and the Indians and Loyalist partisans; it was a war of sporatic, destructive raids on native villages, isolated settlements, and remote garrisons. Although the frontier militia with the support of relatively few Continentals enjoyed great numerical superiority, the British had one initial advantage: control of the Great Lakes allowed them to easily provision their interior garrisons.

Yet British manpower was inadequate. At the outbreak of the war only a single regiment of 500 men garrisoned the posts on the Great Lakes—Niagara, Detroit, and Michilimackinac. The vast region south of the lakes from the Ohio to the Mississippi was devoid of redcoats. Moreover, the British war effort was marred by conflict of authority and rivalry among key officials. Guy Carleton, who as governor of Quebec had direct command over the western posts, did not get along with his superior in London, Lord George Germain, or with Guy Johnson, the Indian superintendent. On the frontier, commanders Henry Hamilton at Detroit and Edward Abbott at Vincennes were jealous of each other. Johnson spent much of his time busily plotting against John and Walter Butler. Some of the British commanders were incompetent or little inclined to prosecute the war on the frontiers. Abbott at Vincennes and, more important, Carleton and his successor as governor of Quebec, General Frederick Haldimand, resisted taking the offensive in the West and insisted on limiting the use of Indians. They employed a purely defensive strategy.[1]

Offsetting the numerical inferiority of the British were the hundreds of Indian warriors who took up the hatchet two years after the war began. Yet the British were to find the unstable, unreliable Indians unsatisfactory as combatants. Moreover, not all of the tribesmen sided with the British; many were initially neutral, and some even enlisted with the Whigs. Only the fierce Mohawk, reduced to a few warriors, and perhaps 500 Seneca of western New York posed an immediate threat on the northern frontier. John Heckewelder and other missionaries successfully frustrated the efforts of the British to win over many of the Delawares on the Ohio. But some Delawares who were at first neutral or had sided with the Whigs were lost to the American cause due to the brutal atrocities committed by the frontier militia. The Indians held the balance of power in the Northwest. Six hundred Delawares and Munsee, 600 Shawnee, 300 Wyandot, 600 Ottawa, 5000 Chippewa, 400 Potawatomi, and 300 Miami ranged from the Ohio to the Great Lakes; 1400 Sauk, Fox, and Iowa warriors resided further west. The aggressive expansion of the frontiersmen inclined the natives to favor the British. In addition, the British, except in the South, were better able to supply them with goods. Yet the Indians were never reliable in combat, and they did not contribute a decisive number of men. Some braves remained at home to protect their villages or to provide for their families. Generally, they took part only in small forays for a limited time during the spring and summer. Moreover, animosities among the tribes often engaged them elsewhere. For example, the Chippewa were fighting the Winnebago and the Menominnee.

Neither were the southern tribes initially much of a military factor. Creeks fought Choctaw, and thus struggling with one another, neither came to the aid of the Cherokee who were attacked by southern militiamen in the summer of 1776. Only the Seminole engaged in the minor raids early in the war that prevented a Whig invasion of East Florida from Georgia. Not until 1779 did the British succeed in patching up the disputes among the major tribes and enlist significant numbers of warriors. Thomas Brown—he and Alexander Cameron served as super-intendents of Indian affairs after the death of John Stuart—then induced the Upper Creeks to join the British, but by that time Spain had entered the war, and the British used the Creeks, Chickasaw, and Choctaw against the Spanish along the Gulf coast rather than against the American frontier. By 1780 when the British were in control of the upper Savannah, they were finally able to supply the Cherokee. But this tribe, decimated by smallpox and two disastrous wars in the past two decades, was no match for the Virginians and North Carolinians who launched punitive expeditions in the last years of the Revolution.[2]

In the face of the British and Indian attacks, the frontiersmen, for the most part, had to rely on their own meager resources, and the back-country militia, particularly in the North, generally proved inadequate to the task. Relatively few Continental troops were stationed in the Mohawk Valley and Vermont and at Fort Pitt. The frontier militia in the North was totally unable to undertake decisive offensive operations and hardly adequate to establish an effective defense against enemy incursions. Penetrating at will, the British partisans and the Indians bypassed the garrisoned forts and massed overwhelming strength against the isolated settlements. They were gone before the scattered militia could gather in force. When settlers from the ravaged New York, Pennsylvania, and Virginia borders fled eastward in despair, the fighting strength of the frontier was further depleted. Frequently, attempts to raise men for offensive action met with local resistance. As Colonel Samuel Hunter from the Susquehanna frontier put it: "The Generality of Inhabitants does not think it prudent to let [the militia] out of the County . . . when the Frontiers is [sic] like to suffer by a cruel savage enemy."[3] Always prone to desert, the militiamen could only be called upon for limited duty. Dissension among the Americans further hampered the war effort. Friction existed between rival military commanders and between Continental officers and civilians at Fort Pitt; and partisans of Pennsylvania in the boundary dispute with Virginia refused to enlist in or support the expeditions raised by Virginians.

When the militia was unable to defend the frontier, the settlers were restricted to seige conditions in blockhouses and stations. At times the Indians cut down stragglers within a hundred yards of the stockades. Life in the confined, unsanitary quarters became a nightmare. In once pastoral Kentucky the stench of the stations reminded one settler of the streets of Edinburgh. At Harrodsburg the springs were watered by ponds above the station so that "the whole dirt and filth of the fort, putrified flesh, dead dogs, horse, cow, and hog excrements" as well as the "sweepings of filthy Cabbins . . . and washing of every sort of dirty rags and cloths" that ran into the "spring poisons the water and

makes the most filthy nauseous potations of the water imaginable. . . ."
Typhoid and dysentery broke out among the settlers.[4]

Since the settlers themselves were in desperate straits, they were
not always willing to provision the garrisons in the forts ranging along
the frontiers. At Fort Pitt where the garrison was often without bread
or meat for days at a time, Colonel Daniel Brodhead sent out requisition
parties, but the inhabitants of the area drove their cattle into the mountains to avoid having them seized. Several times the troops at Fort
Pitt and in the Mohawk Valley mutinied or marched east from their
stations. The difficulty in supplying the western garrisons partially
stemmed from inflation of Continental currency, but profiteering, hoard-
ing, and the evacuation of farmers also made for scarcity. The results
were often disastrous, particularly along the Ohio, for the soldiers and
militia who were scattered throughout a vast region depended on local
supplies or occasional shipments from the East. For a time French merchants in the Illinois country and in Louisiana provided supplies, which
came up the Mississippi and Ohio. Oliver Pollock, an American merchant
at New Orleans devoted to the Whig cause, invested his own fortune
and borrowed on the credit of Virginia, but his meager resources were
quickly exhausted. No further aid was received from Virginia, herself
in serious financial difficulty, and by 1781 threatened by British invasion.
With the collapse of American credit and the Spanish source of supplies
at New Orleans exhausted, the men of the Ohio garrison were often
left destitute. Virginia then withdrew her forces east and south of the
Ohio.[5]

Logistics and trained men were the keys to the military operations
in the West. Although each side suspected and feared the offensive
potential of the other, neither was capable of a sustained offensive that
could have large forces operating at great distances. Almost all informed
American officials agreed that the most effective defense against Indian
incursions would be a large-scale attack on the Indian villages, and
more important, the elimination of such British centers as Niagara and
Detroit. But a sustained offensive would require months of preparation
and campaigning, at least two thousand well-trained men, artillery,
scores of wagons and hundreds of packhorses, thousands of bushels
of grain, hundreds of meat animals, and thousands of pounds of munitions. To control the Northwest the Americans needed a chain of advanced posts in addition to a large, well-provisioned and trained force.
These conditions were not met on the frontier until more than a decade
after the Revolution. After early attempts to take the offensive, with
only one exception each side fought a defensive war limited to harassing
raids conducted by relatively small forces.

Until the British invaded the southern Piedmont later in the conflict, their most sustained efforts on the northern frontier were generally limited to raids designed to gain Tory sympathizers, to destroy foodstuffs— Tryon County, New York, was considered the granary for Washington's army—and to force the American commanders to weaken their position by committing troops for the defense of the back country.

In the North the Americans quickly seized the initiative at the outbreak of the Revolution with the dramatic capture of the British forts on the line of communications with Canada. On May 10, 1775, eighty Green Mountain Boys under Ethan Allen and Benedict Arnold crossed Lake Champlain and surprised the small caretaker garrison at Ticonderoga. Crown Point, the other post on Lake Champlain guarding the route to Canada, fell to Seth Warner two days later. Although the Green Mountain Boys returned to their settlements, the way to Canada was now open to the Continental forces under Arnold and Richard Montgomery. When the gallant Montgomery with 1200 men swept to the St. Lawrence and occupied Montreal, the British line of communications with the interior posts was cut. On the last day of 1775, however, the Americans failed to carry an assault of Quebec and fell back in confusion as far as Ticonderoga. With the British forces under Governor Guy Carleton of Quebec in control of Lake Champlain, the northern frontier was open to attack in 1776. Panic swept the settlers of northern New Hampshire and Vermont where only 300 poorly armed men were available. Many of the pioneers in northern New England began evacuating their towns. Fortunately, Carleton, who had no desire to press the war, dismissed the Indians who had been raised in the interior and retreated.[6] The exposed frontiersmen received a year of grace.

The British also failed to capitalize on the situation in the South during 1776. An expeditionary force under Henry Clinton did not arrive off the Carolina coast in time to aid the back-country Loyalists who subsequently were defeated piecemeal by the Whigs. Neither did the British supply any military aid to the Cherokee following their attacks on the Holston, Watauga, and Carter's Valley settlements in the summer of 1776. Forewarned of the Indians' plans, James Thompson, William Cocke, James Shelby, John Sevier, William Russell, and other frontier leaders withstood the attacks led by Dragging Canoe, Old Abram, and The Raven; the southern states then put into the field an overwhelmingly superior force against the Indian towns. With the Choctaw and the Creeks held inactive by the British Indian agents, the Cherokee fought alone. Colonel Samuel Jack and a force of Georgians destroyed all their towns on the Tugoloo River while Colonel Andrew Williamson and 1100 South Carolinians burned the Lower Towns near the head of the Savannah River and then joined General Griffith Rutherford and 2800 men from North Carolina in attacking the Middle Towns. Rather than endanger their women and children by confronting the numerous whites, the Indians abandoned their villages and retreated. Encountering little resistance, Williamson and Rutherford razed thirty-six towns, leaving the Lower and Middle Cherokee destitute. Later in 1776 Colonel William Christian and 1800 Virginians invaded the Overhill country and forced the Indians to agree to a peace treaty to be signed the following year.[7]

The Cherokee had been urged to attack the Holston-Watauga frontier in 1776 by those tribes along the Ohio who had long resented encroachments by the whites on their lands and who were particularly apprehensive over the fortifications the Virginians had erected along the river. A troublesome band of eighty Mingo at Pluggy's Town on the Scioto, along with a few of their relations among the Wyandot and Shawnee, raided Kentucky during 1776, forcing settlers into three stockaded stations—Boonesborough, St. Asaph's, and Harrodsburg. But the bulk of the tribes along the Ohio and around the Great Lakes were still not committed in 1776; indeed, many had pledged their neutrality to the American commissioners at Pittsburgh. Nonetheless, the few who took to the warpath posed a serious threat to the Kentucky frontier where the number of men available for defense during the year fluctuated between 50 and 200. Beginning in February 1777, however, the Mingo, Wyandot, and Shawnee began striking in greater force at Wheeling, Boonesborough, and the other stations. Two hundred warriors under Blackfish harassed the stations until a relief force of 100 men under Colonel John Bowman arrived from Botetourt and Montgomery counties.[8]

In the summer of 1777 the British intervened decisively. A large number of Indian warriors were used in a major campaign on the New York frontier. General John Burgoyne with a sizable army was to move from Canada down Lake Champlain and the Hudson River to Albany while Colonel Barry St. Leger and Sir John Johnson would strike with another force, mainly Indians, from Oswego to the Mohawk Valley and join Burgoyne on the Hudson. As a diversion Henry Hamilton, the British commander at Detroit, would launch the Indians against the settlements on the Ohio River. On receiving orders in June Hamilton, who had sought up to this point to restrain the western Indians, began recruiting. The northwestern tribesmen, notwithstanding the diplomatic efforts of the Americans, were eager for war. Within a week delegates from the Ottawa, Chippewa, Wyandot, Miami, Potawatomi, Shawnee, and Delawares had pledged to send out parties to be led by French Canadian partisans. Approximately eleven hundred and fifty Indians participated in the northern campaigns in 1777; the great bulk of them, Canadian and Iroquois, were raised by John Butler and Daniel Claus at Niagara. The tribes around the Great Lakes contributed relatively few warriors, and the Shawnee and Delawares generally remained neutral.

Although only a small number of Indians harassed the Ohio frontier

Simon Kenton, a Kentucky frontiersman and Indian fighter. Portrait by an unknown artist. (The Filson Club, Louisville, Kentucky)

during 1777, they succeeded almost completely in tying down the settlers. In Kentucky, where food and clothing were scarce, the situation was desperate. Only the arrival of Bowman's militia from Virginia saved the defenders of St. Asaph's and Harrodsburg from starvation and surrender. Within the walls of beseiged Boonesborough were 200 women and children. They had only a two months' supply of bread by the end of the year when Bowman appealed for aid to General Edward Hand, commandant at Fort Pitt. Conditions along the more heavily populated and fortified upper Ohio were somewhat better. Forts Henry, Randolph, and Pitt at Wheeling, Point Pleasant, and Pittsburgh, as well as other blockhouses in the Monongahela country, provided sanctuary, although twenty-one luckless settlers caught outside Fort Henry in September died in an ambush led by Half King of the Wyandot.[9]

The situation might have been worse in 1777 had the bulk of the Delawares and Shawnee become involved in the war. In two separate incidents, the Ohio River frontiersmen, condemned by some as little less savage than their tawny neighbors, unfortunately antagonized the warriors residing closest to the borders. Late in 1777 several Shawnee, including Cornstalk, a consistent friend of the whites since the outbreak of the war, were wantonly murdered at Fort Randolph. The Shawnee then took up the hatchet against the Ohio frontiersmen whom they called "Long Knives" and early in 1778 began raiding the frontier. The second episode occurred in February when General Edward Hand marched on the Indian towns on the Cuyahoga River with 500 men, chiefly Pennsylvania militia, intending to destroy British stores reputed to be held by the tribesmen. The whites found no hostile Indians, but they did find some Delawares who, confiding in the friendship of the Americans, had settled about forty-five miles from Fort Pitt. At an abandoned village near Newcastle the militia killed an old man, the brother of the friendly Delaware chief, Captain Pipe, two women, and a small boy and captured two squaws. In disgust, Hand asked to be transferred. This "Squaw campaign," as it was derisively called, did nothing to endear the Americans to the Ohio tribes.

Hamilton at Detroit now had willing supporters among the warriors for raids against the Ohio in 1778. Ambitious to capture Fort Pitt, the British commander was restrained by his superiors, however. Both Carleton and his successor at Quebec, General Frederick Haldimand, refused to go beyond the instructions of the previous year limiting operations to mere diversionary raids designed to pin down American manpower, destroy supplies, and win over potential Loyalists in the back settlements.[10] Simon Girty and Alexander McKee, who escaped from Pittsburgh in March, as well as the French partisans at Michilimackinac and Detroit undertook such raids in 1778.

In the spring Kickapoo, Mascuten, and Wea from the upper Wabash and Mingo, Shawnee, and some Delawares struck all along the Ohio frontier from the Cheat and Monongahela to the Kentucky. Point Pleasant, the Kanawha, and the Greenbrier settlements were the focal points for the Mingo and Shawnee raids. For a week during May, 400 Indians beseiged Fort Randolph and then marched up the Kanawha burning and pillaging as they went. Throughout the summer small parties raided Kentucky, and in September, 400 warriors, mainly Shawnee under Black Fish, invested Boonesborough. Greatly outnumbered, the settlers had to resort to guile. After several days of negotiations the leaders agreed to renew their loyalty to George III if the braves withdrew immediately. These negotiations collapsed, however, when the Indians tried to seize the white emissaries. After attempting unsuccessfully to undermine the fort at Boonesborough during a driving rainstorm, the unstable Indians lost heart, gave up the seige, and then broke up into smaller parties to ravage the environs of the other stations.

The situation was more precarious on the Mohawk and Susquehanna frontiers where the major British blows fell during 1777 and 1778. The frontier settlements in the Mohawk Valley were extended along a narrow belt as far west as German Flats (modern Herkimer County) and north beyond Johnstown. To the south they reached the headwaters of the Susquehanna and the valley of Schoharie Creek beyond Middleburg. North of Albany, settlements in Charlotte County were scattered as far as Skenesborough and along the western and eastern shores of Lake Champlain. A large British army under Burgoyne invading from Canada was scheduled to meet 1700 Tories and Indians under Barry St. Leger marching east from Oswego through the Mohawk Valley. On August 3, St. Leger's mixed force beseiged 600 Whigs under Colonel Peter Gansvoort at Fort Stanwix, now called Fort Schuyler. Ticonderoga, hastily evacuated by Arthur St. Clair and the Continentals, had already fallen to Burgoyne. Terror struck the Whig militia of Tryon County. With no outside support they were threatened by two hostile forces and faced a savage foe; some fled, and others declared they would not fight. The Tories now began to show themselves in increasing numbers. As early as July 22 the Schoharie Committee of Safety reported that half the settlers had laid down their arms and were on the verge of joining the invaders.

Early in August General Nicholas Herkimer hastily gathered 800 militia and a party of Oneida Indians and advanced from Fort Dayton for the relief of the garrison at Fort Schuyler. But near Oriskany he fell into an ambush laid by eighty Tories and 400 Indians under John Butler and Joseph Brant. In the bitter, hand-to-hand fighting during a torrential rainfall, both sides lost heavily. With less than 400 men on their feet, the Americans, although in possession of the field, could not pursue the invaders who had lost 150 men, mostly Indians. The heavy casualties suffered by the Seneca may have led them to commit their worse excesses on the New York frontier later in the war. Even now the Indians had little stomach for continuing the seige of Fort Schuyler in the face of an advance by 800 men under Benedict Arnold. From Fort Dayton the audacious Yankee commander sent a half-witted Tory prisoner, Hans Host Schulyer, and a party of Oneida to St. Leger's camp to frighten the susceptible Indians with exaggerated tales of the strength of the approaching American relief column. Disheartened by their losses at Oriskany and the destruction of their supplies during a daring sortie against their camp led by Marinus Willett, the Indians bolted. On August 22, St. Leger raised the seige, abandoned his stores,

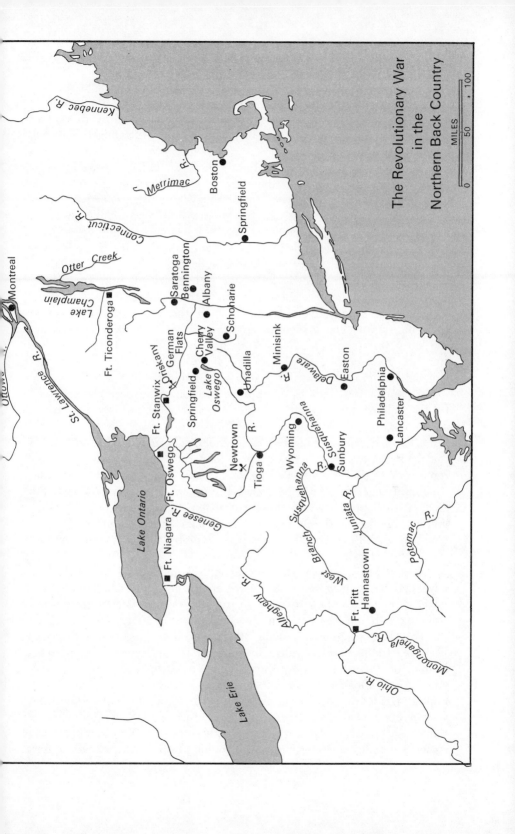

The Revolutionary War
in the
Northern Back Country

MILES

0   50   100

and retreated to Oswego. Brant and a few Mohawks passed through the valley, however, and fought their way to Burgoyne. But here, too, the Indians with the main British force were discouraged by the failure of Burgoyne to win a quick victory and by the restraints the British commander imposed on them.[11]

Burgoyne had used the 500 Indian warriors with his army for their psychological effect on the frontier settlers, and initially his bombastic threats to let loose the braves against the Whigs were effective. Panic-stricken, many settlers hastened to the British camp, and hundreds of others fled from the Vermont Grants. A seemingly minor occurrence, however, nullified Burgoyne's tactics and aroused the fury of the frontier population. A small party of Indians escorting Jane McCrae, fiancée of a Tory officer, senselessly killed the girl. Horrified, Burgoyne reiterated his orders that the braves abstain from indiscriminate warfare. This lost him the support of the bulk of the warriors who deserted early in August. The Whigs made good use of the incident, spreading the story throughout the New York and New England frontiers. Far from his base and short of supplies, Burgoyne dispatched Lieutenant Colonel Frederick Baum with 500 heavily laden German infantry, some Tories, and a few Indians to capture provisions purportedly collected by the Whigs at Bennington. A few miles short of his objective Baum allowed parties of Americans who claimed to be Loyalists to join his force. After they had infiltrated, these Americans enveloped and harassed the flanks of the British force when John Stark and a vastly superior force of Whig militia attacked on August 16. The defeat of Baum and a column sent to his rescue sealed Burgoyne's fate. He recrossed the Hudson in September and slowly retreated. Surrounded near Saratoga and unable to break through the American ring, he surrendered on October 17.[12] Thus ended the only attempt by the British to conquer the northern frontier.

Despite this setback the British and their Indian allies still held advanced bases in western New York and along Lake Champlain from which they were able to harass the frontier, raiding almost at will and leaving death and destruction in their wake. Out of Niagara and Unadilla the Tory leaders, John and Walter Butler, William Caldwell, and Barent Frey, led Indians and Loyalists burning for revenge over the indignities heaped on their families by the Whigs. The struggle on the Mohawk and Susquehanna became a war of savage, unsparing retaliation. British raiding parties initially struck almost with impunity. Operating from Crown Point, 500 men under John Fraser in the fall of 1778 scoured the vicinity of Skenesborough, along both sides of Lake Champlain and some forty miles up Otter Creek, destroying grain, livestock, and houses.

Along the Mohawk and Susquehanna the storm broke in May. A British force routed 300 Schoharie militiamen and burned Springfield; in June they destroyed Andrustown near German Flats. Early in July John Butler with a force of 1100 men, including 700 Indians who were mostly Seneca led by Old King, delivered the most telling blow in the Wyoming District. Defending the eight American forts and blockhouses were a militia regiment and a company of Continentals under the inept Zebulon Butler and Nathan Dennison. Forts Jenkins and Wintermoot surrendered promptly, but the defenders at Fort Wyoming were lured out and ambushed. In a savage battle, the merciless Indians gave no quarter to their armed opponents and killed almost 300 Whigs. The remaining settlers in Fort Wyoming surrendered. There was no massacre of unarmed men, women, or children at Wyoming, but the terrified survivors who fled the valley in the "great runaway" told a different story, one of horror and atrocities. So great was the panic that even Sunbury was abandoned, and the roads to the south and east were thick with settlers fleeing for their lives.[13] Some semblance of order was restored when General Lachlan McIntosh sent more than 300 troops under Colonel Daniel Brodhead to the Susquehanna, and Zebulon Butler with 100 men reoccupied Wyoming in August.

Reinforcements were also sent to the New York frontier when Colonel Peter R. Livingston after a tour of the Mohawk Valley reported that Schoharie, Cherry Valley, Fort Dayton, Stone Arabia, and Johnstown would be deserted unless an adequate force of Continentals was stationed in the region. In an effort to destroy the Indian and Tory bases, Colonel William Butler in October 1778 led 500 men of the 4th Pennsylvania Regiment on a sweeping raid along the upper Susquehanna. They burned the Indian village of Oquaga, destroyed 4000 bushels of corn and a great number of livestock and poultry, and according to the Indians, ravaged and killed the young wife of an Oneida chief. The enraged warriors took their revenge on November 11 when 800 Indians and Tories led by Walter Butler attacked 350 Continentals and 150 militiamen stationed at Cherry Valley, a major supply depot. Despite repeated warnings of the impending onslaught the inept American commanders were unprepared. During the attack on the garrison the uncontrolled Indians massacred over thirty men, women, and children in retaliation for the raids on Unadilla and Oquaga during the previous months. Up to that time there had been no reports by the Americans of atrocities against women and children. In the retreat Walter Butler was able to rescue some of the survivors; he released them under strong guard and sent away most of the Indians in disgrace. Haldimand at Quebec was shocked by the outrage and repeated his orders that the warriors were to be restrained. But the British and Indian raids continued. Passive defense even with the aid of Continentals had proved inadequate to protect the frontier; an offensive was necessary.

Developments on the northern frontier early in 1779 confirmed the lessons of the previous two years. The Indians and Tories under Joseph Brant raided Schoharie, the upper Susquehanna, and later penetrated as far as the Minisink District on the upper Delaware. The American commanders were helpless. From Wyoming Zebulon Butler complained that "it is aggravating to see the savage wretches drive off cattle [and] horses [,] burning and destroying, and we not able to attack them out of the Fort."[14]

The governments of New York, Pennsylvania, and Connecticut, those whose frontier settlers suffered directly, now appealed to the Continental Congress for relief. First, a regiment of Continentals under Colonel Edward Hand took up stations in Northampton and Cumberland counties; another posted at Pittsburgh and Kittanning on the Allegheny covered Bedford and Westmoreland counties, and the militia of Lancaster and Cumberland counties mobilized to defend the western portions of Pennsylvania. Since the lack of provisions and transportation ruled out any move against the British in Canada, Washington decided on a more limited objective—an expedition against the Indian villages and, if possible, the reduction of Niagara. Although American authorities had previously considered an invasion of the Indian country and attacks on the British posts, particularly Detroit, they had done little until 1779. In October 1778 General Lachlan McIntosh had attempted to move against Detroit from Fort Pitt, but rumors of a large Indian force, the lateness of the season, and the fact that the Pennsylvania militia could only be used for two months, forced him to abandon the attempt. He did establish two small posts, however: Fort McIntosh at the mouth of Big Beaver Creek, thirty miles below Pittsburgh on the right bank of the Ohio, and Fort Laurens on the Tuscarawas River.

The British were vulnerable along the Ohio and Mississippi rivers as two raids conducted in 1778 by George Rogers Clark and James Willing demonstrated. Since Willing, the ne'er-do-well son of a Philadelphia merchant family, had spent some time on the lower Mississippi, a Congressional committee had sent him on a raid to plunder the Natchez settlements and possibly to establish commercial connections with the Spanish at New Orleans. With about thirty men he set off from Fort Pitt on January 10, 1778, in a small boat, the *Rattlesnake.* Descending the Ohio and avoiding Choctaw patrols on the Mississippi, he struck the settlers at Manchac on February 21. After plundering the residents, Willing made for New Orleans where he was received by the Spanish governor, Bernardo de Galvez. The settlers at Natchez revolted against Willing's men, however, and with the aid of 100 British troops from Pensacola regained control of the lower Mississippi. Willing's expedition achieved the opposite effect of what Congress probably intended. Instead of facilitating the sending of supplies to the Ohio frontier, it called forth British reinforcements from West Florida and a virtual blockade of the lower Mississippi.[15] Virginia forces were able, however, to establish temporary control over the confluence of the Mississippi and the Ohio in the summer of 1778 when George Rogers Clark and a small band from the Old Dominion and Kentucky seized Kaskaskia.

The ungarrisoned Illinois country was a military vacuum, governed only by a civil magistrate, the Chevalier de Rocheblave, and inhabited principally by Frenchmen with little love for the British. Some merchants such as Thomas Bentley and James Murray who had contacts with the Kentucky and Ohio settlements may have encouraged, or indeed instigated, the American occupation of that region. George Rogers Clark learned of the situation in the Illinois country in 1777 when he sent two spies, Benjamin Lynn and Samuel Moore, disguised as hunters to Kaskaskia. After they returned, Clark traveled to Williamsburg and that winter proposed a scheme for the conquest of the Illinois towns to Governor Patrick Henry. Clark's motives for the secret expedition are not clear. If he intended to conquer the Illinois country as a preliminary step toward the reduction of Detroit, he was dissipating his meager forces against an objective lying in almost the opposite direction. However, Clark professed more immediate aims; he insisted that the Illinois country was essential to the British to control the Indians and send them against the Kentucky stations, to disrupt the American supply line from New Orleans, and to provision their garrison at Detroit.[16] Yet there were relatively few warriors in the Illinois country; those braves who were raiding south of the Ohio lived on, and east of, the Wabash. They looked to Detroit, not to Kaskaskia, for support. Moreover, the British garrison at Detroit was not provisioned from the Illinois country but from its own immediate vicinity and Montreal by way of the Great Lakes. Since there were no British troops in the Illinois country, as Clark well knew, they could not exercise the supposed control over the Mississippi and Ohio that he proposed to break by occupying the French villages.[16]

Whatever Clark's motives—and they may have been to establish land claims or to consolidate Virginia's right to the region north of the Ohio—fortune was with him when he departed on an ill-conceived and hazardous expedition. He carried two sets of instructions: public orders to raise 500 men for service in Kentucky, and private instructions to lead an expedition against the Illinois country. Even without informing his men of their true objective, Clark and his captains could raise only 170 men from Frederick and Fauquier counties, the Monongahela region, and the Holston settlements. After traveling down the Ohio to the Falls, the Holston men deserted when they learned that they were not to defend the Kentucky settlements, as they had been told, but to capture the French villages in Illinois. However, a band of Kentuckians under James Harrod joined the expedition, and Clark with 178 poorly equipped and poorly provisioned men continued down the Ohio. Short of food and uncertain of the location of their objective, near the mouth of the Tennessee by chance they met a party of American hunters who had left Kaskaskia eight days before. One of the hunters, John Saunders, guided Clark's men 140 miles overland to Kaskaskia where the nearly starved Americans arrived on July 4. On route from Virginia Clark had learned of the Franco-American alliance signed earlier that year. This information proved invaluable in winning over the French inhabitants whom the English merchants had already alienated. With no British garrison to oppose him, Clark took over Kaskaskia without a struggle. John Bowman and thirty men occupied Cahokia, and after Father Pierre Gibault and Doctor Jean Baptiste Laffont had won over the inhabitants of Vincennes, Captain Leonard Helm with thirty men established a post there. But the Virginia force was on the point of breaking up. With only 100 men prepared to remain, Clark was able to form but two companies of militia from men among the French inhabitants.

Hundreds of miles from any American base and without supplies, Clark was in a tenuous position. Only the support of Spanish officials across the river at St. Louis and French merchants helped him keep his force intact. One of the wealthiest merchants, Godfrey de Linctot of Cahokia, was invaluable in winning over the neighboring Indians. Clark adopted an audacious pose with the northern Chippewa, Ottawa, and Potowatomi during councils held that summer. If they wanted war, he would oblige them. This was a mere bluff for if the warriors attacked in force, Clark could not have withstood them. The immediate danger came from Detroit to the northeast.

Fortunately for the mixed Franco-American force under Clark, British commander Henry Hamilton was too eager to win a name for himself. Without waiting for orders or for the spring when the Indians would have been available for a protracted campaign, Hamilton decided to move immediately against Clark. He left Detroit with only 162 men, less than one-fifth of them regulars upon whom he could depend. But 350 Indians joined him by the time he arrived at Vincennes. After taking possession of the Wabash village on December 17, 1778, without firing a shot, Hamilton called a halt, and then compounded his error by dismissing the Indians until the following spring. Clark did not wait, how-

George Rogers Clark. Portrait by Jouett. (The Filson Club, Louisville, Kentucky)

ever. On learning from an informer, Francis Vigo, of his adversary's weakened position. Clark raised two companies from the French villages in the Illinois country and on February 5 started overland for the Wabash. After an exhausting trek, Clark with 180 nearly starved men reached Vincennes on February 24. The French inhabitants who had previously withheld their ammunition from Hamilton now joined the American commander. Hamilton's French Canadian militia from Detroit refused to support the British governor and with only thirty able-bodied men in Fort Sackville, Hamilton had no other choice but to surrender. The effect north of the Ohio was immediate. Captain Arent Depeyster, commandant at Michilimackinac, reported: "Mr. Hamilton's defeat has cooled the Indians in General."[17]

Yet Clark had neither the men nor the resources to exploit the situation. That summer John Bowman diverted the bulk of the militia Clark was relying on to join him for an expedition against Detroit in a raid upon the Indian village at Chillicothe in the hope of breaking up an expected attack by 200 Shawnee on the Kentucky settlements. Without adequate munitions, men, or provisions Clark called off his planned attack on Detroit. Establishing his headquarters at Fort Nelson at the Falls of the Ohio, he stationed James Shelby with a small garrison at Vincennes and left Colonel John Montgomery in charge of the Illinois detachment.

The Americans almost immediately consolidated their position. Virginia organized county government for the Illinois country with John Todd as county lieutenant and John Dodge as Indian agent. Clark's victories had provided some measure of security on the lower Ohio, and in 1779 when the Virginia legislature passed a land act regularizing the sale of land in Kentucky, many new settlers flocked to the region. Three hundred large boats arrived at the Falls in the spring of 1780 alone. So great was the influx of pioneers that the price of food shot up tremendously. Settlers and speculators alike rushed to the survey office opened in the area by George May. New stations were soon established: Lynn's Station on Beargrass Creek, ten miles from the Falls; Brashears Station at Floyd's Fork; and Sullivan's, five miles from the Falls. Harrodsburg was also expanded; Robert Patterson led one party to found Lexington and Isaac Ruddle led another to the Old Hickston settlement on the Licking. Martin's Station was established in the same neighborhood. From St. Asaph's came settlers to found Whitely's, Worthington's, Field's, and Pittman's Stations. Parties from east of the mountains settled in other communities. North Carolinians, including relations of the Boones, founded Bryant's Station on the north fork of the Elkhorn, and the McAfees returned from Virginia to reoccupy their old site. Stations dotted all of central Kentucky north and south of the river. Yet despite the relief offered by Clark's military victories in 1778–1779, the expanded settlements below the Ohio were not free of the Indian menace.

At the request of the northern states with exposed frontier settlements, the Continental army undertook a massive campaign in 1779 to crush the Indians. The immediate objectives of the expedition under Major General John Sullivan of New Hampshire were the elimination of the Indians and Tories located chiefly in the Finger Lakes region of New York, the Chemung Valley, and along the upper St. Lawrence, and, if possible, the capture of Niagara. Even if the campaign succeeded only in destroying their foodstuffs, the warriors would be forced to flee to the British posts where they would become an additional liability on the already overburdened supply system. A successful campaign would seriously weaken the British and Indians and relieve the frontier, freeing Continentals and militia to hold the Hudson Highlands. There was still a further objective. By 1779 Washington realized that the war might end in a deadlock with the United States confined to a strip of territory along the Atlantic. A western expedition in conjunction with Clark's operations north of the Ohio might secure for the infant republic the region west of the Alleghenies and south of the Great Lakes.

With these objectives in mind Washington carefully planned the campaign and assigned a considerable number of trained regulars to a three-pronged attack that was designed to converge simultaneously on the British and Indian bases in western New York. On August 10 Colonel Daniel Brodhead led 605 Continentals and volunteers from Fort Pitt up the Allegheny. After establishing garrisons at Kittanning and Mahoning, he penetrated overland into the Indian country but found the villages in northwestern Pennsylvania deserted. Through the incompetence of his guides, Brodhead was unable to join the other American forces and turned back. The columns assembled on the Mohawk and Susquehanna rivers had greater success. In April Colonel Goose Van Schiack and Marinus Willett led 558 men in a preliminary raid from Fort Schuyler through the Onondaga country, taking Indian women and children as hostages to force the warriors to act as scouts for the main American army. During June and July a large force under General James Clinton constructed 200 flat-bottomed boats at Canajoharie, hauled them by wagon over the hills to the head of Lake Otsego, and then floated down to Tioga to meet the main army. After spending five weeks assembling supplies, General John Sullivan's troops ascended the Susquehanna. Aware of the inadequacy of militia, Washington provided Sullivan with veteran, disciplined regulars, scouts, and a detachment of Daniel Morgan's riflemen. When Sullivan left Tioga after the rendezvous with Clinton he had nearly 4000 troops, artillery, and a train of 1200 packhorses.

The British were totally unprepared for this massive offensive. Initially, Haldimand in Canada was uncertain of the American objective and, consequently, was late in sending reinforcements under Sir John Johnson. The British never got beyond Oswego. John Butler with only a few regulars and rangers could not prevail on many Indians, who were already short of supplies, to join him. Convinced that there was no chance of stopping Sullivan by a major engagement, Butler and Joseph Brant favored a harassing withdrawal, but the Delawares and Seneca insisted on making a stand. On August 29, between 600 and 1200 British and Indians behind a crude breastwork faced 3200 Americans at Newton, near modern Elmira. The issue was quickly decided. An artillery barrage and bayonet charge by the Continental regulars against the enemy flank turned the Indian line. With most of his force in flight, Butler withdrew, leaving the field to Sullivan. Casualties were light on both sides, but the Indian country was open to the Continentals.

After burning two nearby towns, on September 3 Sullivan's men continued their march of destruction along the east side of Seneca Lake to Canadesaga and then westward through the Finger Lakes region. By the middle of the month, a shortage of supplies prevented them from pressing on to Niagara and forced them to turn back. They were disbanded at Easton, Pennsylvania, on October 15. Thus went out of existence the only force capable of winning the Northwest for the United States. But the Continentals had destroyed more than forty Indian towns and 160,000 bushels of corn. So complete was the devastation that few Indians returned to their lands. During the exceptionally severe winter that followed many died of starvation, and more than 5000 flocked to Niagara where Guy Johnson's Indian department fed and clothed them. Broken, the Six Nations never recovered.

Except for the immediate protection of the northern frontier, Sullivan's campaign was a practical failure. The braves, incensed over the destruction of their villages, became more impatient than ever with the restraints imposed on them by the British leaders during the almost continuous raids on the frontiers in the following years.[18]

Throughout the northern frontier the Americans had come to a standstill; in some areas they had retreated. Along the Ohio, Clark's victory, the result of audacity, simple luck, and Hamilton's miscalculation, had no lasting effect. Clark simply did not have the resources to hold his conquests or the supplies and munitions to keep the Indians favorably inclined toward the Virginians. With no aid arriving from the Old Dominion, he was not even able to supply his small garrisons at Vincennes and in the Illinois country. By 1779 Oliver Pollock, the merchant at New Orleans who had supplied and financed his force, had exhausted his credit, and $25,000 in bills drawn by Clark were protested by the merchants and authorities at New Orleans. Both Virginia and Continental currency depreciated rapidly in the Illinois villages, particularly after the arrival of eastern speculators. Unwilling to supply or sell goods without some assurance of payment, the French inhabitants turned mutinous and charged the Virginia government with oppression. Colonel John Montgomery, the military commandant, and John Todd, the county lieutenant, were at odds with each other. In disgust, Todd left the region. It was soon apparent that with a shortage of supplies and constant desertion by the troops, Virginia could not maintain garrisons in the Illinois country for long.

In 1779 American authorities were also forced to withdraw the garrisons from several of the posts along the upper Ohio. Constant harassment by the Indians under Captain Henry Bird and Simon Girty, the difficulty in procuring provisions, and the unreliability of the militia compelled Brodhead at Fort Pitt to evacuate Forts MacIntosh and Laurens as well as Fort Randolph at the mouth of the Kanawha.[19] Not only did the Americans abandon key fortifications along the Ohio, but they also lost control of the river, the vital lifeline from New Orleans. In October 1779 the Girtys, Matthew Elliot, and a party of 130 Indians ambushed Colonel David Rogers and sixty men in a flotilla bringing munitions from New Orleans to Fort Pitt. Rogers and forty men were killed, and Colonel John Campbell and five others were taken prisoner. Only one boat escaped.

Once again the frontiersmen along the Ohio were on the defensive as the British from Detroit and Michilimackinac rallied from the defeat of Hamilton and prepared again to let loose the Indians. But Virginia could do little, for in 1780 she faced for the first time a major threat from British forces invading the South.

◁ 8 ▷

Victory and Stalemate,
1780-1782

*D*uring the early years of the Revolutionary War the northern states had been the scene of the heaviest fighting. But failing to conquer New York, Pennsylvania, New Jersey, and Rhode Island, the British in 1779 opened a major theater of operations in the South. With royal troops in the upcountry, they expected that the Loyalists, purported to be a large group in the back country, would rally to the royal standard, freeing the British regulars to defeat the Whigs and to bring the southern states to submission.

For the first time since the abortive Loyalist and Cherokee uprisings of 1775–1776, the back settlements of the Piedmont felt the full impact of the war. In 1779, 1000 troops under Brigadier John Campbell were sent to fortify Pensacola and to hold West Florida and the lower Mississippi while 3000 men under General Augustine Prevost moved from St. Augustine against Savannah. Another force led by Colonel Archibald Campbell marched overland from East Florida against Augusta. The British hoped that Georgia, once secured, would be a base for operations into the Carolinas. Full assistance from the westerners and the Creeks and Cherokee would be essential to control the interior.

124

British military officials were to be disappointed in the support received from the Indians and back-settlers. Chastised some years before, the back-country Loyalists on the whole hesitated to commit themselves again to the royal cause unless British victory was certain.[1] The Creeks and Choctaw, often antagonistic toward one another, well remembered the fate of the Cherokee when they had attacked the frontiers in 1776. John Stuart, who had restrained the tribes earlier, for some years had great difficulty in holding the allegiance of the Indians although his department supported hundreds of destitute Cherokee. Moreover, George Galphin and the other American Indian commissioners, well-supplied with goods from the French West Indies, actively contested with the British for the favor of the Creeks. They were "a mercenary people," according to Stuart. "Conveniency and safety are the great ties that bind them."[2] Stuart, and after his death, Thomas Brown and Alexander Cameron, finally did win over the Choctaw, Chickasaw, some Creeks, and the renegade Cherokee, or Chickamaugas, under Dragging Canoe who had never recognized the Treaty of Long Island (1777) imposed by the victorious whites and had established themselves on Chickamauga Creek along the Tennessee River.

Had Brown and Cameron brought the Indians against the frontiers when the British began their major campaign, they might have held down a considerable portion of the Whig forces; according to Henry Laurens, president of the state council, perhaps as many as 10,000 South Carolina militia assigned for the defense of the seaboard would have been stationed in the back country to meet a large-scale Indian attack. But the British never did employ large bodies of warriors against the southern frontier. Many of the tribesmen were short of food, and their villages had been decimated by smallpox. Moreover, when Spain entered the conflict in 1779, the British diverted most of the Indians for the defense of West Florida. In the ensuing operations only 360 Creeks joined the British forces in Georgia and South Carolina, and between 1500 and 2000 Creeks served in West Florida.

Despite the support of the hundreds of Indians serving in West Florida, the British were unable to hold the province. Operating with greatly superior forces from New Orleans and Havanna, Governor Bernardo de Galvez between 1779 and 1781 cleared the lower Mississippi of British posts and seized Mobile and Pensacola. The latter town was particularly important to the British as a center to supply, and consequently to hold, the Creek Indians. The Spanish, having achieved their objectives of controlling the Gulf coast and the lower Mississippi, were content to maintain their position until the major powers decided the fate of the North American interior during the peace negotiations.

The Spanish were to base their claims to the Mississippi not only on the conquest of West Florida but also on a raid carried far up the Mississippi against the trading post at St. Joseph, presently Niles, Michigan. Initially, the raid on St. Joseph was merely an attempt by Spanish officials at St. Louis to placate the restless local Indians upon whom they depended. In January 1781 Lieutenant Governor Francisco Cruzat dispatched a party of militia and warriors under Don Eugene Poure against the undefended post. On February 12, Poure, in the name of the King of Spain, annexed the region from the St. Joseph to the Illlinois rivers and withdrew. That summer Cruzat informed his superiors of the incident as evidence to authenticate the Spanish claim to territory north of the Ohio River by right of conquest.[4] Clearly the efforts of the Spanish were limited to achieving their own aims on the Mississippi, and except for diverting some British and Indian manpower, they did not materially aid the American cause when the British between 1779 and 1781 directed their main effort against Georgia and the Carolinas.

The British invasion of the South began with the capture of Savannah and Augusta between December 1778 and January 1779 by forces under Prevost and Archibald Campbell. At this stage the American commanders, Generals Robert Howe and Benjamin Lincoln, were unable to prevent a junction between the British and the Creeks or to restrict the invaders to the region south and west of the Savannah River. The British hoped to expand their offensive into the Carolinas and use Loyalist militia to control the Georgia back country. Indeed, with the fall of Augusta in January 1779 some 1400 back settlers enrolled in twenty companies, but these "Crackers" would be loyal to the Crown only if the British were firmly in control and stationed large numbers of troops in the back country.

When it became apparent that British control would not go unchallenged, many of the back settlers began having second thoughts. Some renounced their oaths of allegiance to George III and joined the irregular partisans organized by Elijah Clarke, John Dooly, and John Twiggs. In February 1779 the Whig militia under Clarke, Dooly, and Andrew Pickens of the Ninety-Six District of South Carolina surprised and defeated a group of 700 Tories under Colonel John Boyd at Kettle Creek in Wilkes County. The bloody engagement was a forerunner of the savage fighting that was to take place between Whigs and Tories in the upcountry during the next three years. With this setback the British were forced to temporarily abandon Augusta, and many potential Loyalists in the back settlements were disheartened.

However, later that year the British once more took the offensive. Andrew Williamson handed over Augusta to the redcoats without a struggle in exchange for a royal commission. Four hundred hard-core Whigs in the interior then withdrew across the mountains in a long

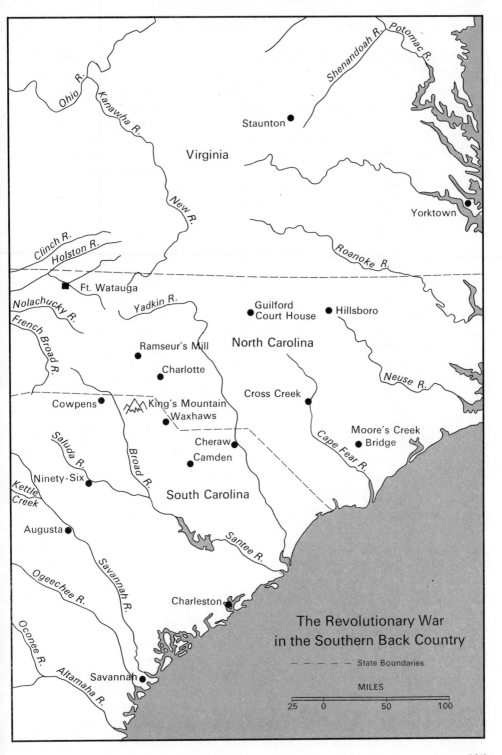

The Revolutionary War
in the Southern Back Country

– – – – – State Boundaries

MILES

25   0   50   100

hard march during the winter of 1779–1780. Apparently considering further resistance to be futile, most of the westerners, except for some eight to nine hundred settlers in Wilkes County, again submitted to British rule. Nonetheless, American control, even after the fall of Charleston in May 1780, continued to exist at various points in Wilkes County and in the Piedmont of South Carolina. The British needed to garrison the back country to control the region, protect potential Loyalists, and to overawe the Whigs under Francis Marion, Thomas Sumter, and Andrew Pickens who remained in the field. Consequently, the royal army established a series of posts from Augusta on the Savannah through the Ninety-Six District and Camden to encourage and protect the loyalists and sent Major Patrick Ferguson to raise a militia.

In some regions, between the Saluda and the Broad rivers where Loyalists were heavily concentrated, Ferguson was successful. Indeed, in the Orangeburg District and near the Little Pee Dee, the Tory militia retained local control until the spring of 1781 when Lord Cornwallis, the British commander in the South, withdrew his main army from the Carolinas. In the Camden and Cheraw districts, however, the Loyalist militiamen were untrustworthy and often deserted to the Whigs. Subsequent military reverses further disheartened the Tories. At Ramseur's Mill near the North Carolina border, the North Carolina militia on June 20, 1780, were able to crush nearly thirteen hundred poorly armed Loyalists, suppressing or driving out the Tory elements in North Carolina. In order to avoid being drafted into the Whig militia some eight hundred Tories gathered on the Yadkin River and escaped to join the main British army.

Despite these setbacks in the interior, Cornwallis on reaching Charlotte by the first week in September 1780 seemed to be almost in complete control. He had put Gate's army to flight at Camden on August 16, and two days later Banastre Tarleton had defeated Sumter.[5] Elijah Clarke and a corps of backwoodsmen failed to capture Augusta that month. For two days they besieged 150 Provincial corpsmen and 250 Indians under Thomas Brown but withdrew before a relief column of Tories raised by Lieutenant Colonel John Cruger at Ninety-Six. The hard-pressed American partisan commanders, Charles McDowell, Isaac Shelby, and Elijah Clarke, once more retreated as Cornwallis sent Tarleton and Patrick Ferguson to the base of the mountains to stamp out resistance and raise Loyalist recruits. Ferguson had with him about 800 militia, raised mainly from the Ninety-Six District, when he marched into Tryon County, North Carolina. Learning that the settlers beyond the mountains had fought against the British and were harboring refugees, he threatened to put their men to the sword and their settlements to the torch. Quickly, the mountain men under Isaac Shelby and John

John Sevier in the uniform of a Revolutionary War general. (Tennessee Department of Conservation)

Sevier gathered at Sycamore Shoals. With the invocation of their minister to strike the British with the "Sword of God and Gideon," the frontiersmen, now heavily reinforced from the Holston and North Carolina settlements, set off. Warned of the settlers' preparations by two Whig deserters, Ferguson recalled his men who had been given leave to visit their families in the area and retreated toward South Carolina. On October 7 while he was encamped on King's Mountain, the Whigs overtook, surrounded, and defeated him. Thirty-two Tories were condemned by a rude court-martial, and nine were hanged before Sevier and Shelby peremptorily put an end to the executions. Many of the Loyalists then joined the American forces to escape death or imprisonment.[6]

With the defeat of Ferguson's force, the western arm of the British advance, Cornwallis postponed his invasion of North Carolina and returned from Charlotte to Winnsboro to regroup. Unable to win a decisive victory over the Americans in the pitched battles of Cowpens and Guilford Court House early in 1781 or to eliminate the Continentals under Daniel Morgan and Nathaniel Green, Cornwallis left his base in South Carolina and struck northward in pursuit of Morgan and to his eventual defeat at Yorktown. While Cornwallis was moving north, some eight thousand troops, mostly Tories and provincial militia, still remained in South Carolina and Georgia. But as early as December 1780 the settlers in the Ninety-Six District became restless under royal control, particularly when Cornwallis proclaimed that all who had previously fought against the British must now actively support the royal forces to win pardon. Resentment in the back country mounted further when Loyalist partisans began to burn and pillage. After having put down their arms, Andrew Pickens and his followers once more took the field against the British. Aiding them were the back-country Whigs from Georgia under Elijah Clarke and William Few. They received a temporary setback from the Loyalists, however, on December 11 at the Battle of Long Canes. By the end of the year the British still retained such key points as Camden, Ninety-Six, and Georgetown.

With the march of Cornwallis into Virginia the British in Georgia and the Carolinas could not, without the support of the back-settlers, maintain their coastal bases and at the same time control the back country and cope with the partisan bands under Pickens, Marion, and Clarke. Greene's mobile, elusive irregulars invested various British outposts. Although repulsed near Camden and Ninety-Six, they took Motte, Granby, Orangeburg, and Georgetown since the British were forced to evacuate much of the upcountry in consolidating their positions. The Whigs finally captured Augusta on June 5, 1781, in an assault that saw the murder of Colonel James Grierson, the back-country Tory whom the Patriots particularly hated. So fearful was Pickens for the safety of the other Tory leaders such as Thomas Brown that he had them transferred across the Savannah for their own safety. In June the Loyalists between the Great Pee Dee and North Carolina laid down their arms, and early the next month the British left Ninety-Six, their last post in the back country of Georgia and South Carolina. Many Loyalists fought their way to Charleston and Savannah to be evacuated at the end of the war, but others flocked to the Whig standard so that they could remain on the frontier and protect their homes and property. By the summer of 1781 the back country was in Whig hands although marauding parties from both sides still roamed the interior.[7]

While the American regular and militia forces were combating the British invasion, the settlers on the outer edge of the frontier faced the menace of Indian raids inspired by Tories and the British Indian

Department. Although the bulk of the Cherokee remained quiet until 1780, and the British used most of the Creek, Choctaw, and Chickasaw warriors against the Spanish along the Mississippi and the Gulf coast, the Chickamaugas under Dragging Canoe on the Tennessee River posed a serious threat to the Holston-Watauga region as well as the new settlements made during the war.

For years the tribesmen had resented encroachments on their lands, and the Chickamaugas in particular had never accepted the extension of the boundary line below Long Island of the Holston west of the Cumberland Gap that William Christian and the other Virginia commissioners had obtained from the Cherokee in the Treaty of Long Island in 1777. Indian hostility notwithstanding, the frontiersmen rushed to the new acquisition particularly when North Carolina established Washington County and opened road connections from the Watauga, Nolichucky, and Holston regions. A strong current of migration, particularly from the Shenandoah, James, and upper Holston valleys of Virginia flowed toward the Tennessee country.

Judge Richard Henderson, after the failure of the Transylvania venture in Kentucky, was prominent in the colonization of French Lick (Nashville). To lead the enterprise he selected the well-known and experienced frontier leaders, James Robertson and John Donelson. During the winter of 1779–1780 Robertson led one party with the livestock overland while Donelson took the women, children, and thirty Negro slaves from Fort Patrick Henry at Long Island by boat. They descended the Holston, traveled to the mouth of the Tennessee, and then came up the Ohio and Cumberland rivers to French Lick. There they established eight stations, the two largest being Eaton's and Nashborough. Henderson, the only lawyer or jurist among the settlers, drafted a compact adopted on May 1, 1780, at a mass meeting of the pioneers. The signers agreed that the settlers of the eight stations were to elect twelve tryers, or judges, to settle disputes relating to property, debts, and land. The compact established no new political institutions, and persons accused of crimes were to be sent to North Carolina for trial in the regular courts. The "Cumberland Compact" related primarily to land since the settlers' claims rested solely on Henderson's Indian purchase of 1775, which Virginia had already disallowed and which, North Carolina was to disallow in 1783.[8]

The most pressing problem during the first years of settlement was defense against the Indians. To the Chickamaugas under Dragging Canoe it might have seemed that the new colony was "almost an act of benevolent providence intent on making their prospective victims more accessible."[9] These renegade Cherokee were quick to launch the attacks the settlers apparently so openly invited by exposing themselves.

Aided by wandering Creeks, Choctaw, Chickasaw, and even Delawares, they plagued the settlements for three years. Cut off from the East, the Cumberland pioneers were confined to their stockades. No new setlers came to join the 300 who had initially founded the colony. Many were killed; others left for Kentucky and the Natchez region or returned to their old homes. Without the determination of James Robertson, the Cumberland stations might well have abandoned in 1782.

The Indian attacks on the Cumberland settlements were part of a more widespread conflict waged after 1779 between the frontiersmen and the southern Indians, particularly the Cherokee. In the struggle to win the allegiance of the warriors, the American cause was handicapped by the encroachments on Indian lands of the white settlers as well as the fact that neither Virginia nor North Carolina were able to fulfill the promises made in the Treaty of Long Island to provide the natives with supplies and munitions. Consequently, when the fortunes of war turned against the Americans during the major British invasion of the South in 1779, the warriors, now more than ever, were inclined to follow the British who could easily supply them. But since the British were not able to control the militia of the North Carolina and Virginia back country during the early stages of the conflict, the Indian towns were left open to invasion when the warriors moved against the frontier settlements. During the later years of the Revolution the border witnessed a series of raids and counter-raids with the whites enjoying an advantage in numbers and resources. The Choctaw were generally lethargic; the Chickasaw were too far removed from the frontier settlements to pose a serious threat; and most of the Creeks joined the British in West Florida against the Spanish. The most direct and immediate menace came from the Upper Creeks and the Chickamaugas along the upper Tennessee River. Yet, at best, the hostile warriors kept a large force of back country militia occupied so that they could not be used against the British armies.

Once the British began their invasion, their agents instituted diversionary raids. In the spring of 1779 Walter Scott and John McDonald led 300 warriors against the Georgia and South Carolina frontiers, but the Indians quickly withdrew before a large force of militia. In the absence of the warriors, the frontier militia, 900 men led by Evan Shelby, John Sevier, and Arthur Campbell, gathered on the Clinch River, constructed boats, and managed to penetrate into the Indian country and surprise the towns. They spent two weeks systematically burning eleven Chickamauga villages. The campaign had little consequence since the women and children escaped, the Indians suffered few losses, and the British continued to supply the warriors. Dragging Canoe simply shifted his men to the impregnable Chattanooga Mountain where with the consent of Alexander McGilvry, the half-breed chief of the Creeks, they established the Five Lower Towns. At this point Thomas Brown enlisted the aid of the Cherokee who had signed the Treaty of Long Island and had hitherto remained quiet. Despite the efforts of Joseph Martin, the Virginia commissioner, to dissuade them, the Cherokee attacked the frontiersmen who had settled beyond the boundary line on Indian hunting grounds.

With little support from the British or the other tribes the Cherokee were no match for the whites. For two years John Sevier, Andrew Pickens, and Robert Anderson led sizable parties of Georgia and Carolina militia against their towns, systematically destroying the Indian settlements. In the fall of 1781 the land-hungry whites began a rush into the upper Tennessee country, and within a year they had penetrated up the French Broad River and into the valley of the Big Pigeon which was within a day's travel of the nearest Cherokee towns. John Sevier refused to carry out the orders of the North Carolina authorities to evacuate the squatters, and the war continued.[10] By the end of 1782 the whites had defeated the Cherokee.

With the evacuation of the British and Tories from Georgia and South Carolina the other Indian tribes did not pose a serious or immediate threat. In the final years of the Revolution the Americans had won a decisive victory in the South. However, this was not the case in the Northwest.

After the high point of the Whig military effort on the northern frontier in 1779, a stalemate existed during the final years of the war. Each side was only able to raid for short distances into the territory of the other, and neither was able to inflict a decisive defeat on the enemy.

From Niagara, Montreal, Oswego, Detroit, and Michilimackinac the British and the Indians, for almost two years swept along the entire northern frontier from the Otter River and Lake Champlain in the northeast to Kentucky and the Illinois country in the southwest. They sought to tie down American manpower, destroy supplies, and offset any drive against the British posts in Canada and the upper country. The years from 1780 through 1782 witnessed in this region the most bloody and desperate fighting of the war. Along the Mohawk and Susquehanna frontier the raiders struck even more frequently than before Sullivan's march through the Iroquois country in 1779. The campaign in 1780 opened in February with a blockade of Fort Schuyler. The next month warriors took the militia garrison at Skenesborough, and in April they attacked Riemendsnyder's Bush, Harpersfield, and Cherry Valley. In May Sir John Johnson with 400 rangers and 200 Indians "visited" his former home, Johnstown. Little Falls felt the sting the next month, and in July the warriors, using different routes, hit Schoharie, Cherry Valley, and German Flats. In August, Johnson with a corps of provincials, 200 Loyalist rangers, and a band of Indians roamed the Mohawk Valley, bringing death and destruction. Always arriving too late at the scene of desolation, the Continentals and militia were unable to defend the settlements against the hit-and-run tactics of the marauders. The single heaviest blow came in October when Brant and Johnson struck the Schoharie and Mohawk valleys. On October 19 at Stone Arabia they defeated 360 militia under Colonel John Brown and then withdrew before General Robert Van Rensselaer arrived with 1000 reinforcements. The region from Fort Hunter to Fort Plain was devastated. During the year the raiders destroyed over 1000 homes, 1000 barns, and 600,000 bushels of grain. Except for a few scattered settlements, above Schenectady the valley was desolate; it had ceased to be a military objective.[11]

The winter offered only a slight respite to the dispirited American militia. In February 1781 the warriors set out again, penetrating almost to Albany and Schenectady, which were now the frontiers, and even into New Jersey. The Americans could no longer maintain their exposed outposts; Fort Schuyler, periodically invested by the warriors, was abandoned and burned. However, the very success of the marauders the previous year now forced them to travel farther to reach their objectives and thus, ironically, made them more vulnerable. In April the Indians destroyed the deserted post at Cherry Valley and pillaged the settlements at Bowman's Creek. But at Coreytown late in June, Colonel Marinus Willett repulsed a sizable force of Indians and Tories led by John Doxstader. Small parties continued to strike during the summer of 1781 in the Schoharie and Mohawk valleys. Then raiders moved in force; Barry St. Leger led a diversionary attack along Lake Champlain, and Major John Ross led an assault of 700 men from Oswego against the Mohawk. After burning Warrenbush on the south side of the river, his followers fought their way back through the Whig militia and Continentals at West Canada Creek and escaped.

No sizable British force moved against the New York frontier during the first months of 1782, and when Joseph Brant prepared to attack in the summer, he was recalled by General Frederick Haldimand. In April the British government ordered the governor of Canada to halt all offensive action in view of the peace negotiations then being conducted in Europe. The British and the Indians still controlled Niagara and western New York when Brant, Johnson, and the other Tory leaders were sent west to help the interior tribes against the whites along the Ohio.[12]

In the western department several factors compromised the American military effort in the last years of the way: the paucity of supplies and munitions, the inadequacy of the Continental forces at Fort Pitt and dependent posts, the rivalry between Virginians and Pennsylvanians, and the exceptionally brutal treatment of hitherto friendly natives. In defiance of all reason and the orders of civil and military officials, frontiersmen from Yohogania and Ohio counties during 1778 and 1779 took over Indian lands for thirty miles along the northern tributaries of the Ohio River. On orders from Colonel Daniel Brodhead detachments from the 8th Virginia Regiment forcibly evacuated the squatters and burned their huts. These encroachments strengthened the position of the Delaware faction under Captain Pipe who favored the British. With the death in 1780 of White Eyes, the leading chief favorable to the Americans, Pipe's party won out, and the American garrisons on the upper Ohio were placed on the defensive.

The American commanders in the western department had great difficulty maintaining their garrisons. Brodhead bitterly complained that it was impossible to recruit men west of the mountains as the frontiersmen would not accept depreciated Continental currency. There was not enough money even to pay the troops already enlisted, and the ragged soldiers of the 8th Virginia Regiment at Fort Pitt went without pay for almost two years. Even more drastic was the problem of food. So short was the supply of beef and bread that Brodhead tried to impress supplies from the settlers, but he had little success. The nearly naked and starving soldiers were often close to mutiny. In the summer of 1781 the Virginia troops put down their arms and were barely persuaded from marching off. During the last year of the conflict General William Irvine could call on only 230 men to defend Fort Pitt and the other posts on the upper Ohio; this was a force too small even to defend the region much less to undertake offensive operations against Detroit or Niagara. The frontier militia was of little help. Indeed, the exasperated Brodhead charged that many of the settlers had migrated west of the mountains "chiefly to avoid militia duty and taxes. . . ."[13]

The frontiersmen were apparently willing, however, to engage in brief expeditions into the Indian country for plunder. In 1781 when Brodhead learned from the Moravian missionary, John Heckewelder, that the Delaware council had decided to break with the Americans, he gathered 150 regulars and an equal number of volunteers, crossed the Ohio, and attacked the Delaware towns on the Muskingum and Tuscarawas rivers. The Americans killed fifteen warriors and captured twenty men, women, and children before the militiamen forced Brodhead to turn back. The booty they collected was sold at Wheeling for £20,000. This brief campaign had little effect. By the following spring the situation on the upper Ohio was bleak. Both Washington and the new commandant at Fort Pitt, General William Irvine, who had less than 300 Continentals, ruled out any offensive action. Yet, according to one observer west of the Allegheny Mountains, Major William Croghan, "The country talks of nothing but killing Indians and taking possession of their lands."

The Christian Delawares at Gnadenhutten on the east bank of the Muskingum presented the frontier forces with an opportunity in 1782. Colonel David Williamson early in March led 300 frontiersmen from the Monongahela to the Indian villages. They seized and bound the Christian Indians; on the pretext of discovering evidence left by hostile warriors at Gnadenhutten, the whites condemned the psalm-singing Delawares and tomahawked some ninety defenseless Indians—twenty-nine men, twenty-seven women, and thirty-four children.

Some frontiersmen were to regret that day. The next summer 500 men under Colonel William Crawford—Williamson having lost the election as commander by only five votes—rode confidently into the Indian country. Possibly they hoped to complete the work begun at Gnadenhutten by finishing off the Moravians at Captives Town. Having previously taken much booty, they now brought with them coils of rope to pack their plunder and secure the horses they hoped to capture.[14] But instead of defenseless Christians they faced a sizable band of warriors under Captain Pipe who were thirsting for revenge, as well as British rangers under Captain William Caldwell. A total of 500 Wyandot, Mingo, Delawares and Munseys held the line. Crawford and his men were decisively defeated on the plain near Upper Sandusky on June 4 and 5. When discipline broke down among the retreating frontiersmen, many were killed, wounded, or captured by the pursuing warriors. Among those taken was the popular, but unfortunate William Crawford; upon him Captain Pipe and the Delawares took their revenge for the Gnadenhutten massacre. The Indians scalped him, laid hot ashes on his head, and roasted him alive over a slow fire. Outraged at such deliberate cruelty, British officials threatened to withdraw their troops if the Indians committed any such acts in the future.[15] The battle at Upper Sandusky proved that it would take a much larger, better trained and disciplined force than Crawford's militia to successfully invade and reduce the Indian country.

General William Irvine was hard pressed enough in protecting the frontier settlements without leading an offensive against the Indian towns. Any expedition against Detroit or Niagara was impossible. On July 13 over three hundred and fifty Tories and Indians under the Seneca, Kiyashuta, destroyed Hannastown, located thirty-five miles east of Fort Pitt on the Forbes Road; and in September the Indians struck again at Wheeling.

It was at this point, late in the summer of 1782, that the British commanders received orders to recall the hostile warriors. The war on the upper Ohio was ended, although the Americans reported continued Indian raids at Sunbury on the Susquehanna.

The inability of the frontiersmen on the upper Ohio to aid offensive operations against the northerwestern Indians greatly prejudiced the chances for any attack George Rogers Clark might launch against Detroit from Kentucky. From 1780 on, Clark and the Kentuckians, beset with problems of insufficient men and supplies, were on the defensive as the British continuously raided the Illinois country and the settlements south of the Ohio. In the spring of 1780 Captain Patrick Sinclair sent a large force of whites and Indians of the lake region from Michilimackinac against the Illinois villages and the Spanish settlement at St. Louis. Warned of the impending siege, the Spanish, Americans, and French were able to ward off the raiders who, owing to the defection of the Fox and Sauk Indians, did not press the assault. The second prong of the British attack was directed against the Kentucky settlements, but the Indians also struck as far east and south as Washington, Montgomery, and Greenbrier counties.

The Kentuckians were left to their own resources when the British and the Indians arrived. One party invested Vincennes, another created a diversion at the Forks of the Ohio, and a third with artillery under Captain Henry Bird in June besieged Ruddle's and Martin's stations on the Licking. The settlers, mostly Germans who spoke no English, quickly surrendered. Short of supplies and fearing that the Indians might get out of control, Bird slipped back across the Ohio taking more than three hundred and fifty prisoners with him. Many of the captives subsequently joined the British forces, and others accepted land and settled near Detroit and Niagara.

The surrender or Ruddle's and Martin's stations dampened the morale of the settlers of the other forts in Kentucky, so much so that John Floyd reported that many were preparing to evacuate. Clark, who had returned to Harrodsburg from Fort Jefferson at the mouth of the Ohio, had great difficulty in raising men, particularly since many seemed more interested in locating land claims than in joining him on a retaliatory expedition. The strong-willed Clark promptly closed the land office, placed a guard on the Wilderness Trail to prevent anyone from leaving the country, and then raised "volunteers." Aided by Benjamin Logan and Thomas Slaughter, he was able to gather 1000 ill-equipped and poorly provisioned men at the mouth of the Licking. Crossing the Ohio on August 1, they followed the trail taken by John Bowman the year before to Chillicothe on the Miami River and then to Piqua on the Mad River. Here the hated Girty brothers with only seventy warriors put up a determined resistance. Short of supplies, the Kentuckians could not continue and, on half-rations, withdrew back across the Ohio.[16]

A chronic lack of provisions—only whiskey seemed to be in abundant supply—prevented the Kentuckians and Virginians from maintaining a sustained offensive north of the Ohio or from supporting garrisons at Vincennes and the Illinois country. The inhabitants resisted all attempts to be forced to accept the worthless Virginia currency, and unable to obtain money, food, or clothing, Clark's troops deserted. He found it impossible to maintain the garrison at Fort Jefferson five miles below the mouth of the Ohio. Encountering repeated attacks by the Chickasaw, Choctaw, and Cherokee in the summer of 1781 and with the garrison under Robert George reduced by desertion, death, and sickness, the Virginians evacuated the post.

The Kentucky settlements were without the protection of outlying forts when the British and Indian parties again began raiding during 1781. With hostile parties penetrating as far east and south as the Sandy and Clinch rivers and Powell's Valley, the militia of the interior counties was confined. The situation was most critical in Kentucky where the garrisons, dispersed over a wide area, could not offer adequate protection against a mobile enemy who struck quickly at scattered points and then disappeared. Nor were the Kentuckians able to mount a counterattack. In the winter of 1780–1781 Governor Thomas Jefferson of Virginia proposed raising 2000 men mainly from Lincoln, Jefferson, Ohio, Monongalia, Hampshire, Ohio, Berkeley, and Greenbrier counties for an expedition against Detroit, but the militia available to Clark for such a campaign fell far short of expectations. Many men refused to leave their homes exposed to attack. Perhaps others felt, as did Colonel Daniel Brodhead at Fort Pitt, that the expedition was merely an excuse for Virginia to acquire more land. Some militia in the Monongahela region, embittered by the dispute over the boundary line with Pennsylvania, refused to contribute men and supplies to Clark's force. One hundred Westmoreland county militia under Alexander Lochry did volunteer, but they were annihilated in August by Joseph Brant in an ambush on the Ohio. The militia of Kentucky simply could not supply the 2000 or more men necessary for the expedition. At best, the three counties, Fayette, Lincoln, and Jefferson, could only muster 1200 men.

Colonel George Slaughter's small force in Fort Nelson at the Falls of the Ohio, destitute of clothing, food, and money, was in a deplorable condition. His patience at a end, Slaughter threatened to evacuate his men. When Clark arrived at the Falls early in September, he found that Benjamin Logan and John Todd had been able to assemble only 700 militia. With the season so far advanced and with so few troops available, the officers decided to merely garrison the stations and to

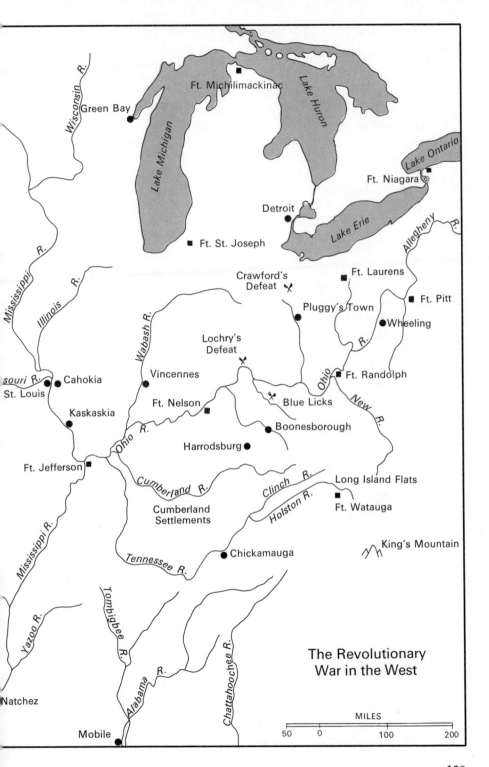

The Revolutionary War in the West

MILES

50 0   100   200

139

apply to Virginia for a force of regulars to capture and hold Detroit.[17] Discouraged, that winter Clark even thought of retiring, but his request was refused so peremptorily that he could not resign with propriety. Yet Clark was no longer the hero in Kentucky that he once had been. "He has lost the confidence of the people," Arthur Campbell snidely reported, "and it is said becoming a Sot; perhaps something worse."[18]

In Kentucky, 1782 was the "year of blood." Ironically, the British and Americans each feared the offensive potential of the other. The British had 400 men at Detroit and 100 soldiers at Michilimackinac, mostly regulars. Nonetheless, apprehensive over an invasion from Kentucky and Fort Pitt, Captain Arent DePeyster at Detroit sent out Indian parties to keep the Americans off balance. The frontier militia of Kentucky, numbering some 1300 men, had an almost impossible task once the raids began: to garrison Fort Nelson at the Falls and at the same time to protect the defenseless women and children in the stations. Many settlers planned to leave. When the British and Indians struck their major blows that summer, the pioneers at McAfee's and Kincheroe's stations on the Salt River evacuated.

In August Alexander McKee, William Caldwell, and Simon Girty led several hundred braves across the Ohio. One party invested Bryant's Station, only five miles from Lexington, but having suffered some casualties and unable to take the post by surprise, the Indians withdrew. By August 20 the raiders reached Blue Licks and took up an advantageous position on a wooded ridge, hoping to ambush the militia pursuing them—182 men from Fayette County under John Todd, Stephen Trigg, and Daniel Boone. The next day the reckless frontiersmen fell into the trap. After drawing the fire of the Kentuckians, the Indians charged the disorganized militia and in the ensuing melee killed 140 of them and captured 100 rifles abandoned by the fleeing whites. Blue Licks was a disaster, for a disproportionately large number of those lost were both militia and civil officers. After recrossing the Ohio the warriors proceeded to Wakitamike where McKee and Girty received orders from DePeyster prohibiting further incursions against the frontier. These instructions had been sent from England earlier that year in anticipation of the peace negotiations in Europe.

The sequel to Blue Licks came in November 1782 when Clark mustered almost all of the militia of Kentucky, 1050 men, crossed the Ohio, and moved up the Great Miami. But he was unable to bring the Indians to an engagement. By the eighteenth day of the campaign Clark's men had killed only twenty Indians; they had not been able to impair the fighting power of the northwestern tribes.[19]

The highpoint of Clark's successes had come in 1779. In the closing years of the Revolution he had been forced to withdraw south of the

Ohio and had not been able to launch an attack against Detroit. At best, he had attempted through raids in force against the advanced Indian villages to form a "roof" for Kentucky. Despite these defensive tactics, in the last years of the Revolution the Indians had inflicted heavy losses on the Kentucky stations. Orders from London, not Clark's forces, brought Indian attacks to a halt late in 1782. The warriors remained in control of the region south of the Great Lakes and protected the British garrisons at Niagara, Detroit, and Michilimackinac. Only a large, well-trained, and well-supplied army—one which did not then exist on the frontier—could have won the Northwest by force. But what Clark and the frontier militia had failed to achieve in the field, the American diplomats in Europe, Benjamin Franklin and John Jay, were to attempt to win at the conference table.

◁ 9 ▷

The West in the Diplomacy of the Revolution

W̰̰̰̰̰̰̰̰̰̰̰̰̰̰̰̰̰̰̰̰̰̰̰̰̰̰̰̰̰

hile frontiersmen and Indians were waging a bloody, but inconclusive struggle in the Old Northwest, in Philadelphia, Madrid, Paris, and London politicans, statesmen, and diplomats were peacefully pondering the fate of the North American interior.[1] Critical to their discussions was the question of the boundaries of the United States vis-à-vis the Floridas and Canada, and impinging on this point were the issues of the navigation of the Mississippi River, the North American balance of power, the Newfoundland fisheries, the debts owed by Americans to British merchants, and the disposition of the American Loyalists and their property. During the preliminary discussions and actual negotiations leading to the Treaty of Paris in 1783 the Americans sought several goals: first independence; second, the right to participate in the Newfoundland fisheries; third, recognition of the charter claims of the states to the region between the Appalachian Mountains and the Mississippi River; and finally, the right of free navigation of the "father of waters." The Americans were to argue for as favorable a boundary as possible concerning West Florida to the south and Canada to the north.

The aims of the contending European powers, Great Britain, France, and Spain, varied. By a treaty signed with the United States in 1778 the French had pledged to fight for the independence of the new nation and had renounced any territory in North America. American independence would satisfy their primary goal of weakening Great Britain. But the French foreign minister, the Comte de Vergennes, hoped that the British would retain the region north of the Ohio as a counterweight against the United States to force the infant republic into a closer dependence on the Bourbon monarchy. On other issues the French supported their Spanish ally in her claims to the region south of the Ohio, the Floridas, and on the exclusion of the Americans from the navigation of the lower Mississippi River. Spain had entered the war against Great Britain as an ally of France, not the United States. Her first concern was Gibraltar; in North America she sought primarily to secure a buffer against possible Anglo-American enroachment on Mexico. Consequently, the Spanish desired the Floridas, control of both banks of the Mississippi south of the Ohio, and the sole right of navigation of the river.

The conflict between Spanish and American interests was painfully evident when Spain, before entering the war, attempted in 1778–1779 to mediate between the belligerent powers. At the request of Vergennes, Congress sought to define its terms for concluding the conflict and its instructions to plentipotentiaries to be sent to Europe. The delegates were by no means agreed on the importance of the West. Some, such as Henry Laurens of South Carolina, were apparently willing to concede the navigation of the Mississippi in exchange for an alliance with Spain; a few such as Governor Morris would accept Spanish control of the Southwest and British retention of the region west of Lake Erie and Lake Michigan if the exigencies of war required such sacrifices. Some delegates were primarily concerned with commercial and fishing concessions of direct benefit to the northern states. Since under their colonial charters the southern states had the most extensive claims to the western lands, their representatives held out strongly for the Mississippi River as the western boundary and for the full right of navigation.[2]

In drawing up terms for negotiations, Congress sought to placate every faction by including conditions to satisfy all sections and states. The cession of Canada and Nova Scotia by Britain to the United States was desirable but was not made an ultimatum. However, Congress stipulated, if Canada was to remain in British hands, it was to be limited to the boundaries specified in the Proclamation of 1763, not those set by the Quebec Act of 1774. Congress claimed the West by the boundaries it proposed for the United States: on the north, a line from Lake Nipising to the Mississippi; on the west, the Mississippi; and on the south, a line following the 31° north latitude, the Chattachoochee, Flint, and

St. Mary's rivers. By acknowledging Spanish control of the Floridas the American government naively hoped to win Spanish recognition of the American right to navigate the Mississippi, a port of deposit for American traders below the 31° north latitude, and the region south of the Ohio.

In October 1780 the delegates adopted a report written by James Madison of Virginia justifying the American claim to the interior and the right of navigation of the Mississippi. Congress based its claim primarily on the right of succession to the sovereignty over the region previously excercised by the British Crown. Only as a secondary argument did Congress cite military conquests. If the Spanish claimed the American interior on the basis of military conquest, the American position could not be denied, for the United States had a more extensive claim: it was already in possession of the *important* posts in the Illinois country and on the Wabash. The Spanish, holding no post north of West Florida except Natchez, had an inferior claim.[3]

The following year the fortunes of war strengthened the Spanish position. In 1781 Virginia was forced to withdraw her garrisons from the mouth and the north bank of the Ohio, and at the same time the Spanish extended their military operations, thereby improving their claims in the winter of 1780–1781. On November 22, 1780, Captain Balthazar de Villiers and a detachment of troops from the Arkansas River took possession of the east bank of the Mississippi. And in February 1781 Captain Eugenio Poure at St. Joseph formally proclaimed Spanish possession of the Illinois country. By the summer of 1781 when West Florida also fell to Spanish arms, the court of Madrid had established a better right than the United States to possession by military conquest. Although the Spanish attack on St. Joseph initially was not undertaken to establish a claim to the region east of the Mississippi, Spanish diplomats used it for that purpose during the negotiations.[4]

The Spanish had another factor operating in their favor, for military developments in the southern states made it highly desirable that Congress placate Spain in order to obtain direct military aid against the British who had invaded Georgia and South Carolina and were threatening to occupy the entire South. Within a month after voting to instruct John Jay, the American plentipotentiary in Madrid, to insist on American retention of the transmontane region and the navigation of the Mississippi River, delegates from the threatened southern states advocated concessions to Spain in the West. Confronted with an ever-deepening military crisis, Congress in 1781 voted to waive the right of navigation and instructed the American ministers in Europe to follow the lead of the French court on the question of the western boundaries. The French ambassador at Philadelphia, who exerted great influence on the Gallican or pro-French faction among the delegates, believed that Congress would make any sacrifice—even acceptance of the Appalachian Mountains as the western boundary—in order to win direct Spanish support and achieve what all considered the essential point, recognition of the independence of the American republic.[5]

Fortunately for the United States, the need for Spanish aid was eliminated when Washington and Rochambeau later that year forced Cornwallis and a British field army to surrender at Yorktown. Happily, the American representatives, John Jay and Benjamin Franklin, in the ensuing peace negotiations in Paris, did not follow their instructions. Instead, they virtually cut themselves off from the Secretary of State for Foreign Affairs, Robert R. Livingston, and negotiated independently on the issue of the boundaries.

The surrender of Cornwallis was decisive; although the British were subsequently to win substantial victories in other theaters of the war, most British politicians and ministers, skeptical for some time, were now convinced that it was impossible to win a military victory in America or reduce the former colonists to obedience. They must make peace. Among the new ministers who took office in March 1782, the Earl of Shelburne was to play the key role in the ensuing negotiations. Long opposed to the war, but reluctant to recognize the independence of America, Shelburne hoped to lay the foundations for future Anglo-American relations, particularly commercial ties, by making concessions to the new nation. A disciple of Adam Smith and an optimistic, but uncritical proponent of free trade, he had no misgivings about seeing the United States in possession of the region between the Appalachian Mountains and the Mississippi River; he hoped that both English-speaking peoples would share in the economic development of the hinterland. Yet Shelburne was not a free agent. During the negotiations of 1782, news of the relief of the besieged British bastion of Gibraltar increased the militantcy and, consequently, the demands of some English ministers. The political situation in London, the balance of power in North America, and the international rivalries all impinged on the boundary negotiations. Moreover, the need to win public concessions for the Loyalists led Shelburne during the summer and fall of 1782 to attempt to retain the region north of the Ohio as a Tory sanctuary.

In 1782 diplomats of four nations, the United States, Great Britain, France, and Spain, undertook to decide the disposition of the North American interior. Initially, John Jay carried on discussions with the Conde de Aranda, Spanish minister to Versailles, and Joseph Mathias Gerard de Rayneval, first secretary at the French Ministry of Foreign Affairs. At the same time, Franklin was negotiating with Richard Oswald, an emissary of Shelburne, and later with Henry Strachey, a British undersecretary of state. Although Franklin, Jay, and John Adams, who later participated in the discussions in Paris, were formally bound by the Congressional instructions of 1781 specifying that they take, as a last resort, the advice of the French Court, that is, Vergennes and Rayneval, Robert R. Livingston strongly urged them to secure the Mississippi River as the western boundary of the United States. Spain, whose claims to the West were based only on military conquest, had no right to the interior, the Foreign Secretary contended. If George III had any right to the backlands, it was as king of the American people. Having ceased to be their monarch, his rights also terminated, and the American government succeeded him as sovereign. Occupation of the region west of the mountains, according to Livingston, constituted the best claim.[6]

Except for the political necessity of terminating the conflict, the British position was not well defined in the spring of 1782. But in April 1782 the ministry sent orders to halt offensive operations from the upper posts along the Great Lakes, and at the discretion of the new commander-in-chief, Guy Carleton, to evacuate the army from the coastal cities. Recognition of American independence was to be a bargaining point, not a condition granted prior to, or during, the peace negotiations. Shelburne was not adverse to American occupation of the hinterland, but he and his colleagues never seriously considered giving up Canada, which Shelburne, for one, considered valuable as a trade corridor to the Mississippi Valley. The subsequent difficulties in the negotiations lay in defining the boundaries between Canada and the United States in the West and in setting aside backlands as a sanctuary for the Loyalists.

It was Richard Oswald, Shelburne's agent, who initially suggested to Franklin in Paris that both nations might share in the economic development of the transmontane region. A Scottish merchant, slaver, and colonial entrepreneur, the naive Oswald did more to plead the cause of the United States than that of Britain. His discussions with Franklin during April and July of 1782 became the basis for later, more formal Anglo-American negotiations. In April Franklin submitted to Oswald a list of the conditions he considered indispensible for peace and another list he considered advisable. On the first list were British recognition of American independence, restriction of the boundaries of Canada—preferably to those in force before the passage of the Quebec Act—and the right of Americans to engage in the Newfoundland fishery. Among the advisable points, Franklin asked for the cession of Canada and suggested that the vacant lands in the back country could be sold to raise money for property destroyed by the British and Indians and to indemnify Royalists for the confiscation of their estates. Franklin was later to regret this last proposal and did not mention it to John Adams who arrived in Paris later.

Shelburne initially rejected the cession of Canada and indicated that the British would not acknowledge American independence without some compensation for the Loyalists. For his part Franklin, in discussing the matter with Oswald on July 10, insisted that the back country be ceded as a necessary condition for peace without any stipulation on the Loyalists. Despite these obvious differences Oswald was optimistic that Franklin would drop his advisable terms and that the provisions he considered necessary for a treaty would not be an obstacle to further negotiations. On August 29 the British cabinet decided on its terms. The ministers would retain Canada, no matter how imprecisely defined, and would not at this time give specific recognition of American independence. On receiving instructions based on these conditions, Oswald was dissatisfied, pointing out that a refusal to grant the Northwest to the Americans would merely raise difficulties. It would be impossible, he argued, to convince Franklin, despite his previous suggestion, to give up the region south of the Great Lakes or to allow it to be sold as compensation for the Loyalists as he had originally suggested in April. If the territory north and west of the Ohio, annexed to Canada by the Quebec Act, was relinquished by Britain, Oswald foresaw no difficulty. Indeed, he hoped the American commissioners would agree to British retention of West Florida with its boundary extended north along the Mississippi at the expense of the claims of Georgia and the Carolinas.[7] What the Scottish dilettante blithely ignored, of course, was how, short of continuing the war, the Spaniards could be persuaded to give up what they had conquered.

The disposition of the back country contemplated by Oswald and Franklin contrasted directly with the aspirations of the court of Madrid. The goals of Spain, who was generally supported by France, were clear and fixed: Gibraltar—then besieged by a combined Bourbon naval force—and the exclusion of Anglo-American influence from both the coast of the Gulf of Mexico and the lower Mississippi. Since Spanish arms had already conquered Mobile, Pensacola, and the British posts on the lower Mississippi, as far as the court of Madrid was concerned, there remained only the formality of affirming perpetual Spanish possession of the surrounding territory. The Conde de Floridablanca, the leading Spanish minister, hoped to have England remain in control of the region north of the Ohio.[8]

The Spanish minister at Versailles, Aranda, persistently pressed these points while confronting Jay during July and August. He had the full support of the wily and ingenious Rayneval who drew up several memoranda on the question of the back country. In contending for the Mississippi as the western boundary, Jay cited primarily the charters granted by the British Crown to the colonies, the royal Proclamation of 1763, and the fact that the Americans had actually settled beyond the Appalachian Mountains. Aranda claimed the transmontane region by right of conquest and as a dependency of Louisiana, which France had ceded to Spain in 1763.

Rayneval "mediating" between the two allies of France, adopted the Spanish position. Lightly dismissing the "ephemeral excursion" of George Rogers Clark against Kaskaskia and Vincennes, he rejected the American contention that the United States had succeeded the Crown of Great Britain to the sovereignty of the region between the Appalachians and the Mississippi, or that the Americans had any rights to the West deriving from the colonial charters. This region was never part of the original colonies, he contended, for it was acquired by the British only by the Peace of Paris of 1763. Spain through her conquests held West Florida and was in military occupation of the region north of the province. The area beyond the Ohio was in British hands. Consequently, Britain and Spain, the two nations in possession, not the United States, were to decide the disposition of the transmontane region. If, indeed, the Americans had settled on the Ohio, the sale of lands along the river by Virginia could not be regarded as effective possession. Finally, Rayneval concluded, since the ruler of both banks of any river controlled the course of that stream, the navigation of the Mississippi below the Ohio belonged exclusively to Spain.

As a "compromise," however, the Frenchman proposed a line running between Mobile and Pensacola on the Gulf of Mexico and roughly up the Alabama, Coosa, and Tennessee rivers to the Ohio as the boundary in the West between Spain and the United States. Jay refused this solution, declaring that he was not authorized to depart from the boundary of the Mississippi River as demanded by Congress.[9]

On Rayneval's departure from Paris early in September for a conference in London with Shelburne, Jay became convinced that the French were seeking to keep the direction of American diplomacy in their own hands until Spain achieved her aims for North America; he thought that they would not support the United States on the issues of the western boundary or the fishery, and that they would be willing to postpone British acknowledgment of American independence until the conclusion of the peace. Indeed, should the belligerents agree to a cessation of hostilities on the basis of *uti possedetis,* the British would retain vital American territory. Consequently, Jay began overtures to Shelburne through Oswald and Benjamin Vaughan, a busybody British politician with little knowledge or sense, for a quick resolution of those issues still outstanding between the Americans and the British that Franklin had previously discussed: navigation of the Mississippi and the disposition of the transmontane region. American rights on these points, Jay suggested, devolved from the laws of nature and the successful Revolution that had vested in the United States the territorial rights of Great Britain. During the first week of October Jay drafted a set of articles subsequently approved by Oswald and Franklin. According to these terms the boundary of the United States would run along the 45° north latitude to the St. Lawrence and Lake Nipising, down the Mississippi River to the 31° , and then east by the Chattahoochee and St. Mary's rivers. Oswald willingly conceded the back country in exchange for some compensation to the Loyalists.

The sticking point to further negotiations was the commission from the British government to Oswald authorizing him to confer with representatives of the *colonies*. Jay insisted that it be with the ministers of the *United States* for he feared Spanish and French duplicity on the boundary question. To negotiate unilaterally, the American ministers needed a clear guarantee of independence from the British. The dispute on Oswald's commission held up negotiations for two months and lost the Ontario Peninsula for the United States. Although the British had initially agreed to restrict Canada to the limits set by the Proclamation of 1763 and a line from Lake Nipising to the Mississippi, in the end they obtained the boundary of the 45° north latitude and the Great Lakes.[10]

Jay's anxieties were not fully justified. Shelburne in his discussions with Rayneval on the boundary question dismissed the American claim to the Mississippi based on charter rights as foolish. Although Rayneval was apparently noncommittal, Shelburne was convinced that the French would support their American ally on the issue of independence, but not on the other issues in contention. The British then made one more effort for the Loyalists. After a cabinet meeting on October 17, the ministers instructed Oswald to secure the region north of the Ohio or a portion of Maine as a refuge for the Tories. They accepted joint Anglo-American navigation of the Mississippi but declined for the present to allow free trade between the two nations. Oswald was to strongly urge the payment of debts owed to British merchants by the Americans, but above all, he was to obtain a definite settlement that would eliminate future disputes. Significantly, Henry Strachey, an undersecretary who was sent to Paris to join Oswald, was instructed to yield to the demands of the Americans on the boundaries rather than defer settlement of the issue to a postwar commission. Shelburne seemed to have been especially concerned about putting up a public front in behalf of the Loyalists for he instructed Strachey that the record of the negotiations in Paris must show "authentically" that every effort had been made in support of the Tories and the British creditors.[11]

The American commissioners, including Adams who had by this time arrived in Paris, refused to accept British retention of the Northwest as compensation for the Loyalists, but they were willing to compromise on the boundary in the North. Instead of the Nipising line they offered the British a choice: either the line 45° north latitude, or the St. Lawrence River and the Great Lakes. The British choose the latter, with the Mississippi limiting American territory on the west. Unable to move the Americans on the other points[12] Oswald and Strachey signed the preliminary treaty on November 30. Once the British and Americans had come to an understanding, Spain and France fell into line. Spain received both East and West Florida but recognized the 31° north latitude, the Flint, Chattahoochee, and St. Mary's rivers, as the southern boundary of the United States.

Unwilling to carry on the war in North America, the British conceded the interior to the United States. Shelburne, the key minister, was predisposed to the concession in the hope that Great Britain would share in the future development of the Mississippi Valley. Only the need for some gesture in behalf of the Loyalists led him to make a halfhearted, last-minute attempt to retain the Northwest. In the end, the British had to content themselves with the Ontario Peninsula south of Lake Nipising where some Loyalists had been settled as early as 1780. Yet the specific boundary established between Canada and the United States was "apparently as much the result of chance as of any deep appreciation of the vital issues involved."[13] The diplomatic agreement notwithstanding, the Northwest still had to be won.

Although the British promptly carried out some provisions of the Treaty of Paris by evacuating their military forces, Indian agents, and traders from the South, they retained the northern posts situated in American territory. Military officials at Niagara, Detroit, and Michilimackinac warned that American occupation would lead to an Indian war and threaten the lives of all whites, British and American. The warriors north of the Ohio refused to accept the peace treaty and would not recognize the right of the British to cede their lands,[14] never conquered by the Americans, to the hated "Long Knives." For them, the war was not over; the struggle was even now continuing in the face of renewed white encroachments on their territory. The problem was all the more acute at the end of the Revolutionary War as the frontiersmen surged west in search of new lands. Fearing another outbreak of hostilities, General William Irvine at Fort Pitt issued orders prohibiting whites from crossing the Ohio. The governments of Virginia and North Carolina also attempted, by force when necessary, to check squatters. From the Ohio to the Savannah the frontiersmen were on the move. It was now the responsibility of the states and the Continental Congress to solve the problems of the West.

lem. Settlers and speculators alike demanded tracts. The need for revenue, particularly following the collapse of Continental and state curren-
cies after 1779, also required a solution. Moreover, as an inducement
to enlist in the eighty-eight Continental regiments raised in the states,
Congress in 1776 had offered first cash and then land bounties to volunteers and recommended to the states that they provide land in proportion
to the volunteers' military contributions. Generally the states with land
available—Connecticut, Georgia, Massachusetts, Pennsylvania, New York,
Virginia, and the Carolinas—awarded certificates to their officers and
soldiers to be redeemed for tracts in specially reserved military districts.
New York set aside over 1,600,000 acres west of the 77th meridian;
Pennsylvania located lands west of the Allegheny River, and North Carolina situated its military reservation between the Tennessee River and
the Virginia boundary where they intersected the Cumberland River.
Virginia assigned the region between the Cumberland Mountains and
the Green, Tennessee, and Ohio rivers. If this area proved insufficient,
Virginia hoped to use lands north of the Ohio.[2] Not all of the soldiers
and officers took up the land to which they were entitled however;
many sold their certificates, or transferred them to settlers and
speculators.

Some states, particularly New York and Vermont, also put up for
sale confiscated Tory lands in the frontier regions. This policy generally
did not benefit the small landholder in the back country. Although much
land changed hands in the Grants through confiscation, the net effect
was to establish the supremacy of the Allens and other influencial Whig
leaders and to replace New York with Yankee speculators. The legislation
passed by New York did not do much for the small holders or tenants
of Tryon and other frontier counties; however, the act of 1779 discouraged sales of lots over 500 acres and gave tenants first choice at an
appraised price of the land they had cultivated. Many of the settlers
in the region had been Loyalists who fled from the state; and with
few exceptions the great tracts in Charlotte and Tryon counties that
came under state control went either to large landholders or speculators.[3]

Regardless of the need for revenue from land sales, most states
offered fairly generous terms to bona fide settlers or to squatters. In
Vermont, grants were made on liberal terms. Unsettled tracts covered
by earlier grants from either New York or New Hampshire could be
repurchased at nine pence an acre. Settlers were entitled to 100 acres
including their improvements. In Maine squatting was prevalent since
many of the small settlers believed that Massachusetts would confiscate
the lands of Tory proprietors. The General Court approved a system
for adjusting the claims between settler and proprietor and a program
for creating townships to discourage migration to other states. As a

special inducement settlers received 100-acre plots in the new townships. Pennsylvania also provided for squatters. Those persons who had occupied and improved land acquired by the Treaty of Fort Stanwix in 1768, but who had been forced to evacuate during the Revolution, had first preference. The state sold 100 acres at £5, and no individual could buy more than 300 acres without special permission. Squatters who occupied their holdings before 1780 could purchase 100 acres at two shillings an acre plus interest.[4]

The governments of some southern states simply continued the old headright or family-right system with a few modifications. By an act of 1777 the head of a family in Georgia was entitled to 200 acres with an additional 50 acres for every member of his family, up to ten persons. Squatters on unallotted soil received an improvement right. North Carolina, seeking to raise revenue, did not offer such liberal terms. Squatters could obtain 640 acres of ungranted land with an additional 100 acres for every member of the family, but payment, 4 shillings 8 pence for every acre, had to be made before January 1779. A pre-emption right was established by an improvement. Due to numerous complaints against speculators the land office was closed in 1781, but it reopened two years later in response to pressures from officers and other speculators. At that time the legislature set aside for military bounties and for sale, at £10 per 100 acres (five dollars in specie), all land from the mountains west to the Mississippi except for a small Indian reservation. Speculators during the next few months bought nearly four million acres before the legislature repealed the statute.[5]

Virginia faced an especially complex problem due to the conflicting claims of settlers and the military, as well as the land companies both within and without the state. Except for the Loyal and Greenbrier companies, the speculating organizations received little consideration from the Old Dominion. In 1776 the state extended its jurisdiction over all land granted by the charter boundaries of 1609 and denied the validity of purchases made from the Indians by private individuals. But Virginia, and subsequently North Carolina, each granted the Henderson Associates 200,000 acres on the Ohio and Green rivers in Kentucky and on the Powell and Clinch rivers in Tennessee in recognition of their expenses in opening the Kentucky and Cumberland valleys. Although some Virginians supported the claims of the Indiana and Walpole (Vandalia) companies, which were syndicates dominated by Pennsylvanians, others led by George Mason strongly opposed them. As head of the Ohio Company of Virginia, Mason led a successful struggle to repudiate the claims of the northern speculators by establishing the exclusive right of Virginia to pre-empt from the Indians all lands within her charter limits. Thereafter the northerners appealed to the authority of the Continental Congress and challenged the right of Virginia to her claims west of the mountains. The ensuing conflict, in part, was between two sets of speculators, those from Virginia, and those from Pennsylvania, Maryland, and New Jersey.

The Ohio Company still had not located the grant made to it before the French and Indian War, and the 800,000 acres surveyed in Kentucky by Hancock Lee, George Rogers Clark, and others for Mason and the company had not yet been patented. It was Mason who proposed the bills for the state's land policy enacted in 1779. By 1778 the depreciation of Virginia currency had convinced many leaders in the Old Dominion that they must obtain funds from the sale of land in order to restore credit. Thomas Jefferson and Mason took the lead, hoping to solve the financial problem, undermine outside speculators, and avoid future confusion by settling those land claims still outstanding. The legislation passed in July 1779 generally recognized three types of claims: settlement and pre-emption rights, military warrants, and warrants purchased from the state treasury. The legislation also distinguished among settlers who occupied their lands before January 1, 1778, those who settled between January 1, 1778, and the enactment of the land laws, and finally those who arrived later. Settlers in the first category received 400 acres at a nominal price and the right to pre-empt an additional 1000 acres at the regular rate, £40 for every 100 acres; those in the second group had the right to pre-empt 400 acres of their holdings at the regular price.

The legislation, however, made no adequate provision for supervising surveys or for protecting the improvements of settlers who took up land after the passage of the acts. The law did establish an order of preference: first, lawful surveys made under warrants based on various proclamations; second, pre-emption rights acquired before January 1, 1778; and third, settlement rights made before 1779. After that it was first come, first serve. In disputed cases, the first settler, or his heir, had preference. The commissioners of the land court had nothing to guide them in supervising surveys except the locations provided by the settlers or claimants. Because of haphazardly drawn boundaries, the courts were kept busy with litigation for half a century. The Virginia law provided for the early settlers and for the speculators, both resident and absentee, and many a settler was able to engage in speculation. Within a year the land court in Kentucky recorded entries and surveys for almost three and a half million acres. Warrants were issued for five to ten times as much land as was then available for entry. Locating these lands was at best a random process with the advantages in favor of anyone familiar with legal procedures and shrewd individuals with connections both in Richmond and Kentucky. Prominent Kentuckians such as John Floyd, George Rogers Clark, and Daniel Boone served

as agents in locating western lands to be purchased by absentee speculators with military or treasury warrants.[6]

Although the land commissioners during the winter of 1779–1780
were able to satisfy the claims of many of the settlers and speculators
in Kentucky, difficulty arose with the immigrants who came to Louisville
from the Monongahela country. Since they arrived after the passage
of the Virginia land act of July 1779 they were not entitled to pre-
emption rights and had to pay the full price of £40 for every 100
acres. Both resident and nonresident speculators had already pre-empted
the choice tracts. In their anger, the recent arrivals at the Falls of the
Ohio threatened to destroy the entry books of the land commissioners.
Unable to obtain cheap land in the immediate vicinity, the disgruntled
settlers at the Falls initially protested to the government at Richmond;
they then appealed to another political authority, the Continental Congress, asking it to assume control of the region south of the Ohio. At
this time their interests ran parallel to those of the northern land companies whose members consisted primarily of merchants and politicians
of the middle states.[7] Since Virginia in 1779 had rejected the claims
of the Indiana, Walpole, and United Wabash and Illinois companies,
organizations with claims to lands both north and south of the Ohio
River, the speculators from the other states sought to have Congress
assume control of the entire region west of the mountains as a national
domain. To do so Congress would have to deprive some states of their
extensive western holdings.

The question of a federal domain had been troubling the delegates
in Congress for years, ever since 1776 when the Articles of Confederation, the first compact between the states following the Declaration of
Independence, proposed to give the Confederation government jurisdiction over the interior. Six of the states, New Hampshire, Rhode Island,
New Jersey, Pennsylvania, Delaware, and Maryland, had definite boundaries fixed by their colonial charters. But the boundaries of several other
states had been vaguely set by their charters, allowing for extensive
claims. Georgia, North Carolina, South Carolina, and Virginia claimed
the Mississippi River as their western boundary. All or portions of the
Old Northwest also fell within the charter limits of Virginia as well
as the limits of New York, Connecticut, and Massachusetts. In addition,
the Bay state had jurisdiction over Maine, and New York claimed Vermont and much of the interior on both sides of the Ohio River on
the basis of its succession to the presumed suzerainty exercised by the
Iroquois Indians over the western tribes. To further complicate matters,
Connecticut was contending with Pennsylvania for jurisdiction over the
Wyoming region, and the Quaker commonwealth still had not settled
its dispute with Virginia concerning their western boundaries.

One way out of the dilemma was to give Congress the power to settle overlapping claims as was first proposed in the Articles of Confederation. But due to the opposition of the "landed" states, those with extensive claims, Congress under the Articles as finally adopted in 1777 was denied jurisdiction. The "landless" states, those with fixed boundaries, particularly Maryland, for years resisted ratifying the Articles until Congress was given authority over the interior and the power to settle boundary disputes.

Significantly, the speculators of the land companies generally resided in New Jersey, Maryland, Delaware, and Pennsylvania. They bitterly opposed Virginia, the state claiming not only the left bank of the Ohio where the Indiana and Vandalia companies had their grants, but also the region north and west of the river where the Illinois and Wabash companies had made their purchases. No doubt the members of these companies played some role in the decision of the "landless" states, Maryland, New Jersey, Pennsylvania, and Delaware, to refuse to ratify the Articles of Confederation until Virginia and the other "landed" states ceded their western holdings to the Confederation government. Yet their role, although important, was not decisive in shaping the voting record in Congress on the issue of the national domain.

The alignments in Congress on the question of the interior lands stemmed, in part, from the disputes over the boundary between Connecticut and Pennsylvania on the one hand, and Virginia and Pennsylvania on the other. Both the Quaker colony and the Old Dominion had sanctioned settlements in the disputed Monongahela Country and had appointed local officials in that region. So intense had been the rivalry that an armed clash was imminent at the outbreak of the Revolution. Moreover, local partisans of the Walpole and Indiana companies hoped to set aside the jursidiction of Virginia. Robert Morris and James Wilson, two Pennsylvania delegates, appealed to the Continental Congress to settle a temporary line, but the Confederation government did nothing except call on the settlers from both states to put aside their differences and respect the property of one another. At the same time Pennsylvania was engaged with the Susquehanna Company and Connecticut over jurisdiction of the Wyoming Valley where the Yankees had begun to settle some years before the Revolution. The controversy lasted throughout the war, and influential land speculators and politicians were to be found on both sides: Eliphalet Dyer, Oliver Wolcott, and Samuel Huntington for the Susquehanna Company and James Wilson, Tench Coxe, James Tilghman, and Robert Morris for Pennsylvania. Some of the principals involved sat in the Continental Congress.

The delegates from Pennsylvania, Connecticut, and Virginia, the states involved in boundary disputes, had to align themselves with delegates from other states on the pervasive question of whether Congress could "dismember" a state. Specifically, could Congress recognize Vermont as an independent state and in so doing deprive New York of a portion of her territory? If so, Congress might well do the same to Virginia by depriving her of the region west of the mountains, particularly the area north and west of the Ohio River, to the advantage of the land companies and the "landless" states. Through the interplay of sectional and political interests, the issues of the national domain, the "landless" states, the land companies, the boundary disputes, and the independence of Vermont were intertwined. Seeking to prevent an unfavorable precedent, Virginia and the other "landed" states of the South supported New York on the question of Vermont, while the "landless" middle states voted with the New England governments. Also influencing the delegates was the awareness that recognition of the independence of Vermont would increase the voting power of the New England block at the expense of the southerners. The men leading the independence movement in Vermont—the Allens, Thomas Chittenden, and Jonas Fay—shrewdly built up support for their position both in New England and among the congressional delegates from New Jersey, Pennsylvania, and Maryland by awarding liberal land grants to influential officers and politicians.

The delegates from New England realized that once the problem of western lands had been settled, they could not rely on Pennsylvania and Maryland to support them on the issue of Vermont, for these states and the southern representatives feared the dominance of the eastern section. Consequently, the New Englanders sought to postpone any decision on western lands until the Vermont question was resolved in their favor. In addition, Rhode Island voted with the middle states on the question of the national domain since she was apprehensive over an attempt by Congress to raise money by taxing goods entering her ports; her leaders saw in the western lands an alternative source of Congressional revenue.[8]

The politicians of the smaller states such as New Jersey, Delaware, and Maryland wanted the western lands as a fund for revenue and a source for military bounties for their officers and soldiers. The influence of the land companies was particularly strong among the delegates from these states. Some of the speculators took pains to distribute shares to the delegates and politicians, including George Reed of Pennsylvania and Delaware, Thomas Johnson, Charles Carroll of Carrollton, Samuel Chase of Maryland, Robert Morris, James Wilson, George Ross, and the Reverend Doctor William Smith of Pennsylvania as well as Silas Deane of Connecticut, and Conrad Gerard and John Hoker, the French envoy and consul respectively in Philadelphia. The latter two men had influence with the pro-French faction in Congress.

Yet these speculators did not place their land interests above all else. Hoping to secure independence, Wilson, Morris, and Johnson were willing in 1781 to give up the American claim to the interior, if necessary, to win the support of France and Spain when the British threatened the South. Moreover, some politicians in New Jersey and Maryland who had no interest in the land companies still insisted that Virginia and the other "landed" states cede their western lands before ratification of the Articles of Confederation; they believed that the western territories should be the common property of all the states. Maryland, Rhode Island, New Jersey, and Delaware wanted Congressional control in order to provide bounties for their troops. True, Virginia in 1779 had offered to furnish land north of the Ohio for troops from those states that had no unappropriated lands for this purpose, but on the condition that Congress reject the claims of the land companies and confirm to the Old Dominion the territory south of the Ohio. Virginia forces under Clark at that time had no more than a toe hold in the Illinois country, and there was little to indicate that the British would be forced to give up the Northwest.

Barraged with repeated petitions and memorials from the land companies over a number of years, neither side was able to muster the votes of nine states required for a decision. The break came when New York decided to give up her tenuous claim in the interior and her apparently hopeless position in Vermont to obtain confirmation of her more contiguous western regions. In February 1780 New York ceded her title to the West to Congress, and in October Connecticut followed suit. Adverse military developments forced many Virginians to realize that they too would have to make concessions. The state could not hold the area beyond the Ohio, and British forces were moving north from South Carolina and beginning to raid the Chesapeake Bay region. For the first time, Virginia needed direct military aid from the middle states. Even the land speculators in Virginia, the Lees, Walkers, and George Mason, saw the need for some concessions. It was Mason who devised the formula that would protect the immediate goals of the Virginia speculators. In January 1781 the Virginia legislature adopted his proposals that the Old Dominion cede to Congress the territory north and west of the Ohio River, but with the stipulations that Virginia land titles be confirmed, the claims of the outside land companies disallowed, and Virginia's title to the region east and south of the Ohio recognized. Virginia's offer was ingenuous and her concession more apparent than real. In exchange for territory over which she had no control, the state demanded Congressional guarantees for her retention of the left bank of the Ohio, an area in which Mason and the land speculators associated with him were seeking more than 800,000 acres.

Following the conditional cession by Virginia, Maryland finally ratified the Articles of Confederation the following month. She was the last state to do so. Whatever the influence of the land speculators, ratification was brought about more by the pressure exerted by the French Minister, Luzurne, who sought to strengthen the American union, and consequently, the American contribution to the war effort against the common foe, Great Britain. Luzurne was not without influence, for in view of British depredations in Chesapeake Bay, French naval aid was essential to Maryland.

With ratification of the Articles and the cessions by New York, Connecticut, and Virginia, the land companies resumed their efforts in Congress; the United Illinois and Wabash Company sought confirmation of purchases from the Indians north of the Ohio and the Indiana and Walpole groups for tracts on the left bank of the river. A committee consisting mainly of delegates from Pennsylvania, Maryland, and New Jersey was appointed to consider the companies' memorials; but despite the influence of Wilson and Morris, the committee in November 1781 rejected the private purchases of the Illinois and Wabash Company, acquisitions made without governmental authority. It did support the grants to the Indiana and Walpole groups for the British government purportedly had sanctioned their claims. Since Congress had succeeded the British Crown as sovereign, it, not Virginia, had jurisdiction over the land south and east of the Ohio. The committee further recommended that Congress not accept the cession of the Northwest on the conditions demanded by Virginia. The real issue was the region lying west of the mountains and south of the Ohio River, an area claimed in whole or part by the Indiana and Walpole associates.

Inadequate attendance in Congress and the dispute over Vermont delayed a quick resolution of the problem, but by 1783 new developments had altered the situation. Although the New Yorkers continued to protest the admittance of Vermont into the Confederation, they realized that they would have to relinquish jurisdiction and allow commissioners to settle disputes over property rights in the Grants. Moreover, the severe financial crisis facing Congress made it imperative that the Confederation government have a source of revenue. The sale of western lands was clearly the only alternative considering the difficulty in getting all of the states to agree to an amendment of the Articles of Confederation giving Congress taxing powers. By this time it was evident that the peace treaty with Great Britain would leave the Northwest to the United States; consequently, there would be enough land to satisfy the veterans of the "landless" states. Finally, a lobby of officers backed by Washington himself was beginning to exert pressure for lands. Slighting Pennsylvania, New Jersey, and Delaware, whose delegations reflected the interests of the land companies, Congress created a new committee to consider the problem of western lands. Without specifically acquiesing to the demands made by Virginia in 1781, the committee generally accepted the conditions posed by the Old Dominion. Over the continued objections of the delegates from New Jersey and Maryland, Congress in September 1783 agreed to accept the cession of the Northwest on the terms stipulated by Virginia thirty-two months before. In December the state legislatures accepted the Congressional settlement and the following March, over the solitary objection of New Jersey—Maryland not being represented at the time—the Virginia deed was executed in Congress.[9]

The way was cleared for the other "landed" states to cede their western holdings to the federal government and for Congress to develop a policy for the national domain. The program incorporated in the Land Ordinance of 1785 paralleled the British order-in-council of 1774. Both provided for systematic disposal of regularly surveyed lands at public auction in order to raise revenue and prevent confusion over land titles.

◁ **11** ▷

Government and Law in the Back Country

*T*he American Revolution had little effect on either political practices or the structure of government in the back country. Dominated by the provincial governments before the war, the frontier communities after 1776 were controlled by the new states that replaced the colonial regimes. The adoption of new constitutions following the issuance of the Declaration of Independence by the revolutionary Whig leaders did not significantly alter property qualifications for voting or the proportion of back-country representation in the state legislatures and did not result in greater local rule for the interior. Alterations in political practices that foreshadowed the egalitarian society of the nineteenth century such as the widening of the franchise were not to begin until the last decade of the eighteenth century; national, not regional, in origin and scope, they were brought about by the functioning of party machinery, a phenomenon of the 1790s.[1] Except in Vermont, no permanent, independent political communities were organized during the Revolution although dissident elements in southwestern Virginia, Kentucky, and southwestern Pennsylvania agitated for separate statehood.

At times some settlers, those living in the more remote areas far from the center of state government and subsisting on a marginal economy, suffered from disabilities attributable to disputed or insufficient land titles and the inadequacy of local government. Ambitious magnates in these marginal regions were able to take advantage of this discontent to propose independence from Virginia and Pennsylvania and the creation of separate back-country states. Such was the case in 1779–1780 in southwestern Virginia where Arthur Campbell, lieutenant of Montgomery County, capitalized on disputes between settlers and the Loyal Company of Virginia over land titles. Campbell took the lead in this movement at the time the Continental Congress resolved to claim the trans-Appalachian region. Through the influence of John Donelson, he also sought to include the dissatisfied Kentucky settlers in the movement. Campbell's efforts in southwestern Virginia came to naught when the Virginia Superior Court resolved the dispute between the Loyal Company and the settlers of the region. It was the secessionist sentiment in frontier Kentucky that grew to have wider appeal and was, consequently, more serious.

Dissatisfaction in Kentucky had existed for some years among various groups. As early as 1775 the settlers who had come from Virginia to Harrodsburg had protested the claims of both the Henderson Associates and the surveyors attempting to locate lands under military warrants for magnates from Virginia. Led by John Gabriel Jones and George Rogers Clark, they had successfully appealed to the Virginia Convention, which then established Kentucky County. The Virginia land laws passed in July 1779 generally had satisfied the settlers who were already in Kentucky, but those who came later, particularly from Pennsylvania and North Carolina, were not granted settlement or pre-emption rights. They had to pay the full price for land and compete with agents of eastern speculators who were pre-empting the choice locations. Moreover, the single unit of county government was inadequate for the far-flung stations, and the nearest higher court lay over the mountains in Richmond. Capitalizing on the discontent, ambitious leaders such as John Donelson, John Kincaid, and John Todd prevailed on the dissatisfied pioneers to petition Congress to erect a new state for the region south of the Ohio River. Naturally, the northern speculators cited these complaints when they asked Congress to deny Virginia jurisdiction over the region and recognize a new government that might honor the claims of their land companies. The Virginia legislature was not blind to the legitimate grievances of the settlers, however, and in the early 1780s it provided for county courts in Kentucky, granted 400 acres of land for every indigent family, established more effective local government by dividing Kentucky into three counties, Lincoln, Fayette, and Jefferson, and set up a district court.[2]

Northern speculators also capitalized on the dissatisfaction among settlers in the Monongahela country by pushing for a new frontier state beyond the Alleghenies called Westsylvania. Significantly, the boundaries of the new state were to be those of Vandalia, the colony sought from the British government before the Revolution, and among those who fomented the secessionist movement were the followers of George Croghan and Thomas Cresap. Aggressive and ambitious, both of these early pioneers in the Monongahela country were associated with the Vandalia group, and both claimed large tracts in the region on the basis of Indian deeds, transactions recognized by neither Virginia nor Pennsylvania.

In 1776 the secessionists proposed calling a convention to form a new state and to appeal to the Continental Congress for recognition, but they were checked by Virginia officials, John Neville, John Campbell, and John Gibson. Four years later when it appeared that Virginia and Pennsylvania might settle their boundary dispute, the dissident leaders associated with the land companies again seized the opportunity to agitate. For two years they stirred up the settlers, arguing that they need not pay Pennsylvania taxes since the entire region would become a new state. In Westmoreland and Washington counties armed bands drove off tax collectors and refused to take the oath to the Quaker commonwealth. Pennsylvania finally acted to halt the secessionist movement in the West by decreeing the death penalty for those advocating separation and sent secret agents, among them the Reverend James Finley, to counteract the propaganda of the malcontents and win over the settlers. Finley's efforts, the threat that the settlers' land might be sold, and the cool reaction to the proposed new state by Congress finally quieted the Westerners.[3]

Two separate governments were established in the back country during the Revolution; however, only one, the Transylvania colony set up in 1775 by Richard Henderson and his associates, was short-lived. The experiment grew out of the rivalry among the leaders of the various Kentucky stations in 1775. In order to avoid deciding among the stations and having his authority challenged by those dissatisfied with his decision, Henderson issued a call to the settlers from the four stations, Boonesborough, Harrodsburg, Boiling Spring, and St. Asaph's to send representatives to confer with him as proprietor. The assembly meeting at Boonesborough on May 23 followed procedures that paralleled to a remarkable degree those followed by the Virginia House of Burgesses or any provincial house of representatives in its relation with the colonial governors. At the suggestion of Henderson, John Lythe, James Douglas, and Isaac Hite proposed a plan of government for the infant colony. The settlers were annually to elect delegates to the assembly and nominate judges and sheriffs who were to be appointed by the proprietor. This frontier compact, similar in most respects to the colonial and county governments of Virginia and North Carolina, lasted less than a year for Virginia assumed jurisdiction over the Kentucky region and in 1776 established county government.[4]

The only new, permanent government established in the back country during the Revolutionary era resulted from an attempt by the Allen faction in Vermont to secure their lands claims against New York. Many of the settlers there initially did not desire independence; some preferred New York rule and others wanted a merger with New Hampshire. Despite these differences the majority of the Vermonters found the New York constitution of 1777 wholly unacceptable. It allowed the Grants only nine of the seventy seats in the assembly and only three of the twenty-four places in the state senate. At the same time most Vermonters realized the need for unity in preparing for the invasion by Burgoyne's forces. In July delegates representing the towns in all sections of the Grants met in a six-day session and adopted the constitution that Pennsylvania had promulgated the year before. It had been advanced by a friend of the Allens, Doctor Thomas Young of Philadelphia. The document, never submitted to the people for ratification, theoretically emphasized majority rule and the supremacy of the representative legislative branch elected by manhood suffrage. The legislature also had the power to appoint and impeach the elected governor and council. Yet the government did not always function democratically under this constitution. The Green Mountain faction ruled with what the Allens called a "private cabinet." Operating through the council, the Allens and their cohorts often presented the assembly with a *fait accompli* to which the legislature invariably acquiesced since the regime for some years did not impose any taxes. Rather, it financed the state government through the sale of "Tory," that is, New York, estates.[5]

During the Revolution all of the states, except Connecticut and Rhode Island, adopted new constitutions, but the political position of the back country was, at best, only slightly improved, not significantly altered. The basic structure of government on the frontier was retained.

Although the settlers in some western regions before the Revolution had complained of under-representation in the provincial legislatures apportioned on the basis of population and taxable wealth, there had been few grievances, or serious differences, between the eastern and western sections of Georgia, Maryland, and Virginia. Although the newer counties in the interior of Virginia were large, and its eastern region retained a predominance in the legislature, the westerners generally accepted this control and often chose easterners to represent them. In the three states there was little evidence during the Revolution of western resentment against eastern over-representation or misrule. The new Georgia constitution and subsequent legislation gave the back counties, Camden and Glynn, one representative each. In response to complaints that the seat of government was too far removed from the back country, the Georgia executive council in 1783 agreed to meet in Augusta during three months of every year.[6] In neighboring South Carolina the revolutionary leaders, realizing the need to win back-country support, increased the region's representation in the provincial Congress; although the interior districts under the constitution promulgated in 1776 still returned a minority of the representatives, provision was made for reapportionment in 1785 and every fourteen years thereafter on the basis of the number of inhabitants and taxable property within each district. In the constitution adopted for North Carolina in 1776 each county was equally represented, and several articles in the new compact reflected reforms previously demanded by the upcountry Regulators: abolishment of imprisonment for debt, the end of plural officeholding, and the regulation of fees charged by public officials.[7]

In Pennsylvania where under-representation for the interior counties had long been a sore point, the back-country politicians perhaps played a more important role in the formation of the constitution than in any other state. By the fundamental law adopted in 1776 the representation of each county was proportional to the number of taxable inhabitants. A twelve-member supreme council elected by the voters—adult male freemen who paid taxes and their sons over twenty-one years of age— was to appoint all officials except for a few classes elected by the assembly. The voters were to select two or more candidates for the local offices of justice and sheriff, and the council was to commission one from among those nominated. The political division over the constitution and the subsequent political alignments in the state did not reflect an east-west conflict. Nor were the western political leaders extremists. Many a well-to-do western politician, formerly associated with the eastern political group that had dominated the provincial government, was chosen by the back settlers to represent them. James Rankin of York, James Potter of Northumberland, Thomas Smith of Bedford, James Allen of Northampton, and John Harris and John Burd were moderates—men of substance, not radical fire-eaters. Thomas Smith, the Scottish-born lawyer who represented Bedford in the constitutional convention, was disgusted with the leveling tendency of the delegates. He charged that they adopted democratic principles to win popularity and political office. Indeed, some of the moderate leaders who served as officials in the back counties opposed the new government controlled by the extremists of Philadelphia by boycotting public offices and refusing to turn over their official records. By 1777–1778 a block of twenty conservatives in the assembly—three from York, four from Cumberland, six from Bedford, and one each from Northampton and Westmoreland counties—was challenging the radicals who favored the constitution. The old political forces, including westerners, were coming back. The new constitution of 1776 did not significantly increase the relative strength of the back country. In the May 1780 assembly, the first since the Revolution that was apportioned on the basis of taxables, Bedford, Northumberland, and Westmoreland lost a total of ten seats. Philadelphia and the three eastern counties returned 60 percent of the seats; previously they had controlled only 40 percent.[8]

The operation of the county, the unit of government most directly affecting the lives of the frontier settlers, was largely unchanged by the alterations in the state governments. During the Revolution the states, as the provincial regimes earlier expanded the county system to cover new settlements. They subdivided old counties and created new ones. Pennsylvania formed Washington County for her southwestern settlements, and Virginia in 1776 divided the district of West Augusta into Ohio, Monongalia, and Yohogania counties and four years later created Lincoln, Fayette, and Jefferson counties for the Kentucky settlements. At the outbreak of the Revolution the settlers who had gone down the Holston to the Indian lands in the Watauga region found themselves outside the jurisdiction of Virginia and beyond the established government of North Carolina. Fearing a threat to their land titles and other property, they selected "tryers" to adjudicate disputes and adopted the Virginia form of county government. Finally in 1776, they successfully petitioned North Carolina for a regularly constituted government. Initially, the region was called Washington District, but was subdivided in 1778 into Washington and Sullivan counties. Much the same situation prevailed in the Nashville settlements founded in 1780. The adult freemen from the various stations set up a tribunal of notables to settle disputes over property and land; in other respects they utilized the procedures of the Virginia and North Carolina counties. After three years North Carolina established Davidson County for the region. In both the Watauga and Cumberland settlements there were few attempts at innovations; rather, the settlers and tryers seem to have made a conscious effort to adopt a familiar system. Thus there was an easy transition from "compact" to county government under North Carolina.[9] Indeed, the most prominent settlers among the frontiersmen who had been elected to the tribunals were appointed as justices of the new county courts.

Generally a frontier or back-country elite, less stable perhaps, but just as powerful as the magnates who dominated the eastern counties, controlled the county courts in the interior. The back country had its own gentry; they were vigorous, often well-educated men who owned large tracts of land and some slaves and indentured servants, and thus enjoyed a higher social and economic status than the great majority of their neighbors. Differences in class were recognized and accepted since most settlers generally followed the leadership of their "betters"; in turn, the gentry held the positions of authority expected of them. In the back country as elsewhere once a man achieved a measure of wealth, status followed; with status came privilege, and with privilege came responsibility, office, and power. Arthur Campbell, a magnate in frontier Botetourt County, Virginia, thought it only natural for the "people of the lowest Class" to show respect for their constituted superiors. The gentry, acknowledged leaders in their communities, received the highest civil and military offices; they were commissioned as militia officers, lieutenants of the county, justices of the peace, sheriffs, surveyors, clerks of the courts, and recorders. Plural office holding was common.[10]

The lower orders did not often challenge the system; rather, contests were waged among members of the gentry themselves who competed for positions of prestige and honor and sought to use their influence with the provincial, and later the state, governments to obtain appointments. In Bedford and Westmoreland counties, Pennsylvania, Arthur St. Clair and Robert Hanna vied with one another for the right to locate the new county seat as a mark of their prestige and influence. St. Clair was not untypical of the frontier gentry. Born and educated in Scotland, he had studied medicine and served as an officer in the Royal American Regiment. In 1762 he resigned his commission, entered trade, and after moving to western Pennsylvania, acquired large tracts of land and a host of local offices in Bedford, and later Westmoreland, counties; he acted as justice of the peace, prothonotary, recorder of deeds, and registrar of wills.

If they were not candidates for all the offices themselves, the gentry in the newly settled regions were influential in electing representatives and in securing appointments of friends to local positions. In Tryon and Charlotte counties on the New York frontier, such magnates as the Johnsons, the Butlers, Philip Schuyler, Philip Skene, and Beverly Robinson dominated the local scene. Generally the Johnsons were associated with one faction in provincial politics while Schuyler was allied with another in opposition. Although the Butlers and the Johnsons were eliminated during the Revolution, Schuyler, as the leading Whig in the back country, continued to exert influence with the governor and the council of four senators who, under the constitution of 1777, annually appointed sheriffs and coroners. Loan officers, county treasurers, and clerks were selected by the legislature, and town clerks, road supervisors, assessors, constables, and tax collectors were locally elected. During the chaotic years of the Revolution, the Tryon County Committee of Safety supervised the election of these local officers.

In Virginia control of local government rested with the justices of the peace who were members of the wealthiest families in their communities. Although nominally commissioned by the governor, they had established the practice of holding office for life and recommending men for vacancies to the county court. Although subject to public sentiment, they were not compelled to act against their own wishes, and directly or indirectly, chose the other county officials—clerks, sheriffs, coroners, and militia officers—even when these officials received their commissions from the governor. In the backcountry, powerful families as a matter of course held the highest posts in county government and the militia. In newly created counties such as Botetourt and Fincastle their leadership was as decisive and complete as was that of the older families in the East. As the frontier population flowed down the valley and across the mountains, the most prominent families were often in the first wave. The Prestons and Campbells became the dominant leaders of southwestern Virginia. Their former neighbors in the valley occupied a similar position in other regions, the Seviers in eastern Tennessee and the Zanes and Lewises in the trans-Allegheny region. Even in the Carolinas, despite the animosities engendered by the pre-revolutionary Regulator movements, family status counted in the back settlements where the farmers acknowledged the leadership of the local gentry. In the settlements west of the mountains the important families, those well-endowed in land, slaves, and indentured servants, also held high offices.

The power the gentry exercised on the county courts was considerable, for the justices dealt with a range of problems affecting almost every facet of life on the frontier. The activities of the county courts from New York south had much in common with, and paralleled to a remarkable degree, the functions of comparable courts not only on the seaboard but in England as well. Indeed, there existed on the frontier a transplanted system of local English government in which the gentry served without charge. The courts functioned as administrative bodies for the provincial, and later the state, governments in holding elections, supervising roads, and licensing ferries and ordinaries; as judicial bodies in lesser criminal and civil actions; as social agencies in caring for orphans, illegitimate children, and apprentices; and as the guardians of public morality, in addition to setting rates, registering deeds, determining land titles, and probating wills. For the conduct of routine business, the court met every month on a day set by law, and every three months as the court of quarter sessions to deal with criminal cases.[11] Since law enforcement was a major function of the courts, lawyers soon made their appearance. In less than a year after the formation of Bedford County, Pennsylvania, its court admitted at least ten attorneys, among them James Wilson, David Sample, and George Brent. Walter Butler practiced law at an early date in Tryon County, New York, and in 1773 John Gabriel Jones was admitted to the bar in Fincastle County.

The punishments imposed by the county courts included fines, ducking, lashing for both men and women, mutilation, and hanging. At times, punishment could be swift and brutal. In Washington County, North Carolina, a horse thief was arrested on Monday, tried on Wednesday, and hanged on Friday of the same week. Another man convicted for the same offense received thirty-nine lashes, lost both ears, and was branded with a "H" on both cheeks. In the back country of Pennsylvania counterfeiters were also hanged. Servile classes generally were at a disadvantage before the courts, and punishments were particularly harsh for Negro slaves. John Bowman's slave, Will, "not having the fear of God before his eyes, but being move[d] & seduced by institution of the Devil" had raped a white woman and was hanged. Sawney, a slave belonging to Robert Breckinridge, received the same punishment for merely stealing four guns, a hog, and a harp. Yet in 1774 the Fincastle court allowed Roma, a Negro slave accused of feloniously attempting to kill his master, William Campbell, to testify in his own defense and then judged him not guilty.[12] Indentured servants also suffered harshly. In Botetourt County, two servants, a man and a woman, were sentenced to two years additional service as punishment for fleeing from their masters. In Westmoreland County, Pennsylvania, James Kincaid accused his indentured girl of stealing a few articles from him. She was fined and received fifteen lashes on her bare back. Since Kincaid complained that he had lost four-days service and had gone to considerable expense in prosecuting the girl, the court ordered her to serve her master for two more years. This case was not exceptional. Yet the courts also protected the servant from unjust treatment by the master. In the district of West Augusta William Freeman accused his master, John Collins, of abusing and beating him. After hearing both parties, the court judged Collins guilty and ordered him to be jailed until he posted bond for good behavior.

The county courts enforced morality not only on slaves and indentured servants, but on free whites as well. The Botetourt court in 1771 ordered a settler, the putative father of an illegitimate child, to be taken into custody until he gave security to the churchwarden of the parish for the maintenance of the infant. Punishment was also meted out for unlawful cohabitation, fornication, quarreling, blasphemy, and breaking the Sabbath. The courts acted as social agencies in requiring that parents educate their children in a Christian manner. In Jefferson County, Kentucky, the orphaned infant, Thomas George, was bound out to William Spangler who was to instruct his ward in "the art & mystery of a Blacksmith," and as required by law, to teach him to read, write, and cipher. At the request of Ann Hammon, the Yohogania court ordered that her five-year-old son be apprenticed to Isaac McMichael. McMichael was to teach the boy to read, write, and cipher "as far as the rule of three" and to initiate him into the "Mystery of Husbandry." At the age of twenty-one, the youth would receive a new suit of clothes, a Bible, a grubbing hoe, and an axe.[13] Thus equipped, he would presumably be ready to go forth into the world.

The courts also played a significant role in the economy of the back country. Among their functions were the regulation of fees and the licensing of public inns, ferries, saw and gristmills, taverns, and ordinaries. In 1770 the Botetourt court set the rates ordinaries could charge for a gallon of liquor and spirits: ten shillings for West Indian rum, two shillings, six pence for country (American) rum, ten shillings for Teneriff wine, and five shillings for French and peach brandy. The rates for overnight lodgings in clean sheets were: one to a bed, six pence, two per bed, three pence, three farthings, and more than two, no additional charge. The courts certified the amount of hemp grown by planters and farmers on the Virginia frontier so that they could receive the bounties offered by the government. In order to market hemp, grain, and other agricultural produce, roads in the back country were essential. The county courts were responsible for laying out and maintaining these by-ways, except in New England where, after incorporation, the towns assumed this function. In the unincorporated towns, road maintenance was the responsibility of the proprietors. Evidently there were some disputes between absentee proprietors and the settlers over roads and bridges in remote regions such as the Ware District of Maine and in the newer towns of New Hampshire and Vermont.[14] But in New York and the back country to the south there was apparently little difficulty since the courts assigned surveyors to lay out the roads and appointed overseers to supervise the tithables who constructed the roads and kept them repaired.

A survey of the court minutes of the frontier counties reveals to a surprising degree not only the extent to which government regulated life in a society traditionally thought to be almost free of restraint, but that the forms of government in the pioneer settlements followed closely the traditional mold of the seacoast. At this time there were few, if any, innovations associated with a frontier setting. The familiar, traditional county courts were soon set up in the early settlements. Such innovations as did occur after 1776 seemed to be common to both the interior and the coastal regions and resulted from the general political developments that followed the break with the mother country.

Indeed, there seemed to be little dissatisfaction among the back settlers with the basic framework of government. After all, the Watauga and Cumberland pioneers consciously adopted the county system they had known in the Piedmont and the East, and the South Carolina Regulators in the 1760s fought to have effective county government established for the upcountry where none had existed. In neighboring North Carolina the settlers struggled to reform, but not to abolish, the county courts.

The expansion of the frontier during the Revolutionary era did not bring any leveling tendency in political life. Whatever may have been the case on later frontiers—settled when a more democratic trend was affecting the political structure of the nation as a whole—between 1763 and 1783 the back-country gentry retained their grip on local government. Their power was not often challenged.

In addition to intimately revealing the political structure of the frontier, the records of the county courts also shed light on the economic development of the pioneer settlements, particularly the extent to which local government performed economic functions such as constructing and maintaining local roads. Although primitive by European standards and much criticized by foreign travelers, they facilitated the development of the economy of the hinterland and aided the rise of commercial, and even export, agriculture.

◁ **12** ▷

The Economy and Society of the Back Country

*T*he economy of the back country was based predominantly on relatively small-scale agriculture, particularly the family farm, and on related forest and animal industries. Most pioneers who were cultivating a variety of crops did not remain subsistence farmers for long. Within a short time they were able to produce beyond their immediate needs and send their surpluses to nearby marketing centers and the coastal cities. During the Revolutionary era an ever-increasing volume of grain, livestock, meat, and lumber flowed from the interior to overseas markets in Europe and the West Indies, constituting a vital facet of the American farm economy from the earliest years of colonization.

Despite many common characteristics, significant differences existed among frontier farmers—in the labor force, in land holding, and especially in techniques of cultivation. The various national groups, specifically the predominent Germans and Scots-Irish, sought different types of land and cultivated their holdings in distinct ways. Both groups settled on land resembling the soil they had known in Europe. The Scots-Irish generally did not compare favorably with the Germans as farmers;

172

they were not as productive, were less interested in livestock husbandry, and did not practice soil conservation. Choosing the well-watered foothills and the shale soils, they partially developed their holdings and then sold out to new arrivals before moving on to another frontier region. In contrast, the Germans settled in the heavily wooded limestone regions and valleys that required more effort to clear. They tended to settle permanently and to systematically develop their land. There were, admittedly, some German farmers who exerted a minimum of effort, but these were exceptional. The great majority of the Conestoga Germans, or "High Dutch" as they were known in Pennsylvania, diligently cultivated and improved their farms. Their performance was contrasted to the poorer methods of the "Low Dutch" settlers of the Mohawk Valley who farmed "à la mode de Hollander." A few of the landed magnates on the New York frontier who had sufficient resources attempted to introduce improved agricultural methods to these "Low Dutch" settlers but with little success.

Throughout the frontier, farming was generally inefficient. With fresh land readily available there was little need to cultivate the soil intensively by expending time, money, and effort. In this respect, farming in the interior did not differ from the practices on the seaboard. Livestock was allowed to run at large, and there were few settlers, except the Germans, who fertilized the soil with manure. Sickles, harrows, rakes, and other farm implements were the type that had been used by farmers for centuries. Plows were inefficient; their moldboards were so shallow that they stirred only the top inches of the soil. Much animal power was expended in drawing these heavy, cumbersome implements, limiting the work capacity of both animals and men.[1]

Instead of using their time, energies, and resources in intensive cultivation of smaller plots that would have conserved the land and led to greater returns, frontier farmers practiced extensive cultivation, quickly exhausted their fields, and then opened new plots. Consequently, back-country farmers possessed relatively large holdings in land. The farms of the North Carolina back country were of considerable size in relation to what could be worked at any given time. In Orange County more than three-quarters of the "smaller" holdings ranged from 100 to 500 acres with only 5 percent less than 100 acres. In the interior of South Carolina the average holding seems to have been about 175 acres. Here it was unprofitable to hold unimproved land for long since it was taxed at the same rate as improved soil. In New England the size of farms in the newly opened sections during the 1760s averaged about 300 acres, which was considerably more than the units in the coastal regions. In the North the larger farms were generally located in the interior.[2] Many of the farmers probably held more land than

Eighteenth-century farm implements. (Photo by the Pennsylvania Historical and Museum Commission, Harrisburg, Pennsylvania)

they could immediately cultivate in order to be able to speculate or to pass their holdings on to their sons.

The pioneer family most often supplied its own labor, although planters used tenants, indentured servants, and slaves. However, smaller farmers also employed hired or bonded workers and servile blacks. Indeed, slavery was established from the outset on the frontiers in the northern colonies, New York and Pennsylvania, and in the southern Piedmont. It was used on a significant scale in the frontier provinces of East and West Florida by planters who migrated from Georgia and the Carolinas. Significant numbers of slaves were held in Westmoreland, Fayette, Washington, Allegheny, and Bedford, the western counties of Pennsylvania, until the state abolished the institution of slavery in 1780. Many slave holders, originally Virginians, then moved their human property down the Ohio River to the Kentucky settlements where they swelled the already significant slave population. A census taken in 1777 at Boonesborough, Harrodsburg, and St. Asaph's merely two years after their founding revealed that Negroes already constituted 10 percent of the total population.[3]

Much the same situation prevailed in the older frontier settlements of Virginia and North Carolina from where the majority of the Kentuckians had come. The fact that the Negro slaves constituted only a small percentage of the population during the initial period of settlement in the southern upcountry did not necessarily reflect the distaste of the pioneers for servile labor; it indicated that there was merely an initial lack of capital with which to purchase slaves. A sound male slave in Botetourt County, Virginia, in 1772 cost eight pounds, one pound more than a horse and three pounds less than a rifle. In time as the pioneer farmers acquired more wealth, they were able to purchase Negroes. Those who could afford slave labor favored it as much as the coastal planters. The presence of slavery during the initial period of settlement on the southern frontier was "both a symptom and a portent of the ultimate" composition of society and the economy once the frontier stage was passed.[4]

Just as frontier farmers followed the general agricultural practices of the eastern colonies, so some continued the familiar methods of clearing the land. In the North, the New England, or "Yankee system," of cutting down and burning timber prevailed. But the English and Scots-Irish pioneers of the middle and southern regions adopted the Indian practice of "girdling" rather than cutting down the trees. The dead timber allowed sunlight to reach the crops. Underbrush and saplings were grubbed out, and in a few years the branches and then the deadened trunks fell. This method initially saved labor, provided firewood, and did not destroy the humus in the soil, but it cut down efficiency since the pioneer farmer had to cultivate around the trees and thus reduce his yield. The Germans almost invariably used the Yankee method of cutting down and burning the forest, thereby gaining more land for immediate, and more efficient, cultivation. But this process consumed more time and labor, and the burning destroyed the humus in the soil.

Once they had cleared the land, the pioneers, generally planted Indian corn as their first crop. In the southern Piedmont several varieties of native peas were also sown; rye was grown on the New England frontier and wheat in the Mohawk Valley. Within a few years the back-country farmers were harvesting a variety of crops: wheat, barley, rye, oats, millet, potatoes, pumpkins, turnips, squash, peaches, and apples. In addition, some frontier farms in the South were producing tobacco, hemp, and flax. For the first five or ten years the farmer took a meager income out of the land because he was concerned with the immediate problem of providing sustenance for his family. Yet by expanding his cultivated land and improving his holdings, he could produce capital to allow him to convert to diversified, commercial farming.

Initially, he would sell his surplus to newly arrived settlers in the neighborhood. James Whitelaw noted in the Vermont Grants that the pioneer farmers were charging later arrivals "pretty high" prices for foodstuffs: four shillings sterling a bushel for wheat and rye and three shillings per pound for mutton and beef. Within a generation after the initial settlements, the frontier regions were engaged in a fairly complex export trade. Wagons loaded with a ton of grain and drawn by as many as four horses carried produce to the rivers from where they could be shipped to the ports on the coast.[5]

Throughout most frontier regions, roads led to the heads of the navigable rivers flowing into the Atlantic. The routes were constructed and maintained through a variety of interests. In response to a petition from the towns of Lancaster, Northumberland, and Shelburne, the General Assembly of New Hampshire in 1773 provided funds for the construction of a road to the Connecticut River. At about the same time through the influence of Philadelphia and Baltimore merchants, roads were laid out closely linking the interior of Pennsylvania to the ports of the two cities. The mercantile interests of the eastern cities, realizing that the prosperity of the seaboard depended to a great extent on the growth and economic expansion of the back country, took a favorable view of spending provincial funds for internal transportation improvements.

In the decade preceding the Revolution, the Pennsylvania assembly began matching local subscriptions from interested persons and voted sums ranging from £200 to £1000 for roads and river navigation. Two major roads linked the trans-Allegheny settlements of Pennsylvania with the East: the Forbes, or Philadelphia, Road to the Delaware River and the Braddock, or Virginia, Road to the Potomac. The Great Wagon Road also led from Philadelphia west to the Cumberland Valley and then south to the valley of Virginia. West of the Blue Ridge the settlers had learned by trial and error that roads could be constructed under a system of local responsibility, and the Virginia assembly had granted the county courts extraordinary powers to construct them. Through Vestal's, Gregory's, Snicker's, and Thornton's gaps roads led from the great north-south wagon road through the Blue Ridge east to Alexandria, Colchester, Frederick, and Falmouth. The Great Wagon Road then turned southeast into the Carolina Piedmont. Here lesser roads led to the coastal region. An ever-increasing volume of agricultural produce and livestock was being brought to market on these highways.[6] The settlements west of the mountains were still too sparse, and the rugged

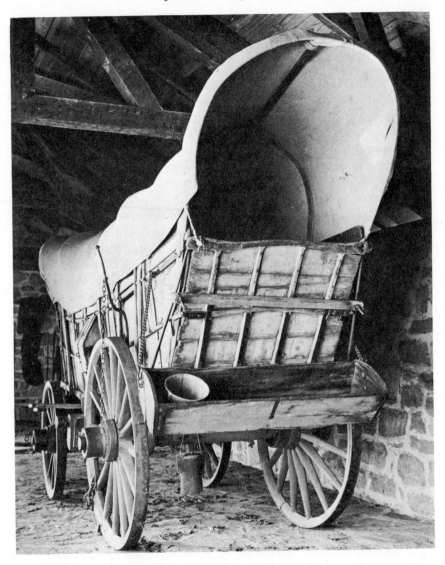

An eighteenth-century Conestoga wagon. (Photo by the Pennsylvania Historical and Museum Commission, Harrisburg, Pennsylvania)

terrain too formidable, to allow construction of an extensive overland transportation system, although in addition to the Forbes and Braddock roads, two more roads were built. They connected the Watauga and Nolichucky settlements with the valley of Virginia.

A more common means of communication beyond the Appalachians was water transport on the river networks that laced the region. In the late 1760s the Philadelphia firm of Baynton, Wharton and Morgan had sizable river craft constructed at the Forks of the Ohio. As early as 1782 Jacob Yoder, a settler in the Monongahela country, left Redstone with a boatload of flour and passed down the Monongahela, Ohio, and Mississippi rivers to New Orleans. With the proceeds of his sales he purchased furs; he then exchanged the skins for sugar at Havana and finally marketed his West Indian produce at Philadelphia. That same year General William Irvine, the commandant at Fort Pitt, granted permits for at least ten boats to each carry more than thirty tons of wheat and flour to the Kentucky stations and New Orleans. The pioneers in the Bluegrass and Nashville regions who had settled there during the war had been hard pressed enough to defend themselves much less to raise food, but by 1783 enterprising settlers such as John Todd, Walker Daniel, George May, and Isaac Hite were forming trading ventures in the Kentucky Basin, and French merchants and traders from both Philadelphia and New Orleans were operating in the transmontane settlements, buying up wheat and flour to be exported from New Orleans.[7] These developments in the last years of the Revolution clearly indicated the pattern of future economic and commercial trends.

East of the mountains in the back settlements of the southern Piedmont the trend toward commercial agriculture began earlier. There the development of overland transportation made possible the emergence of small inland trading towns with thirty to fifty houses and the extension of trade with the seaports. From Augusta on the Savannah to Sunbury on the Susquehanna a line of minor towns situated at the crossroads and junctions of roads and rivers served as collecting and marketing points for produce destined to be shipped by wagon or river craft to the eastern ports. Ninety–Six, Cheraws, Camden, Hillsboro, Salem, Salisbury, and Charlotte in the Carolinas were all located on the Great Wagon Road as were the towns of the valley of Virginia to the north. Hillsboro, which tapped the settlements of Orange County, North Carolina, was connected by road with Cross Creek near the Cape Fear River. By river craft produce was shipped from Cross Creek to Wilmington on the coast. Augusta in Georgia, Brunswick in North Carolina, and Falmouth in Virginia received a large volume of produce by comparable systems of roads and rivers. North of the Potomac in the back country of Pennsylvania were the hamlets of Carlisle, Bedford, Northumberlandtown, Sunbury, Reading, and Lancaster; all were linked by road with the Delaware River ports. Baltimore and New York City also competed with Philadelphia. The merchants of the eastern cities were instrumental in marketing western produce. In the southern Piedmont, Scottish merchants were particularly active in sending buyers and agents into the upcountry. James Hogg, for example, worked as the representative of his brother's Wilmington firm at its branch store in Cross Creek.[8] The produce the eastern merchants marketed—wheat, corn, flour, beef, pork, tobacco, and hemp—revealed the variety of crops and livestock produced and the increasing emphasis on commercial agriculture.

Among the farm animals raised by pioneer farmers for sale and export were cattle and swine. In fact, livestock raising was a major industry, particularly on the southern frontier, although farmers in various sections of the Piedmont used different techniques. When the pioneers of Virginia moved into the back country, they brought with them fifty to seventy-five head of cattle as part of general, or mixed, farming. Cattle raising as a separate industry was to be found in Georgia and the Carolinas where herds of several hundred to several thousand head ran on the open ranges and in the cane and woods. When it came time to brand calves or to select cattle for market, the animals were driven into a ranch or "cowpen," an enclosed area of 100 to 400 acres. The "cowpen" was a South Carolina Piedmont innovation that was extended first into North Carolina and by the 1760s across the Savannah River. Negro and white riders annually rounded up thousands of cattle, which were then taken to market at Savannah, Charleston, Wilmington, Alexandria, Baltimore, and even as far north as Philadelphia and New York City. The beef and pork, with other agricultural exports, ultimately were shipped to the West Indies and Europe.[9]

Farmers earned money in other ways. After burning off the forest covering to clear the land, pioneers in New England, New York, and Pennsylvania boiled down the wood ashes and obtained potassium carbonate, or potash, which they sold to be used for the manufacture of soap and glass. In the 1760s Sir William Johnson established a potash factory in the Mohawk Valley and employed German workmen under the management of Robert Adem. The beginnings of small industry were also to be found in other areas. The pioneers of Kentucky in 1778 refined salt on a large scale; those in Schoharie in 1777 produced sulphur. As early as 1772 the smiths along Redstone Creek were mining coal banks, and one coal mine was already open at Stewart's Crossing (modern Connelsville, Pennsylvania) on the Youghiogheny. Gristmills, sawmills, and fulling mills for processing the cloth spun in most pioneer homes were also established. In 1769 Cherry Valley, a settlement with only forty or fifty homes, boasted a pearlash work, a sawmill, three gristmills, a gunsmith, and a blacksmith who turned out ploughshares, coulters, and other agricultural implements.

Lumbering was a major occupation in the back country, especially in those sections of North Carolina and northern New England where the soil was too poor or too heavily timbered to cultivate. By 1771 the industry was well established in the Carolina Piedmont and in Vermont. That year an estimated 150,000 staves and boards were shipped down the Champlain Valley by the St. Lawrence River to Quebec. In Pennsylvania white pine, cherry, and walnut planks turned out at the saw pits at Middletown were sent down the Susquehanna to the eastern ports. This sector of the frontier economy was clearly commercial in nature.

By the outbreak of the Revolution some frontier regions such as the valley of Virginia, only partly settled before the French and Indian War, had developed a fairly diversified economy. The lower valley boasted distilleries, wineries, and at least four ironworks—Zane's, Bird and Miller's, Vestal's, and the Bloomery. Zane's Works annually produced several hundred tons of cooking utensils, stoves, plows, and other implements. Like the upper valley where significant settlement did not begin until the late 1760s it also exported large quantities of hemp, wheat, flour, corn, rye, oats, barley and beans.[10] This was a portent of the future economic development of the more recently settled frontier regions in the Carolinas, Pennsylvania, New York, and the Ohio Valley. Although not as far advanced, these regions were shortly to show comparable economic and social gains.

To Hector St. John Crevecoeur, the French aristocrat traveling on the Susquehanna River in 1774, it seemed that America, particularly the frontier environment, had wrought a marked change in the European immigrant, transforming him into a new man, the American.[11] This concept of the frontier as a "melting pot," a crucible, was perhaps more the romantic notion of an eighteenth-century European aristocrat and intellectual than it was a reality.

Although many national groups settled in the same general area on the frontiers, they invariably established separate, distinct communities and remained divided by cultural attitudes, social heritage, language, and religion. Each national and ethnic group clung to its heritage and resisted amalgamation; marriage between individuals of different nationalities was not the rule. As late as 1789 Paster Roschen warned the Germans of the Carolina Piedmont against marrying with the English or Scots-Irish: "Dissensions and feeble children are often the result." Germans, he claimed, "owe it to our native country to do our part that German blood and the German language are preserved. . . ." The Germans often referred contemptuously to "the dumb Irish," and the Ulstermen, for their part, were no more generous in their opinions of their Teutonic neighbors. Often it took several generations, long after the frontier stage had passed, for the various national and ethnic groups to adopt the English language and for the Germans, for example, to anglicize their names from "Weiss" to "White" or from "Stein" to "Stone" or to adopt the English equivalents "Carpenter" for "Zimmermann" and "Taylor" for "Schneider." The Germans, the "Switzers," the Scots, as well as the French Huguenots of the Carolina back settlements, spoke a different language and were far less assimilable than the Scots-Irish. Unlike urban life with its daily demands for intermingling, the isolated rural existence fostered the mutual exclusiveness of the various national and ethnic groups. Moreover, the regular arrival of kinsmen and friends from the Old World further reinforced their European attitudes and values.

No typical "frontiersman" or common frontier characteristics or traits emerged from the experiences of the early stages of settlement. All too often the Scots-Irish are taken as representative, but they were only the most numerous minority on the frontier. They tended to be undisciplined, emotional, aggressive, fiercely intolerant, restless, and in the southern back country, indolent. However, the Scots-Irish were also noted as being deeply religious, well indoctrinated in theology, hospitable, and courteous to strangers. The Germans in contrast were sedentary, pacific, law-abiding, stolid, and devoted to the social ideal of a well-ordered community, characteristics that set them apart not only from the Scots-Irish but also from the pioneers of English stock in southwestern Pennsylvania and Virginia who were noted for their tendencies toward profanity, dissipation, drinking, and gambling.[12]

Although small farmers constituted the great majority of the frontier population, class and social distinctions were to be found as gentlemen, soldiers, lawyers, professional men, land speculators, merchants, embryonic entrepreneurs, artisans, and men of substance and culture moved to the back settlements. Among the westerners existed a very wide range of social position, from abject poverty to considerable holdings in land, slaves, and personal property. In every frontier region there lived a small number of leading men from distinguished families, such as Adam Steven, William Fleming, Arthur St. Clair, and Philip Skene, who were differentiated from the majority of the population by culture, attainment, property, and education. The ordinary settlers looked up to them, and in turn they "supplied an initial overlay of culture to a nascent, bucolic society" of rustic farmers. In his travels among the Pennsylvania back settlements Philip Fithian found many "Persons of Character & Fortune." One, John Harns, residing west of the Juniata, lived "elegantly." His "Parlour" contained three large windows "each with twenty-four Lights of Large Glass." Squire William Browne, a farmer in the Kishacoquillas Valley of Pennsylvania, owned both a gristmill and a sawmill and ran an "extensive business." Samuel Culbertson, the son of another prosperous farmer, attended the college at Princeton and returned to western

Michael Brown stone house, Rowan County, North Carolina, 1766. (North Carolina State Department of Archives and History, Raleigh)

Pennsylvania as "a Doctor of Physick."[13] Such were living conditions among the frontier elite, but not among most of the early pioneers who often came to the new settlements with a minimum of the world's possessions and began their new life in a rustic hut or log cabin.

These primitive dwellings had been common in the heavily timbered regions of northern Europe for centuries before the first Scandinavians in 1638 and the Germans about 1710 used them in America. The Germans built this type of structure initially on the frontier of Pennsylvania and in the valley of Virginia. By the time of the Revolution, the log cabin was universally adopted by the backwoodsmen of whatever nationality and had become the earliest dwelling constructed on the frontier. With interstices plugged with a mixture of clay, grass, or moss and roofed with clapboard and bark, the log cabin was a simple, direct, and economical answer to the initial housing needs of the frontiersman of the wooded region who had only a few tools—an axe, adz, gimlet, auger, hammer, and saw. The simplest cabins were one- or two-room structures, often with dirt floors, but if covered, then with puncheons or split logs. Before glass was available, the settler covered the windows

William Marn's log cabin, Saluda, Polk County, North Carolina, 1790. (North Carolina State Department of Archives and History)

with skins, heavy shutters, or oiled paper. As the pioneer prospered, he replaced his log cabin with a log house of square hewn timbers, shingled roofs, a stone chimney, glass windows, and planked floors. Later he might have erected a clapboard and stone house, patterning it after structures in the East.[14]

During the initial frontier stage, most settlers enjoyed a simple standard of living. The pioneer family generally made clothing of animal skins or coarse linen and homespun wool cloth. Their homemade furniture was also rough and simple—a bedstead from a split tree, three-legged stools, crude tables, a few pewter dishes, forks, and knives for eating, and iron pots for cooking over an open fireplace. Meals often consisted of mush and milk or hog and hominy, occasionally supplemented by vegetables from a small garden or fish, venison, and bear meat. Practically all members of the family shared in the preparation and production of food. The women also wove cloth and fashioned garments from locally grown flax or from wool sheared from the family's sheep. Every pioneer family turned out its own leather. In time the settlers generally bettered their position and enjoyed a higher standard of living. Their homes could boast of featherbeds, pillows, linen sheets, tablecloths, looking glasses, china and delftware. On the southwestern Virginia frontier, the leading pioneers' wives decked themselves in silks, satins, and velveteens on Sundays; the men wore black, blue, brown, and scarlet broadcloths. It was not uncommon for choice wines to be

The MacKay House, residence of an Augusta Indian trader, Robert MacKay, from 1770 to 1775. (Georgia Historical Commission, Atlanta)

served at meals. By 1783 the "ladies" in the Kentucky stations were already anxious for the traders and merchants to import alum and copperas "of every kind" to be used as dyes and cosmetics.[15]

As the settlements developed, small hamlets grew up, and taverns or ordinaries for travelers were established at key trading points or at county seats, the scene of much activity on court days. More than one tavern was often found in small back-country villages with only thirty to fifty crude dwellings. According to one traveler, Carlisle, Pennsylvania was populated in 1762 mostly by people who kept dramshops and public houses. Hillsboro, North Carolina, in the 1760s had two or three ordinaries, an equal number of stores operated by Scottish merchants, a church, a courthouse, and a jail. Pittsburgh was perhaps the largest of the frontier hamlets even though the war had retarded its growth. By 1783 it housed about one hundred families in as many rude wooden cabins. With the cessation of hostilities its officers and merchants turned to trade with the settlements located down the Ohio River and imported dry goods from Philadelphia and Baltimore in exchange for whiskey, wheat, flour, and skins. The town boasted four attorneys at law and two doctors. But as yet there was no resident minister.

Generally, manners in the back country tended to be rustic, although a few persons attempted to follow the standards of the more polished society of the East. Most settlers engaged in physical sports and entertainment: foot and horse racing, cockfighting, house-raising, corn shucking, and shooting matches, all accompanied by the consumption of great quantities of strong drink. Heavy drinking and the general lack of morality, particularly in the South Carolina back country and in other regions where there were few restraints imposed due to the absence of churches and local courts, impressed many observers. The behavior of the recently arrived Presbyterians and Germans in Pennsylvania seemed to have been exemplary, however. While attending the funeral of a young infant in the Virginia settlements on the Monongahela, Nicholas Cresswell, an English traveler, noted that "At the Grave the parents and Friends W[e]pt and drank Whiskey alternately." One day Cresswell visited a prominent settler "at his Mistress's. The woman is common to him, his brother, half brother, and his own son and is his wife's sister's daughter at the same time." Shocked by these bizarre relationships, the priggish Englishman concluded that the settlers were a "vile set of brutes."[16]

Despite the rustic setting, the leading pioneers in the frontier communities often attempted to emulate the customs and conventions of upper class society on the seaboard. At Fort Pitt the officers of the British garrison and the important traders held dances every Saturday and entertained the prettiest ladies, who were sometimes Indian squaws. They also organized a "Monday club" for drinking and storytelling. A later American garrison there also attempted to observe the social amenities. On hearing that the "Gentlemen and Ladies of Stewart's Crossing" intended to visit them, the officers of the 8th Virginia Regiment erected a grand bower in the orchard, prepared a barbeque, and scheduled a ball in the rooms of Colonel John Gibson for the visiting officers and their wives and daughters.

The frontier gentry also sought to imbibe the learning of cultivated society as well as its mannerisms. Throughout the back country were to be found lawyers, physicians, teachers, and ministers—men of professional standing and general intellectual achievement. Although constituting only a small minority, they were to insure that learning would be transplanted and would flourish in the new setting. Lawyers arrived at an early date. William Grubbins, admitted to the Davidson County bar in 1785, attempted in his dress, attitudes, and law books "to re-create the life" of the lawyers he had known on the North Carolina seaboard[17] as did the lawyers of frontier Hillsboro in the 1760s when they used English texts and legal references. Few doctors, much less trained physicians, were to be found in the back country, although Loudoun and Carlisle in Pennsylvania could each boast of one as early as 1764. William Fleming, a former surgeon in the British army, settled on the Virginia frontier and rode throughout the countryside with a saddlebag of instruments and drugs. Apparently, there was some suspicion of doctors. Sir William Johnson complained that most of the "ignorant" settlers in the Mohawk Valley would "rather employ their own Quacks" than trust a trained physician. Even James Sterling, the merchant of Detroit, when seized by a "rascally distemper," preferred to "beat it out the field by pure force of Medicines & Bleeding." If a man died before the age of 100, Sterling speculated, "it must be by the blow of a stone hammer, or the infallible Medicines of some Quack Doctor."[18]

It is tempting to conclude that in a rustic society with little time for reading or cultural refinements there was a dearth of books and learning. Although generally valid, this conclusion is nonetheless misleading. George Croghan, the Indian trader, could hardly spell, but he did read and appreciate Sterne's *Tristram Shandy*. While wintering in Kentucky, Alexander Neely read aloud to Daniel Boone and other long hunters from Swift's *Gulliver's Travels*. Throughout the back country there were a few men of learning, culture, and literary taste. When Philip Fithian dined with Doctor Francis Aleson, Jr., and John Barber at the home of William Scull in the frontier hamlet of Sunbury, Pennsylvania, "Books & Literary Improvements" were the topics of conversation. On the Virginia frontier William Fleming had a library of 152 books in 214 volumes, including texts on practical subjects as well as historical and literary works. William Few in Hillsboro possessed a set of the *Spectator* among his library holdings; and Joseph Robinson, who migrated to the New Acquisition in South Carolina and settled on the Broad River in 1775, owned a library of sixty volumes in English, Latin, Greek, and Hebrew on mathematics, law, and divinity. These men were exceptions; however, many of the pioneer German families brought books, mainly religious works, from Europe, and once they had settled in the back country, obtained books and newspapers from the presses of their brethren in Pennsylvania. The Scots-Irish pioneers insisted that every child be able to read the Bible and the Shorter Catechism. Their Presbyterian ministers distributed books and tracts and helped found schools in the interior. Even before the outbreak of the Revolution they had established a chain of church schools along the frontier from New England to Georgia.[19]

Except in the South Carolina Piedmont where local government and church organizations were late in arriving, schools were set up at an early date through a variety of means. On the New England frontier the towns traditionally assumed the responsibility for education. However, in regions without a conventional village pattern, education was conducted initially on a haphazard basis. Still, the settlers showed concern that their children should not grow up without at least a rudimentary education, particularly, religious instruction. Mrs. William Coomes, an educated Catholic woman, ran a school at Harrodsburg during the earliest days of the settlement, teaching the children of the station the alphabet and arithmetic. A school was founded at McAfee's Station in 1777 and another at Boonesborough two years later. As early as 1761 the inhabitants of Pittsburgh subscribed £60 annually for a schoolmaster to teach their children. About twenty "Scholars" attended classes. In the 1760s Sir William Johnson helped support a "free School" at Johnstown in the Mohawk Valley.

Various Protestant religious organizations were a great influence in furthering education through the missionaries and ministers they sent into the back parts. For the Scots-Irish Presbyterians, education, specifically the ability to read the Bible, was essential for the laity as well as in the training of ministers. The Synod of New York and Pennsylvania in conjunction with the Presbyterian College of New Jersey (later, Princeton) played a key role. Their influence extended as far south as the back country of North Carolina where in the 1760s schools and log-cabin colleges under Doctor David Caldwell and the Reverend Henry Patillo were opened in Orange and Granville counties. In Virginia the Reverend John Brown had established a classical school in Augusta County before 1763, and by the outbreak of the Revolution, the Hanover Presbytery had founded Augusta Academy. Western Pennsylvania enjoyed schools of higher learning at an early date due to the efforts of ministers and teachers such as John McMillan, John Brown, John Smith, and Thaddeus Dodd. Out of their efforts west of the Allegheny Mountains came Cannonsburgh Academy, Washington Academy, and finally, Jefferson College. As early as 1780 the governments of New York and Virginia took steps to establish advanced schools—Clinton College at Schenectady for the education of the youth of Albany, Tryon, and Charlotte counties in the liberal and useful arts, and Transylvania Seminary at Lexington for the youth of the Kentucky frontier. Three years later the North Carolina assembly chartered Martin Academy, which had been founded by Samuel Doak, a former teacher at Hampden-Sydney. In 1777 Doak had crossed the mountains and come down the blazed trails to the Holston settlements. At Salem in Washington County he established a log-cabin college, Martin Academy, the first school of higher education in Tennessee and the first literary institution in the Mississippi Valley. Another early Tennessee teacher was Zachariah White who, like so many of the pioneer schoolmasters, taught in a primitive, rustic environment but employed in the Latin, or Classical, schools the texts and methods that were also used in the English and Scottish institutions.[20]

In establishing schools the pioneers sought to train ministers in their particular faith. The variety of Protestant sects represented among the back-country population in part reflected the diversity of national origin but also stemmed from the emotional upheaval of the revivalist Great Awakening of the 1720s and 1730s that had splintered many church groups throughout provincial America. On the frontier were to be found Congregationalists from New England, Anglicans from the seaboards of Virginia and the Carolinas, Scots-Irish Presbyterians, Baptists, and Quakers from all sections, French Huguenots, and Lutheran and Reformed Protestants from Germany and the Swiss cantons. The most numerous sects in the new settlements were the Presbyterian, Baptist, and German Lutheran and Reformed; however, these churches could claim only a small proportion of the population as adherents, for religion did not play a dominant role in frontier life during the initial years of settlement. The settlers of some sections, Pennsylvania for example, were perhaps more devout than those in South Carolina; and the Scots-Irish and Germans of Pennsylvania took their religion more seriously than did the Virginia frontiersmen of English descent. The Baptist, Presbyterian, and Lutheran churches could impose moral restraints only on their own members, a small portion of the population. As late as 1783 one traveler found no churches in Pittsburgh and only a few visiting preachers ministering to the German pioneers. There appeared to be no sign of morality or regular order among the other settlers of English extraction. Indeed, it seemed that the Presbyterian ministers feared to come to Pittsburgh lest "they should be mocked or mistreated." Richard Henderson condemned the first settlers of Boonesborough as a "set of scoundrels who scarcely believe in God or fear a devil. . . ." David Rice, a Presbyterian minister who settled in Kentucky in 1783, found the situation little changed at that time. He could scarcely find one man and only a few women who supported "a creditable profession of religion."[21] The settlers in the South Carolina back country and in Vermont were notorious for loose living and freethinking.

Differences in religion as well as in national origin tended to divide the back-country population. Congregationalists, Anglicans, Lutherans, Presbyterians, and Baptists often formed separate, distinct communities and maintained closer relations with their coreligionists in the East than with their neighbors of different persuasions. Sectarian animosities at times were strong on the frontier. Although there were instances of different sects using the same church building, some Presbyterians in western Pennsylvania objected to hearing a sermon by David Jones simply because he was a Congregationalist. Charles Woodmason, an Anglican missionary in the South Carolina backparts, complained that the Scots-Irish Presbyterians had hired "lawless Ruffians to insult me, which they did with Impunity. . . ." Exclaiming that they wanted no "D—d Black Gown Sons of Bitches," the Presbyterians even threatened Woodmason. When he persisted in holding services, in marrying couples who had not had the benefit of clerical sanction for their union, and in baptizing children, they often interrupted his services by "hallooing and whooping without Doors like Indians."

Despite adversity, indifference on the part of many pioneers, and open opposition by others, dedicated itinerant ministers of various Protestant denominations such as James Hawes, Benjamin Odgen, Lewis Craig, Charles Woodmason, Nicholas Christian, and Charles Beatty brought religion to the frontier. Traveling many miles on horseback from one community to another, they preached to whoever would listen and wherever they could—in houses, in barns, and even out-of-doors on the open ground. During one open-air service on the Juniata River in 1766 the congregation was forced indoors by rain. Two rattlesnakes had also sought the same refuge, but the "providence of God appeared very remarkable in preserving us from the venom of these creatures," Beatty recorded.[22]

Various religious organizations in the East and in Europe—for example, the Anglican Society for the Propagation of the Gospel, the Presbyterian Synod of New York, and the Congregational General Association of New England—sent ministers into the back country to proselytize and bring the established religious forms, practices, and churches to the frontier settlers.

The early Baptist ministers, by no means a majority among the frontier clerics, were a contrast to the more formal, educated clergy of the other sects and were peculiarly suited to the bucolic population of the new settlements. After hearing the sermon of a self-taught Baptist preacher from western Virginia, John Adams concluded that the parson had "No Learning—No Grace of Action or Utterance—but an honest Zeal. He told us several good Stories." Following the division into Separate and Regular Baptists during the revivalism of the Great Awakening, separatist societies spread quickly into the southern colonies, especially among the lower order of settlers. Their ministers, often men with little education, were sometimes jailed by the civil authorities, particularly those in Virginia, who claimed that in their preaching and teaching they disturbed the peace. Despite such obstacles, the New Light Separatists, carrying an extremely emotional message, made many converts among the isolated farmers. By the beginning of the Revolution they had become an aggressive, recognized force in Pennsylvania and throughout the South and were active among the settlers migrating westward. By 1780 eight Baptist ministers, accompanied by many of their followers, who had belonged to churches east of the mountains moved to the Holston, Watauga, and Kentucky settlements. Of the first twenty-five preachers to settle in Kentucky, twenty seem to have been Separatist Baptists from Virginia and North Carolina. Among them were Lewis Gray, Thomas Tinsly, and William Hickman. The Baptists were the first to extend the organized work of the church across the Allegheny Mountains and for several years were the strongest religious group in the transmontane region. From the first the Baptists west of the mountains maintained close relations with parent organizations in the Piedmont such as the Sandy Creek Association of North Carolina and Virginia formed in 1760. The earliest Baptist association beyond the mountains, the Redstone Association, was established in 1775 with the six churches—Great Bethel, Goshen, Ten Mile, Turkeyfoot, Pike Run and Yough—that had been founded in the Monongahela country between 1770 and 1774 by Henry Crossly, Isaac and James Sutton, and William Wood.[23]

In the North, the Warren Association of Rhode Island, one of the most active of the Baptist missionary centers, in 1767 sent itinerant preachers to the New England frontier. This was not the only religious organization to take an active interest there. Seven years later the Congregational General Association of New England, noting the lack of ministers among their coreligionists in the western and northwestern settlements, also resolved to send missionaries by raising money in the various Connecticut churches. German settlers in Rowen and Mecklenburg counties, North Carolina, sent to Hanover, Germany, for a pastor and a supply of ministers, but their request was not immediately fulfilled due to the outbreak of the Revolutionary War. However, the parent organizations of the Lutheran and Reformed churches in Pennsylvania were able to send ministers to the southern back country. Before the Revolution the Anglican bishops in England and the Society for the Propagation of the Gospel sent missionaries and ministers to the Floridas, the Georgia and South Carolina back settlements, and the Mohawk Valley. Anglican churches were scattered throughout the interior. Indeed, St. Thomas' Episcopal Church, probably built in 1770, may have been the first church west of the mountains in Pennsylvania.

Recent arrivals from northern Ireland to the frontier brought with them Presbyterian religious institutions and practices. Although ministers initially were not available in the new settlements, parents often indoctrinated their children in the Longer and Shorter Catechism. In the Ligonier Valley of Pennsylvania, according to one observer, almost every family carefully studied the Westminster Confession of Faith. Families pooled their resources and applied to the New Side Synod of New York and Philadelphia for ministers. At first, the Synod sent out traveling missionaries such as Charles Beatty and George Duffield, but by the start of the Revolution the Presbyteries of New Castle, Donegal, and New York had licensed James Powers, John McMillan, Thaddeus Dodd, and Joseph Smith who were permanently established west of the Allegheny Mountains.[24] Responding to appeals from Scots-Irish pioneers, the Synod of New York and Philadelphia in 1768 sent ministers to the southern back country. By 1771 the Presbytery of Orange was organized for North Carolina. Across the mountains two churches at Ebbing and Sinking Creek in the Holston settlements in 1773 offered Charles Cumming, a native of Ireland, £90 a year to act as their minister. The settlers in Lincoln County, Kentucky, persuaded David Rice, the "father of Presbyterianism in Kentucky," at the close of the Revolution to settle near Danville. In 1778 Samuel Doak, a graduate of the College of New Jersey, arrived in eastern Tennessee. Among the others who followed was Gideon Blackburn.

Gideon Blackburn, John McMillan, Samuel Doak, Thaddeus Dodd, the other ministers and teachers, and the physicians and lawyers were among the "potent minority of culture bearers" who transmitted and preserved civilization on the Revolutionary frontier. Despite the influence the wilderness environment might have on a primitive culture, its effect on an advanced society was not decisive. The crude conditions of frontier existence temporarily influenced the back-country society in the earliest stages, but settlers clung tenaciously to the culture, values, and traditions they brought with them. The pioneers themselves were directly or indirectly the products of European, particularly the British, influence, "the oldest, the most persistent, and the most vigorous strain in [the American] heritage."

The frontier settlers of the Revolutionary generation developed little that was new, certainly not democracy; they did not pioneer new systems of government, religion, or agriculture. At best, they adapted old techniques to a wilderness environment, and in the end, they altered this environment. Teachers like Zachariah White who taught in a fort stockaded against hostile Indians used textbooks of English origin. Although frontier ministers may at times have preached in open fields, or crude log cabins, the "basic tenents of their theology were, like the hymns of Watts and Wesley, of European origin."[25] During the initial stages of development in the southern back country and elsewhere on the frontier, the lack of a unified tradition, an underdeveloped economy, and the conditions of landholding led to a rough sort of egalitarianism, but once the frontier stage had passed and the backwoods society had begun to crystalize, the patterns of the established society of the East

NOTES

Chapter 1: Background and Setting

[1] Lewis D. Stilwell, "Migration from Vermont (1776–1860)," *Vermont Historical Society, Proceedings*, new ser., V (1937), pp. 67–71.

[2] Alfred P. James, "The First English-Speaking Trans-Appalachian Frontier," *Mississippi Valley Historical Review*, XVII (June 1930), pp. 57–61; Hugh T. Lefler and Paul Wagner, eds., *Orange County, 1752–1952* (Chapel Hill, N.C., 1953), pp. 14–15; and Robert L. Meriwether, *The Expansion of South Carolina, 1729–1765* (Kingsport, Tenn., 1940), pp. 160–162.

[3] For the Great Cherokee War of 1759–1761, see Lawrence Henry Gipson, *The British Empire before the American Revolution*, 12 vols. (Caldwell, Idaho, and New York, 1936–1965), IX, 55–87.

[4] Thomas Gage to Hugh Lord, August 30, 1772, Thomas Gage Papers, William L. Clements Library, Ann Arbor, Michigan; Anthony F. C. Wallace, *King of the Delawares: Teedyuscung, 1700–1763* (Philadelphia, 1949), pp. 258–262; Gipson, *British Empire Before the American Revolution*, IX, 92–96; Majorie G. Reid, "The Quebec Fur-Traders and Western Policy, 1763–1774" *Canadian Historical Review*, VI (March 1925), pp. 17–18; and Myles M. Platt, "Detroit Under Siege, 1763," *Michigan History*, XL (December 1956), pp. 491, 496.

[5] The best work on the Indian war of 1763–1765 is Howard H. Peckham, *Pontiac and the Indian Uprising* (Princeton, 1847). See also Gipson, *British Empire before the American Revolution*, IX, 94 ff.; and Francis Parkman, *The Conspiracy of Pontiac and the Indian War after the Conquest of Canada*, 2 vols. (Boston, 1887).

[6] Compare John C. Dillin, *The Kentucky Rifle* (4th ed., New York, 1959), p. 50 with Don Higginbotham, *Daniel Morgan, Revolutionary Rifleman* (Chapel Hill, 1961), p. 20 and George A. Cribbs, *The Frontier Policy of Pennsylvania* (Pittsburgh, 1919), pp. 102–103.

[7] See John K. Mahon, "Anglo-American Methods of Indian Warfare, 1676–1794," *Mississippi Valley Historical Review*, XLV (September 1958), pp. 258–275; Charles M. Stotz, "Defense in the Wilderness" in "Drums in the Forest," *Western Pennsylvania Historical Magazine*, Special Bicentennial Issue, nos. 3–4, XLI (Autumn 1958), pp. 99–101; and Edward G. Williams, ed., "The Orderly Book of Colonel Henry Bouquet's Expedition against the Ohio Indians, 1764," *ibid.*, XLII (March, June, September 1959), pp. 9–34, 179–200, 283–302.

[8] See, for example, Bouquet to Benjamin Franklin, August 10, 1764, Franklin Papers, American Philosophical Society, Philadelphia, I, part ii, no. 92; and Bradstreet to Gage, April 6, May 28, June 4, 1764, Gage Papers, Clements Library. On the Conestoga murders and back country discontent in Pennsylvania see Brook Hindle, "The March of the Paxton Boys," *William and Mary Quarterly*, 3d ser., III (October 1946), pp. 461–486.

[9] Peckham, *Pontiac and the Indian Uprising*, pp. 255–263; and Nicholas B. Wainwright, *George Croghan, Wilderness Diplomat* (Chapel Hill, N.C., 1959), pp. 201–222.

[10] For a discussion of British policy in the pre-Revolutionary decade see Helen

Louise Shaw, *British Administration of the Southern Indians, 1756–1783* (Lancaster, Pa., 1931); Jack M. Sosin, *Whitehall and the Wilderness* (Lincoln, Neb., 1961); and John R. Alden, *John Stuart and the Southern Colonial Frontier* (Ann Arbor, Mich., 1944).

[11] William W. Abbott, *The Royal Governors of Georgia, 1754–1775* (Chapel Hill, 1959), pp. 90–91; and Wilbur R. Jacobs, ed., *Indians of the Southern Colonial Frontier. The Edmund Atkin Report and Plan of 1755* (Columbia, S.C., 1954).

[12] Clarence E. Carter, "British Policy toward the American Indians in the South, 1763–1768," *English Historical Review*, XXXIII (January 1918), pp. 38–40, 45–46.

[13] Taitt to John Stuart, October 19, 1772, Gage Papers, Clements Library; Alden, *John Stuart*, pp. 210, 341–343; and Sosin, *Whitehall and the Wilderness*, pp. 212–218, 248–249.

[14] On the frontier military posts see William A. Hunter, *Forts on the Pennsylvania Frontier, 1753–1758* (Harrisburg, 1960); and Stotz, "Defense in the Wilderness," *passim.*

[15] The Earl of Halifax to Jeffrey Amherst, October 11, 1763, Public Record Office, London, Colonial Office, 5/214:690; and Sosin, *Whitehall and the Wilderness*, pp. 32–33, 42–51, 60–64.

[16] Alden, *John Stuart*, pp. 183–185, 199, 201–202; Shaw, *British Administration of the Southern Indians*, pp. 24–25; and Carter, "British Policy toward the American Indians in the South," pp. 51–53.

[17] See Peter Marshall, "Imperial Regulation of American Indian Affairs" (Ph.D. dissertation, Yale University, 1959), pp. 181–184; Ray A. Billington, "The Ft. Stanwix Treaty of 1768," *New York History*, XXV (April 1944), pp. 182–194; Thomas P. Abernethy, *Western Lands and the American Revolution* (New York, 1959), pp. 33–34; Wainwright, *George Croghan*, pp. 239–258; and Sosin, *Whitehall and the Wilderness*, pp. 172–179.

[18] Kenneth Coleman, *The American Revolution in Georgia, 1763–1789* (Athens, 1959), pp. 7–8; Alden, *John Stuart*, pp. 280–283, 301–307; St. George L. Siousatt, "The Breakdown of the Royal Management of Lands in the Southern Provinces, 1773–1775," *Agricultural History*, III (April 1929), p. 75; and Louis DeVorsey, Jr., "The Virginia-Cherokee Boundary of 1771," *East Tennessee Historical Society, Publications*, XXXIII (1961), pp. 17–31.

Chapter 2: Pressures for Expansion

[1] William L. Langer, "Europe's Initial Population Explosion," *American Historical Review*, LXIX (October 1963), pp. 1–17.

[2] Catherine S. Crary, "The Humble Immigrant and the American Dream: Some Case Histories, 1746–1776," *Mississippi Valley Historical Review*, XLVI (June 1959), pp. 46–66; George R. Mellor, "Emigration from the British Isles to the New World, 1765–1775," *History*, XL (February and June 1955), pp. 68–71, 77.

[3] Ian Charles Cargill Graham, *Colonists from Scotland; Emigration to North America, 1707–1783* (Ithaca, N.Y., 1956), pp. 1–89, 185–186; Duane Meyer, *The Highland Scots of North Carolina, 1732–1776* (Chapel Hill, N.C., 1961), pp. 54–100; and "Journal of the Managers of the Scotch-American Company of Farmers," Vermont Historical Society, *Proceedings* (1928), pp. 181–203.

[4] Edward R. R. Green, "Scotch-Irish Emigration: An Imperial Problem," *Western Pennsylvania Historical Magazine*, XXXV (December 1952), pp. 203–208; and Mildred Campbell, "English Emigration on the Eve of the American Revolution," *American Historical Review*, LXI (October 1955), pp. 1–20.

[5] William S. Sachs, "Agricultural Conditions in the Northern Colonies Before the Revolution," *Journal of Economic History* (Summer 1953), pp. 274–290.

[6] Harry J. Carmen and Rexford G. Tugwell, eds., *American Husbandry* (New York, 1939), pp. 63, 123; John G. Gagliardo, "Germans and Agriculture in Colonial Pennsylvania," *Pennsylvania Magazine of History and Biography*, LXXXIII (April 1959), pp. 192–201; and Albert L. Olson, *Agricultural Economy and Population in Eighteenth-Century Connecticut* (New Haven, 1935), pp. 4–10.

[7] John E. Goodrich, "Immigration to Vermont," Vermont Historical Society, *Proceedings* (1909), pp. 65–85.

[8] Willard F. Bliss, "The Tuckahoe in the Valley" (Ph.D. dissertation, Princeton University, 1946), pp. 70–105; and Willard F. Bliss, "The Rise of Tenancy in Virginia," *Virginia Magazine of History and Biography*, LVIII (October 1950), pp. 427–441.

[9] Deane to James Wilson, April 1, 1783, New York Historical Society, *Collections*, Publication Fund, XXIII (1891), p. 149.

[10] Marshall D. Harris, *Origin of the Land Tenure System in the United States* (Ames, Iowa, 1953), pp. 251–252.

[11] Herbert C. Laub, "British Regulation of the Crown Lands in the West: the Last Phase, 1773–1775," *William and Mary Quarterly*, 2d ser., X (January 1930), pp. 52–55; and St. George L. Sioussat, "The Breakdown of the Royal Management of Lands in the Southern Provinces, 1773–1775," *Agricultural History*, III (April 1929), p. 68.

[12] Lewis D. Stilwell, "Migration from Vermont (1776–1860)," Vermont Historical Society, *Proceedings*, new ser., V (1937), pp. 83–84.

[13] On the conditions for land tenure in New York see Don R. Gerlach, *Philip Schuyler and the Revolution in New York* (Lincoln, Neb., 1963), pp. 323–327.

[14] Stevenson Whitcomb Fletcher, *Pennsylvania Agriculture and Country Life, 1648–1840* (Harrisburg 1950), pp. 15, 23.

[15] Clarence W. Alvord, "The Daniel Boone Myth," Illinois State Historical Society, *Journal*, XIX (April 1926), pp. 21–22, and Brent Altsheler, "The Long Hunters and James Knox, Their Leader," *Filson Club History Quarterly*, V (October 1931), pp. 169–180.

[16] For a general discussion see Wayne E. Stevens, *The Northwest Fur Trade, 1763–1800* (Urbana, Ill., 1928).

[17] See, for example, Nicholas B. Wainwright, "An Indian Trade Failure: The Story of Hockley, Trent, and Croghan Company," *Pennsylvania Magazine of History and Biography*, LXXII (October 1948), pp. 343–375.

[18] Croghan to General Thomas Gage, August 8, 1772, Thomas Gage Papers, William Clements Library, Ann Arbor, Michigan; Sterling to John Duncan, August 26, 1762, James Sterling Letterbook, p. 70, Clements Library.

[19] Ernest Cruikshank, "Early Traders and Trade-routes in Canada and the West, 1760–1783," Royal Canadian Institute, *Transactions*, III (1886–1892), pp. 253–274; W. Steward Wallace, "The Pedlars from Quebec," *Canadian Historical Review*, XIII (December 1932), pp. 387–402; and Marjorie G. Reid, "The Quebec Fur-Traders and Western Policy, 1763–1774," *Canadian Historical Review*, VI (March 1925), pp. 15–32.

[20] For a good analysis of the southern merchants see J. A. Brown, "Panton, Leslie and Company: Indian Traders of Pensacola and St. Augustine," *Florida Historical Quarterly*, XXXVII (January 1959), pp. 328–336.

[21] Max Savelle, *George Morgan Colony Builder* (New York, 1932), pp. 6, 17–20, 25–26, 37, 51; Charles M. Thomas, "Successful and Unsuccessful Merchants in

the Illinois Country," *Journal of the Illinois State Historical Society,* XXV (January 1938), pp. 429–437.

[22] For the role of the land speculators in the expansion of New York see Nicholas B. Wainwright, *George Croghan, Wilderness Diplomat* (Chapel Hill, N.C., 1959), pp. 243–244.

[23] David Alan Williams, "Political Alignments in Colonial Virginia, 1698–1750" (Ph.D. dissertation, Northwestern University, 1959), pp. 320–335, 357–358.

[24] On the Virginia companies see Thomas P. Abernethy, *Western Lands and the American Revolution* (New York, 1959); and Alfred P. James, *The Ohio Company: Its Inner History* (Pittsburgh, Pa., 1959).

[25] Wainwright, *Croghan, Wilderness Diplomat,* pp. 254–255.

[26] For the Walpole, Illinois, and Wabash companies see Jack M. Sosin, *Whitehall and the Wilderness: The Middle West in British Colonial Policy, 1761–1775* (Lincoln, Neb., 1961), pp. 181–210, 259–267.

[27] See the deposition of Samuel Wilson, Draper Collection, 1CC161, Wisconsin State Historical Society, Madison, Wisconsin; and John P. Brown, *Old Frontiers: the Story of the Cherokee Indians from Earliest Times to the Date of Their Removal to the West, 1838* (Kingsport, Tenn., 1938), p. 165.

Chapter 3: Expansion in the North, 1763–1775

[1] Rising Lake Morrow, *Connecticut Influences in Western Massachusetts and Vermont* (New Haven, Conn., 1936), pp. 11–14.

[2] Kathryn Harrod Mason, "Harrods's Men—1774," *Filson Club History Quarterly,* XXIV (July 1950), pp. 321–323; and John Gerald Patterson, "Ebenezer Zane, Frontiersman," *West Virginia History,* XII (October 1950), p. 9.

[3] See, for example, Alex M. Hitz, "The Wrightsborough Quaker Town and Township in Georgia," Friends Historical Association, *Bulletin,* XLVI (Spring 1957), pp. 12–16; and Edward R. R. Green, "Queensborough Township: Scotch-Irish Emigration and the Expansion of Georgia, 1763–1776," *William and Mary Quarterly,* 3d ser., XVII (April 1960), pp. 181–197, 199.

[4] E. P. Panagopolous, "The Background of the Greek Settlement in the New Smyrna, Colony," *Florida Historical Quarterly,* XXXV (October 1956), pp. 107–114; and John Pell, "Philip Skene of Skenesborough," New York State Historical Association, *Quarterly Journal,* IX (January 1928), p. 29–30.

[5] Charles H. Ambler, *George Washington and the West* (Chapel Hill, N.C., 1936), pp. 152–156; and Ruth Higgins, *Expansion in New York with Special Reference to the Eighteenth Century* (Columbus, Ohio, 1931), p. 91.

[6] Duncan Fraser, "Sir John Johnson's Rent Roll of the Kingsborough Patent," *Ontario History,* LIII (September 1960), pp. 176–182. On Duane's activities see Edward P. Alexander, *A Revolutionary Conservative: James Duane of New York* (New York, 1938), pp. 58–66.

[7] Fairfax Harrison, *Virginia Land Grants, A Study of Conveyancing in Relation to Colonial Politics* (Richmond, Va., 1925), p. 140, note 2.

[8] Ralph H. Records, "Land as a Basis for Economic and Social Discontent in Maine and Massachusetts to 1776" (Ph.D. dissertation, University of Chicago, 1936), pp. 183–188; and Shelburne Papers, Clements Library, 66:433, 507.

[9] Walter Thompson Bogart, "An Introductory Study of the Lease Lands of Vermont" (Ph.D. dissertation, Stanford University, 1948), pp. 64–66; Florence May Woodward, *The Town Proprietors in Vermont: The New England Town Proprietary in Decline* (New York, 1936), pp. 50–51, 59–81.

[10] John E. Goodrich, "Immigration to Vermont: Was Immigration to Vermont stimulated in the years 1760–90 by persecution on the part of the 'Standing order' in Massachusetts and Connecticut?" Vermont Historical Society, *Proceedings*, (1909), pp. 65–68, 83–85; Lewis D. Stilwell, "Migration from Vermont (1776–1860)," *ibid.*, new ser., V (1937), pp. 64, 74–78.

[11] Hiland Hall, "New York Land Grants in Vermont, 1765–1776," Vermont Historical Society, *Collections*, I (Montpelier, 1870), pp. 158–159.

[12] Chilton Williamson, *Vermont In Quandary, 1763–1825* (Montpelier, 1949), pp. 11–15, 22–23, 26–30, 36–39; and Winn Lowell Taplin, Jr., "The Vermont Problem in the Continental Congress and in Interstate Relations, 1776–1787" (Ph. D. dissertation, University of Michigan, 1956), pp. 9–10.

[13] Higgins, *Expansion in New York*, pp. 73–94; and Albert T. Volwiler, "George Croghan and the Development of Central New York, 1763–1800," New York State Historical Association, *Journal*, IV (January 1923), pp. 21–40.

[14] The best, but far from adequate, treatment of the Paxton Boys is Brooke Hindle, "The March of the Paxton Boys," *William and Mary Quarterly*, 3d ser., III (October 1946), pp. 461–486.

[15] Julian P. Boyd, "Connecticut's Experiment in Expansion; the Susquehanna Company, 1753–1803," *Journal of Economic and Business History*, IV (November 1931), pp. 38–69.

[16] Norman B. Wilkinson, "Land Policy and Speculation in Pennsylvania, 1779–1800" (Ph.D. dissertation, University of Pennsylvania, 1958), pp. 70–72.

[17] Alfred P. James, *The Ohio Company: Its Inner History* (Pittsburgh, Pa., 1959), pp. 122, 150.

[18] See Consul W. Butterfield, ed., *Washington-Crawford Letters, Being the Correspondence between George Washington and William Crawford, from 1767 to 1781 Concerning Western Lands,* (Cincinnati, Ohio, 1877), pp. 19–26.

[19] Percy B. Caley, "Lord Dunmore and the Pennsylvania-Virginia Boundary Dispute," *Western Pennsylvania Historical Magazine*, XXII (June 1939), pp. 87–100.

Chapter 4: Expansion in the South, 1763–1775

[1] Mrs. Dunbar Rowland, comp., "Mississippi Colonial Population and Land Grants," Mississippi Historical Society, *Publications*, centenary ser., I (1916), pp. 409–418; and Cecil Johnson, "The Distribution of Land in British West Florida," *Louisiana Historical Quarterly*, XVI (October 1933), pp. 539–553.

[2] [Albert C. Bates, ed.], *The Two Putnams, Rufus and Israel, in the Havana Expedition of 1762, and in the Mississippi River Exploration 1772–1773, with Some Account of the Company of Military Adventurers* (Hartford, Conn., 1931), pp. 9–45, 186, 200, 261–262.

[3] Wilbur H. Siebert, "Slavery and White Servitude in East Florida, 1726–1776," *Florida Historical Quarterly*, X (July 1931), pp. 8–9, 12–19; and Charles L. Mowat, "The First Campaign of Publicity for Florida," *Mississippi Valley Historical Review*, XXX (December 1943), p. 376.

[4] James Etheridge Callaway, *The Early Settlement of Georgia* (Athens, Ga., 1948), pp. 58–60, 63–66.

[5] Robert L. Meriwether, *The Expansion of South Carolina, 1729–1765* (Kingsport, Tenn., 1940), pp. 242–260.

[6] The best treatment of the Regulator movement is in Richard M. Brown, *The South Carolina Regulators* (Cambridge, 1963).

[7] Adelaide L. Fries, ed., *Records of the Moravians in North Carolina* [1752–1783], 4 vols. (Raleigh, 1922–1930), I, 456, 378.

[8] John Butler to William Butler, August 14, 1771, Regulator Papers, Southern Historical Collection, University of North Carolina Library, Chapel Hill, North Carolina. For the Regulator movement see chapter IV in Hugh T. Lefler and Paul Wagner, eds., *Orange County, 1752–1952* (Chapel Hill, 1953).

[9] W. S. Laidley, "The Frontier Counties of West Virginia," *West Virginia Historical Magazine*, III (January 1903), pp. 14–18.

[10] Shelby Papers, vol. I, doc. 400, Library of Congress, Washington, D.C.; and Faye Bartlett Reeder, "The Evolution of the Virginia Land Grant System in the Eighteenth Century" (Ph.D. dissertation, Ohio State University, 1937), pp. 120–125.

[11] Samuel C. Williams, "Henderson and Company's Purchase Within the Limits of Tennessee," *Tennessee Historical Magazine*, V (April 1919), p. 27; and James G. Ramsey, *The Annals of Tennessee to the End of the Eighteenth Century* . . . , 3d ed., (Kingsport, Tenn., 1926), pp. 106–107, 133–139.

[12] John Ferdinand Dalziel Smyth, *Tour in the United States of America*, 2 vols. (London, 1784), I, 125–126; John Stuart to Thomas Gage, May 26, 1775, Thomas Gage Papers, Clements Library, Ann Arbor, Michigan; deposition of Samuel Wilson, Draper Collection, 1CC161, Wisconsin State Historical Society, Madison; and Williams, "Henderson and Company Purchase Within the Limits of Tennessee," *Tennessee Historical Magazine*, V (April 1919), pp. 8–10.

[13] Alfred P. James, *The Ohio Company: Its Inner History* (Pittsburgh, Pa., 1959), pp. 159–162; and Kenneth P. Bailey, *The Ohio Company of Virginia and the Westward Movement, 1748–1792* (Glendale, Calif., 1939), pp. 274–275.

[14] John Brown to William Preston, May 5, 1775, Reuben Gold Thwaites and Louise Phelps Kellogg, eds., *The Revolution on the Upper Ohio, 1775–1777* (Madison, 1908), p. 10.

[15] Robert Spencer Cotterill, *History of Pioneer Kentucky* (Cincinnati, 1917), pp. 90–92; and also "Journal of Colonel Richard Henderson Relating to the Transylvania Colony," in Walter Clark, *The Colony of Transylvania*, booklet no. 9 of *Great Events in North Carolina History*, III (January 1904), pp. 18–20, 25–26.

[16] William Lester, *The Transylvania Colony* (Spencer, Ind., 1936), pp. 97–103.

Chapter 5: The Struggle with the Indian Tribes, 1773–1776

[1] Croghan to General Thomas Gage, June 17, 1764, Thomas Gage Papers, Clements Library, Ann Arbor, Michigan; and Fauquier to the Earl of Halifax, June 14, 1765, Public Record Office, London, Colonial Office, 5/1345:160.

[2] John R. Alden, *John Stuart and the Southern Colonial Frontier* (Ann Arbor, Mich. 1944), p. 307; John Stuart to Frederick Haldimand, June 24, 1774, Gage Papers, Clements Library; Charles Grant to Gage, August 27, 1767, *ibid.*; and *Minutes of the Provincial Council of Pennsylvania, 1693–1776*, 10 vols. (Harrisburg 1851–1852), IX, 305–306, 350.

[3] *Minutes of the Provincial Council of Pennsylvania*, IX, 416–419, 438, 444–449, 462–464; George Croghan to Gage, February 17, 1768, Gage Papers, Clements Library; John Penn to Gage, January 21, February 11, 1768, *ibid.*; and Thomas Wharton to Benjamin Franklin, February 9, 1768, Benjamin Franklin Papers, II, Part 2, no. 112, American Philosophical Society Library, Philadelphia, Pa.

[4] Alden, *John Stuart and the Southern Colonial Frontier*, p. 218; W. Stitt Robin-

son, Jr., "The Legal Status of the Indian in Colonial Virginia," *Virginia Magazine of History and Biography,* LXI (July 1953), p. 250; and Andrew Lewis to Francis Fauquier, May 9, June 3, 1765, in H. R. McIlwaine and J. P. Kennedy, eds., *Journals of the House of Burgesses of Virginia* (*1619–1776*), 13 vols. (Richmond, 1905–1915), [vol.] *1761–1765,* pp. xx, xxiii–xxiv.

⁵ Entry for May 14, 1771, diary of Alexander McKee, enclosed in Captain Charles Edmunstone to General Thomas Gage, August 24, 1771, Gage Papers, Clements Library.

⁶ John Stuart to Thomas Gage, May 12, 1774, Gage Papers, Clements Library; Stuart to Frederick Haldimand, February 10, 1774, *ibid.;* James Wright to Haldimand, May 20, 1774, *ibid.;* Stuart to Haldimand, February 3, 1774, Frederick Haldimand Papers (transcripts), Public Archives of Canada, Ottawa, vol. 12, pp. 261–267; and Alexander Cameron to Stuart, February 4, 1774, *ibid.,* vol. 12, p. 282.

⁷ Killbuck's speech, undated, is filed among the documents for the year 1771, Gage Papers, Clements Library.

⁸ Alexander Cameron to John Stuart, June 18, 1774, enclosed in Stuart to Gage, July 3, 1774, Gage Papers, Clements Library.

⁹ See the depositions of Isaac Thomas, February 12, 1774, and Thomas Sharp, October 5, 1773, in William Ogilvy to Frederick Haldimand, June 8, 1774, Gage Papers, Clements Library; Alexander McKee to Haldimand, June 28, 1773, Haldimand Papers, Public Archives of Canada, vol. 10, p. 103; and George Croghan to Thomas Wharton, October 15, December 9, 1773, "Letters of Colonel George Croghan," *Pennsylvania Magazine of History and Biography,* XV (1891), pp. 435–436.

¹⁰ On the origins of Dunmore's War and the Indian crisis of 1774, see my article "The British Indian Department and Dunmore's War, 1774," *The Virginia Magazine of History and Biography,* LXXIV (January 1966), pp. 34–50.

¹¹ Arthur St. Clair to Governor John Penn, August 8, 1774, William Henry Smith, ed., *The Life and Public Services of Arthur St. Clair . . . with his Correspondence . . . ,* 2 vols. (Cincinnati, 1882), I, 338–339; Guy Johnson to Thomas Gage, September 29, 1774, Gage Papers, Clements Library; John Stuart to Gage, May 12, November 19, 1774, and January 18, 1775, *ibid.;* John Stuart to Frederick Haldimand, June 25, 1774, *ibid.;* John Stuart to Haldimand, February 3, November 20, 1774, Haldimand Papers, Public Archives of Canada, vol. 12, pp. 263, 397.

¹² Walter H. Mohr, *Federal Indian Relations, 1774–1788* (Philadelphia, 1933), pp. 32–35.

¹³ On the activities of the Massachusetts Whigs see the address to the Six Nations in Peter Force, ed., *American Archives,* ser. 4 and 5, 9 vols. (Washington, 1837–1854), 4th ser., I, 1350; and the Massachusetts Provincial Congress to the eastern Indians, May 15, 1775, in Frederic Kidder, *Military Operations in Eastern Maine and Nova Scotia during the Revolution . . . from the Journals of Col. John Allan . . .* (Albany, 1867), pp. 51–52. For the British efforts see Guy Carleton to Gage, May 3, June 4, July 27, August 5, 1775, Gage Papers, Clements Library; Gage to Carleton, May 20, 1775, *ibid.;* Gage to John Caldwell, May 10, 1775, *ibid.;* Gage to Richard Lernoult, May 20, 1775, *ibid.;* Gage to Arent De Peyster, May 20, 1775, *ibid.;* and Gage to Caldwell, May 20, 1775, *ibid.* See also Marc Jack Smith, "Joseph Brant, a Mohawk Statesman" (Ph.D. dissertation, University of Wisconsin, 1946), pp. 17–19.

¹⁴ See Guy Johnson to Lord George Germain, November 25, 1776, in Force, *American Archives,* 5th ser., III, 839; Sir William Howe to Germain, June 7, 1776,

Germain Papers, Clements Library; Brant's message of December 26, 1776, Haldimand Papers, Public Archives of Canada, vol. 39, pp. 360–361; and Carleton to Lernoult and John Butler, February 9, 1777, *ibid.*, vol. 39, pp. 356–357, 358–359.

[15] On this episode see Percy B. Caley, "The Life Adventures of Lieutenant-Colonel John Connolly: The Story of a Tory," *Western Pennsylvania Historical Magazine*, XI (April 1928), pp. 101–106; Clarence M. Burton, "John Connolly, A Tory of the Revolution," American Philosphical Society, *Proceedings for 1909*, new ser., XX (October 1909), pp. 86–87; Connolly's proposals to Gage, September 11, 1775, Gage Papers, Clements Library; Gage's reply, September 11, 1775, *ibid.*; Gage to Lernoult, September 10, 1775, *ibid.*; Gage to Carleton, September 11, 1775, *ibid.*; and Gage to Captain Hugh Lord (at Kaskaskia), September 12, 1775, *ibid.*

[16] On the activities of the British Indian agents in the South see John Stuart to Sir Henry Clinton, March 15, May 6, 1776, Clinton Papers, Clements Library; Thomas Brown to Stuart, February 24, 1776, *ibid.*; Clinton's memorandum, May 9, 1776, *ibid.*; John Stuart to Thomas Gage, October 3, 1775, Force, *American Archives*, 4th ser., IV, 316; and Henry Stuart's account, August 25, 1776, William L. Saunders, ed., *Colonial Records of North Carolina*, 10 vols. (Raleigh, 1888–1890), X, 771–785.

[17] On the Cherokee War of 1776 see John P. Brown, *Old Frontiers: The Story of the Cherokee Indians from Earliest Times to the Date of Their Removal to the West, 1838* (Kingsport, Tenn., 1938), pp. 140–163; Robert S. Cotterill, *The Southern Indians: The Story of the Civilized Tribes Before Removal* (Norman, Okla. 1954), pp. 42–45; and Elby A. Boosinger, "The Cherokee Indians in the Revolutionary War" (M. A. thesis, University of Nebraska, 1951), pp. 37–50.

[18] Kenneth Coleman, *The American Revolution in Georgia, 1763–1789* (Athens, Ga., 1959), p. 141; and Charles L. Mowat, *East Florida as a British Province 1763–1784* (Berkeley, Calif., 1943), p. 113.

[19] Willett to Philip Schuyler, April 29, 1778, Ayer Collection, Newberry Library, Chicago. The bulk of this chapter is based on Jack M. Sosin, "The Use of Indians in the American Revolution," *Canadian Historical Review*, XLVI (June 1965), pp. 101–121; Nelson Vance Russell, "The Indian Policy of Henry Hamilton: a Re-evaluation," *ibid.*, XI (March 1930) pp. 20–37; Howard Swiggert, *War Out of Niagara, Walter Butler and the Tory Rangers* (New York, 1933), pp. 44, 48; Philip M. Hamer, "John Stuart's Indian Policy during the Early Months of the American Revolution," *Mississippi Valley Historical Review*, XVII (December 1930), pp. 351–366; and Philip M. Hamer, "The Wataugans and the Cherokee Indians in 1776," East Tennessee Historical Society, *Publications*, III (January 1931), pp. 108–126.

Chapter 6: Whigs, Tories, and Neutrals: Political Allegiances during the Revolution

[1] See "The Case of Hugh Kelly and James Fleming . . . ," British Army Headquarters [Guy Carleton] Papers, no. 5178, Public Record Office, London. The latest general treatment of Loyalism, William Nelson, *The American Tory* (Oxford, 1961) is grossly inadequate for the back country.

[2] Richard B. Harwell, ed., *The Committees of Safety of Westmoreland and Fincastle. Proceedings of the County Committees*, Virginia State Library, *Publications* no. 1 (Richmond, Va., 1956), pp. 90–92; Walter R. Hoberg, "Early History of Colonel Alexander McKee," *Pennsylvania Magazine of History and Biography*, LVIII

(January 1934), pp. 31–34; Wilbur H. Siebert, "The Loyalists of Pennsylvania," Ohio State University, *Bulletin*, XXIV, *Contributions in History and Political Science*, no. 5 (Columbus, Ohio, 1920), pp. 13, 15–16; and Zackwell Morgan to Edward Hand, August 29, 1779, Edward Hand Correspondence, Force Transcripts, Library of Congress, Washington, D.C.

³ John Alonzo George, "Virginia Loyalists, 1775–1783," *Richmond College Historical Papers*, I, no. 2 (June 1916), pp. 182–211; and Ephraim Douglas to General William Irvine, n.d., in *Pennsylvania Magazine of History and Biography*, I, (1877), p. 52.

⁴ Alexander C. Flick, *Loyalism in New York during the American Revolution* (New York, 1901), pp. 78–79, 109–110; Siebert, "Loyalists of Pennsylvania," Ohio State University, *Bulletin*, XXIV (1920), pp. 13–14, 19–20; and Richard K. McMaster, "Parish in Arms: A Study of Father John McKenna and the Mohawk Valley Loyalists, 1773–1778," United States Catholic Historical Society, *Historical Records and Studies*, XLV (1957), pp. 107–125.

⁵ Mary G. Nye, "Tories in the Champlain Valley," Vermont Historical Society, *Proceedings*, IX (September 1941), p. 200; and Wynn Underwood, "Indian and Tory Raids on the Otter Valley, 1777–1782," *Vermont Quarterly*, new ser., XV (October 1947), pp. 206, 209.

⁶ Henry Steele Wardner, "The Haldimand Negotiations," Vermont Historical Society, *Proceedings*, new ser., II (1931), pp. 3–29; Winn Lowell Taplin, Jr., "The Vermont Problem in the Continental Congress and in Interstate Relations, 1776–1787" (Ph.D. dissertation, University of Michigan, 1956), pp. 194–208; Chilton Williamson, *Vermont in Quandry: 1763–1825* (Montpelier, 1949), pp. 88–126; and Clarence W. Rife, "Vermont and Great Britain, A Study in Diplomacy, 1779–1783," Ph. D. dissertation, Yale University, 1922.

⁷ The most comprehensive treatment of South Carolina Loyalism is Robert Woodward Barnwell, Jr., "Loyalism in South Carolina, 1765–1785" (Ph.D. dissertation, Duke University, 1941). But see also Kenneth Coleman, *The American Revolution in Georgia, 1763–1789* (Athens, Ga., 1959), p. 75; and particularly Gary D. Olson, "Loyalists and the American Revolution: Thomas Brown and the South Carolina Back Country, 1775–1783" (M.A. thesis, University of Nebraska, 1965), pp. 8–40.

⁸ Peter Force, ed., *American Archives*, 4th and 5th ser., 9 vols. (Washington, D.C., 1837–1853), 4th ser., II, 115–117; Johnston to Joseph Hewes, June 27, 1775, Hayes Collection, North Carolina Archives, Raleigh, North Carolina.

⁹ Johnston to Joseph Hewes, March 10, 1776, *ibid.;* Hugh F. Rankin, "The Moore's Creek Bridge Campaign, 1776," *North Carolina Historical Review*, XXX (January 1953), pp. 26–58; and Robert O. DeMond, *The Loyalists in North Carolina During the Revoluion* (Hamden, Conn., 1964), pp. 46–50, 84–99. See also the undated, anonymous journal of a Highland officer among the Sir Henry Clinton Papers for February 1776 in the Clements Library, Ann Arbor.

¹⁰ Campbell to Henry Clinton, March 4, 1779, British Army Headquarters, no. 1797, Public Record Office, London; Tonyn to Guy Carleton, October 11, 1782, *ibid.*, no. 5850; Coleman, *Revolution in Georgia*, pp. 143–145; Wilbur H. Siebert, "The Loyalists in West Florida and the Natchez District," Mississippi Valley Historical Association, *Proceedings*, VIII (1916), pp. 102–122; and Thelma Peters, "The Loyalist Migration from East Florida to the Bahama Islands," *Florida Historical Quarterly*, XL (October 1961), pp. 123–141.

¹¹ Lord George Germain to Guy Carleton, March 26, 1777, Germain Papers, Clements Library; Frederick Haldimand Papers, vol. 100, pp. 436, 441, transcripts,

Public Archives of Canada, Ottawa; and John Bakeless, *Daniel Boone* (New York, 1939), pp. 232, 250.

Chapter 7: The Initial Years of the War, 1776–1779

[1] Howard Swiggert, *War Out of Niagara, Walter Butler and the Tory Rangers* (New York, 1933), p. 281. See also, for example, Haldimand to Henry Clinton, August 4, 1778, British Army Headquarter papers, no. 1289, Public Record Office. London.

[2] Randolph G. Downes, "Creek-American Relations, 1782–1790," *Georgia Historical Quarterly*, XXI (June 1937), pp. 36–38.

[3] Samuel Hazard, ed., *Pennsylvania Archives*, 1st ser., 13 vols. (Philadelphia, 1852–1856), VI, 175–176.

[4] See Meriwether Peirce to John Fox, May 30, 1779, Frederick Haldimand Papers, vol. 100, p. 355, transcripts, Public Archives of Canada, Ottawa; and the journal of Colonel William Fleming, in Newton D. Mereness, ed., *Travels in the American Colonies* (New York, 1916), pp. 621, 630.

[5] William Dana Hoyt, Jr., "Colonel William Fleming on the Virginia Frontier, 1755–1783" (Ph.D. dissertation, Johns Hopkins University, 1940), pp. 173–181; and James G. Randall, "George Rogers Clark's Service of Supply," *Mississippi Valley Historical Review*, VIII (December 1921), pp. 250–263.

[6] On Carleton's controversial action see Alfred L. Burt, "The Quarrel between Germain and Carleton: An Inverted Story," *Canadian Historical Review*, XI (June 1930), pp. 202–220.

[7] Elby A. Boosinger, "The Cherokee Indians in the Revolutionary War" (M. A. thesis, University of Nebraska, 1951), pp. 52–59.

[8] Randolph C. Downes, *Council Fires on the Upper Ohio: A Narrative of Indian Affairs in the Upper Ohio Valley until 1795* (Pittsburgh, 1940), pp. 190–191, 195–203; and Robert S. Cotterill, *History of Pioneer Kentucky* (Cincinnati, 1917), pp. 111–118.

[9] Hamilton to Lord George Germain, June 3, July 14, September 5, 1777, Public Archives of Canada, Q ser., vol. 14, pp. 79, 94–95, 225; Hamilton to Carleton, July 3, 1777, *ibid.*, vol. 14, pp. 41–42; John Butler to Carleton, June 15, July 28, *ibid.*, vol. 13, p. 317, vol. 14, p. 146; Bowman to Hand, December 12, 1777, Draper Collection, 18ZZ50, Wisconsin State Historical Society, Madison; and George Morgan to John Hancock, July 31, 1777, Papers of the Continental Congress, item 163, p. 258, National Archives, Washington, D.C.

[10] Carleton to Hamilton, March 14, 1778, Haldimand Papers, vol. 121, p. 22; Haldimand to Hamilton, August 6, 1778, *ibid.*, vol. 121, pp. 25–26; and Hamilton to Carleton, April 25, 1778, *ibid.*, vol. 122, pp. 36–39.

[11] Freeman H. Allen, "St. Leger's Invasion and the Battle of Oriskany," New York State Historical Association, *Proceedings*, XII (1913), p. 169; Ernest Cruikshank, "Joseph Brant in the American Revolution," Canadian Institute, *Transactions*, V (1898), pp. 250–253; Marc Jack Smith, "Joseph Brant, a Mohawk Statesman" (Ph.D. dissertation, University of Wisconsin, 1946), pp. 26–27; Mabel G. Walker "Sir John Johnson, Loyalist," *Mississippi Valley Historical Review*, III (December 1916), pp. 334–336.

[12] James Austin Holden, "Influence of the Death of Jane McCrae on Burgoyne's Campaign," New York State Historical Association, *Proceedings*, XII (1913),

249–310; and Carl Berger, *Broadsides and Bayonets, The Propaganda War of the American Revolution* (Philadelphia, 1961), pp. 64–66.

[13] Swiggert, *War Out of Niagara*, pp. 112–118; Charles Minor, *History of Wyoming* (Philadelphia, 1845), pp. 216–218; and John Butler to Colonel Mason Bolton, July 8, 1778, Sir Henry Clinton Papers, Clements Library, Ann Arbor.

[14] Swiggert, *War Out of Niagara*, pp. 139–165; Haldimand to John Butler, December 25, 1778, Haldimand Papers, vol. 62, p. 359; and Zebulon Butler to Edward Hand, March 23, 1779, Edward Hand Correspondence, Force Transcripts, Library of Congress, Washington, D.C.

[15] John Caughey, "Willing's Expedition Down the Mississippi," *Louisiana Historical Quarterly*, XV (January 1932), pp. 5–36; and Wilber H. Siebert, "The Loyalists in West Florida and the Natchez District," Mississippi Valley Historical Association, *Proceedings for 1914–1915*, VIII (1916), pp. 106–110.

[16] George Rogers Clark to John Clark, June 15, 1779, James Alton James, ed., *George Rogers Clark Papers, 1771–1784*, 2 vols. (Springfield, Ill., 1912–1916), I, 336.

[17] Depeyster to Haldimand, June 1, 1779, *Wisconsin Historical Society, Collections*, XI (1883), p. 133; Abraham P. Nasatir, "The Anglo-Spanish Frontier in the Illinois Country during the American Revolution," Illinois Historical Society, *Journal*, XXI (1928), pp. 302–303; and Orville John Jaebker, "Henry Hamilton: British Soldier and Colonial Governor" (Ph.D. dissertation, Indiana University, 1954), pp. 149–156.

[18] Alexander C. Flick, "New Sources on the Sullivan-Clinton Campaign in 1779," New York State Historical Association, *Journal*, X (July, October 1929), pp. 185–224, 265–317; and Obed Edson, "Brodhead's Expedition Against the Indians of the Upper Allegheny 1779," *Magazine of American History*, III (November 1879), pp. 649–675.

[19] Clarence W. Alvord, *The County of Illinois*, Illinois State Historical Library, *Publications* (Urbana, Ill., 1907); Carl E. Boyd, "The County of Illinois," *American Historical Review*, IV (July 1899), pp. 628–631; and Lois E. Graham, "Fort McIntosh," *Western Pennsylvania Historical Magazine*, XV (May 1932), pp. 93–119.

Chapter 8: Victory and Stalemate, 1780–1782

[1] On the very complex subject of the political loyalty of the southern back settlers see Gary D. Olson, "Loyalists and the American Revolution: Thomas Brown and the South Carolina Back Country,' 1775–1783" (M. A. thesis, University of Nebraska, 1965); Robert Woodward Barnwell, Jr., "Loyalism in South Carolina, 1765–1785" (Ph.D. dissertation, Duke University, 1941); and Paul H. Smith, *Loyalists and Redcoats: a Study in British Revolutionary Policy* (Chapel Hill, 1964), pp. 102–103, 136–143, 145–148.

[2] Stuart to Sir William Howe, February 4, 1778, Henry Clinton Papers, Clements Library, Ann Arbor, Michigan.

[3] Cameron to General Augustine Prevost, October 15, 1779, British Army Headquarters Papers, no. 2372, Public Record Office, London; and Thomas Brown to Lord George Germain, May 25, 1780, Germain Papers, Clements Library.

[4] John W. Caughey, "The Natchez Rebellion of 1781 and Its Aftermath," *Louisiana Historical Quarterly*, XVI (January 1933), pp. 57–65; Lawrence Kinnard, "The Spanish Expedition against Fort St. Joseph in 1781, A New Interpretation," *Mississippi Valley Historical Review*, XIX (September 1932), pp. 173–181.

[5] Kenneth Coleman, "Restored Colonial Georgia, 1779–1782," *Georgia Historical Quarterly*, XL (March 1956), pp. 6–18; Doyce B. Nunis, Jr., "Colonel Archibald Campbell's March from Savannah to Augusta, 1779," *Georgia Historical Quarterly*, XLV (September 1961), pp. 275–276; and Smith, *Loyalists and Redcoats*, pp. 102–103, 136–143.

[6] William K. Boyd, *The Battle of King's Mountain, North Carolina Booklet*, VIII (April 1909), pp. 300–313; Samuel C. Williams, "The Battle of King's Mountain as Seen by the British Officers," *Tennessee Historical Magazine*, VII (April–July 1921), pp. 51–56, 104–110; and Lord Rawdon to Major General Leslie, October 24, 1780, Germain Papers, Clements Library.

[7] Kenneth Coleman, *The American Revolution in Georgia, 1763–1789* (Athens, Ga., 1959), p. 135.

[8] Prentice Price, ed., "Two Petitions to Virginia of the North of Holston Men, 1776, 1777," East Tennessee Historical Society, *Publications*, XXI (1949), pp. 97–98; Harriette Louise (Simpson) Arnow, *Seedtime on the Cumberland* (New York, 1960), pp. 211–237, 243–244, 249; Samuel Cole Williams, *Tennessee During the Revolutionary War* (Nashville, 1944), pp. 79–80, 104–108; William S. Lester, *The Transylvania Colony* (Spencer, Ind., 1935), pp. 256–267.

[9] Robert S. Cotterill, *The Southern Indians: The Story of the Civilized Tribes Before Removal* (Norman, 1954), pp. 50–51.

[10] Elby A. Boosinger, "The Cherokee Indians in the Revolutionary War" (M.A. thesis, University of Nebraska, 1951), pp. 65–69, 73–83; and Randolph C. Downes, "Cherokee-American Relations in the Upper Tennessee Valley, 1776–1791," East Tennessee Historical Society, *Publications*, VIII (January 1936), pp. 38–40.

[11] Marc Jack Smith, "Joseph Brant, a Mohawk Statesman" (Ph.D. dissertation, University of Wisconsin, 1946), pp. 43–45; Howard Swiggert, *War Out of Niagara, Walter Butler and the Tory Rangers* (New York, 1933), pp. 204–220.

[12] Smith, "Joseph Brant," pp. 51–52; Swiggert, *War Out of Niagara*, pp. 238–242; Haldimand to Lord George Germain, November 23, 1781, Haldimand Papers, transcripts, Public Archives of Canada, Ottawa, vol. 55, pp. 125, 127; and the Earl of Shelburne to Haldimand, April 22, 1782, *ibid.*, vol. 45, p. 40. See also Marinus Willett's account in the Edward Ayer Collection, Newbery Library, Chicago.

[13] Brodhead to Joseph Reed, January 22, 1781, Draper Collection, 3H47, Wisconsin State Historical Society, Madison.

[14] William Croghan to Michael Gratz, April 20, 1782, William V. Byars, ed., *B. and M. Gratz, Merchants of Philadelphia, 1754–1798* (Jefferson City, Mo., 1916), p. 208; Randolph G. Downes, "Indian War on the Upper Ohio, 1779–1782," *Western Pennsylvania Historical Magazine*, XVII (June 1934), pp. 106–111.

[15] See Caldwell to Arent DePeyster, June 11, June 13, 1782; Lt. John Turney to DePeyster, June 7, 1782; and DePeyster to Alexander McKee, August 6, 1782, Haldimand Papers, vol. 198, pp. 68–69, 87, 102, 116, 117.

[16] See Haldimand Papers, vol. 54, p. 327, vol. 100, pp. 410–417, 428, 436–437, 441, vol. 122, pp. 529–531; John Floyd to William Preston, August 25, 1781, Draper Collection, 17CC130.

[17] Brodhead to Joseph Reed, January 21, 1781, Draper Collection, 3H47; Downes, "Indian War on the Upper Ohio," pp. 107–111; and Charles G. Talbert, "A Roof for Kentucky," *Filson Club History Quarterly*, XXIX (April 1955), pp. 145–147.

[18] G. R. Clark to Jonathan Clark, February 16, 1782, Draper Collection, 32J3;

and Campbell to William Davies, October 3, 1782, William P. Palmer, ed., *Calendar of Virginia State Papers and Other Manuscripts 1652—April 15, 1869, Preserved in the Capital at Richmond*, 11 vols. (Richmond, 1875–1893), III, 337.

[19] Talbert, "A Roof for Kentucky," pp. 145–165; and McKee to DePeyster, August 28, 1782, Haldimand Papers, vol. 102, pp. 154–157.

Chapter 9: The West in the Diplomacy of the Revolution

[1] For a map depicting the various boundary lines proposed for the North American interior during the negotiations see Charles O. Paullin, *Atlas of the Historical Geography of the United States* (Washington, 1932), plate 89.

[2] See Paul C. Phillips, "American Opinion Regarding the West, 1778–1783," Mississippi Valley Historical Association, *Proceedings*, VII (1913–1914), pp. 286–305.

[3] Report of October 17, 1780, Papers of the Continental Congress, item 25, I, 239–241, National Archives, Washington, D.C.

[4] Samuel F. Bemis, *Diplomacy of the American Revolution*, 2d ed., (Bloomington, Ind., 1956), p. 101 and note 17; Abraham P. Nasatir, "The Anglo-Spanish Frontier in the Illinois Country during the American Revolution," Illinois State Historical Society, *Journal*, XXI (1928), p. 348; and Theodore C. Peace, "1780–The Revolution at Crisis in the West," *ibid.*, XXIII (January 1931), p. 679.

[5] George Dangerfield, *Chancellor Robert R. Livingston of New York, 1746–1813* (New York, 1960), pp. 138–143; and Edmund C. Burnett, *The Continental Congress* (New York, 1941), p. 477.

[6] Livingston to Jay, April 16, 1782, Henry P. Johnston, ed., *Correspondence and Public Papers of John Jay*, 4 vols. (New York and London, 1890–1893), II, 188; and Livingston to Franklin, January 7, 1782, Francis Wharton, ed., *The Revolutionary Diplomatic Correspondence of the United States*, 6 vols, (Washington, 1888–1889), V, 87–90.

[7] Oswald's minutes on his instructions of August 29, 1782, Shelburne Papers, 50:224–239, Clements Library.

[8] See Floridablanca's confidential summary to Aranda, May 29, 1782, Archivo Historico National, Madrid, Estado, leg. 4079, apartado 2, Randolph G. Adams Peace Transcripts, Clements Library.

[9] See Florence G. Watts, ed., "The Rayneval Memorandum of 1782," *Indiana Magazine of History*, XXXVIII (June 1942), pp. 167–207; Samuel F. Bemis, "The Rayneval Memorada of 1782 on Western Boundaries and Some Comments on the French Historian Donoil," American Antiquarian Society, *Proceedings*, new ser., XLVII (1937), pp. 15–92; Aranda's account in Archivo, Historico National, Madrid, Estado, leg. 3885, expl., doc. 6, Adams Peace Transcripts, Clements Library; and Jay's account, in Wharton, *Revolutionary Diplomatic Correspondence*, VI, 22–28.

[10] Vincent T. Harlow, *Founding of the Second British Empire, 1763–1793* (London, 1952) p. 297; but compare Bemis, *Diplomacy of the American Revolution*, p. 226.

[11] See Strachey's notes, October 20, 1782, Shelburne Papers, 87:194, 205–206, Clements Library.

[12] By the terms of the agreements incorporated into the final treaty British creditors were to meet with no lawful impediment in collecting debts owed them, and the Congress was to recommend that the states take proper action on confiscated Loyalist property.

[13] Donald G. Creighton, *The Commercial Empire of the St. Lawrence, 1760–1850* (Toronto, 1937), pp. 79–92.

[14] Alfred L. Burt, "A New Approach to the Problem of the Western Posts," Canadian Historical Association, *Report for 1931* (Ottawa, 1932), pp. 61–75; and Frank Hayward Severance, "The Peace Mission to Niagara of Ephraim Douglas in 1783," Buffalo Historical Society, *Publications,* XVIII (1914), pp. 117–134.

Chapter 10: State and Congressional Land Policy

[1] Dwight L. Smith, "Provocation and Occurrence of Indian-White Warfare in the Early American Period in the Old Northwest," *Northwest Ohio Quarterly,* XXXIII (Summer 1961), p. 136.

[2] Rudolf Freund, "Military Bounty Lands and the Origins of the Public Domain," *Agricultural History,* XX (January 1946), pp. 8–18; Phyllis Ruth Abbott, "The Development and Operation of An American Land System to 1800" (Ph.D. dissertation, University of Wisconsin, 1959), pp. 114–115; and Paul V. Lutz, "Land Grants for Service in the Revolution," *New York Historical Society Quarterly,* XLVIII (July 1964), pp. 221–236.

[3] Chilton Williamson, *Vermont, in Quandary, 1763–1825* (Montpelier, 1949), p. 77; and Catherine Snell Crary, "Forfeited Loyalist Lands in the Western District of New York-Albany and Tryon Counties," *New York History,* XXXV (July 1954), pp. 241–248.

[4] Henry Tater, "State and Federal Land Policy during the Confederation Period," *Agricultural History,* IX (October 1935), pp. 180–181; and Norman B. Wilkinson, "Land Policy and Speculation in Pennsylvania, 1779–1800" (Ph. D. dissertation, University of Pennsylvania, 1958), pp. 7–9.

[5] Kenneth Coleman, *The American Revolution in Georgia, 1763–1789* (Athens, Ga., 1959), pp. 209–217; Thomas P. Abernethy, *From Frontier to Plantation in Tennessee* (Chapel Hill, N.C., 1932), pp. 49–54; and William H. Masterson, *William Blount* (Baton Rouge, 1954), pp. 55–70.

[6] Samuel Mackay Wilson, *The First Land Court of Kentucky, 1779–1780* (Lexington, 1923), pp. 4–12; and Thomas P. Abernethy, *Western Lands and the American Revolution* (New York, 1959), pp. 218–220, 224–225.

[7] See Herbert C. Laub, "Revolutionary Virginia and the Crown Lands (1775–1783)," *William and Mary Quarterly,* 2d ser., XI (October 1931), p. 310; James R. Robertson, ed., *Petitions of the Early Inhabitants of Kentucky to the General Assembly of Virginia, 1769 to 1792,* Filson Club, *Publications,* vol. XXVII (Louisville, Ky., 1914), no. 8, p. 45; William Dana Hoyt, Jr., "Colonel William Fleming on the Virginia Frontier, 1755–1783" (Ph. D. dissertation, Johns Hopkins University, 1940), pp. 151–153. See also *The Certificate Book of the Virginia Land Commission of 1779–1780,* Supplement to the Kentucky Historical Society, *Register* for 1923; and the journal of one land commissioner, William Fleming, in Newton D. Mereness, ed., *Travels in the American Colonies* (New York, 1916), pp. 637–655.

[8] Winn Lowell Taplin, Jr., "The Vermont Problem in the Continental Congress and in Interstate Relations, 1776–1787" (Ph. D. dissertation, Michigan University, 1956), pp. 121–122, 211–221, 251; and Edmund C. Burnett, *The Continental Congress* (New York, 1941), pp. 541–545.

[9] Merill Jensen in two articles, "The Cession of the Old Northwest," *Mississippi Valley Historical Review,* XXIII (June 1936), pp. 27–48; and "The Creation of the National Domain, 1781–1784," *ibid.,* XXVI (December 1939), pp. 323–342

overemphasized somewhat the influence of the Pennsylvania, New Jersey, and Maryland speculators in the dispute over Congressional land policy while he ignored the role of the Virginia speculators in the policy of the Old Dominion. For correctives to Jensen's extended treatment see Thomas C. Cochran, *New York in the Confederation: An Economic Study* (Philadelphia, 1932), pp. 74–76, 79–80; Burnett, *The Continental Congress*, pp. 494–500, 537–540, 597; Kathryn Sullivan, *Maryland and France, 1774–1789* (Philadelphia, 1936), pp. 18–22, 87–90, 95–97; St. George L. Siousat, "The Chevalier De La Luzerne and the Ratification of the Articles of Confederation in Maryland, 1780–1781," *Pennsylvania Magazine of History and Biography*, LX (October 1936), pp. 391–418; and Freund, "Military Bounty Lands and the Origins of the Public Domain," *Agricultural History*, XX (January 1946), pp. 8–18.

Chapter 11: Government and Law in the Back Country

[1] See Chilton Williamson, *American Suffrage; from Property to Democracy, 1760–1860* (Princeton, 1960).

[2] George Morgan to William Trent, September 12, 1780, Draper Collection 46J59, Wisconsin State Historical Society, Madison; and James Road Robertson, "New Light of Early Kentucky," Mississippi Valley Historical Association, *Report for 1915–1916*, IX (1917), pp. 90–98.

[3] See the Papers of the Continental Congress, item 48, pp. 243–256, National Archives, Washington, D.C.; and Robert L. Brunhouse, *The Counter-Revolution in Pennsylvania, 1776–1790* (Harrisburg, 1942), pp. 265–269.

[4] See the Journal of Colonel Richard Henderson relating to the Transylvania colony, in Walter Clark, *The Colony of Transylvania, North Carolina Booklet, Great Events in North Carolina History*, vol. III, no. 9 (January 1904), pp. 12–31; and the journal of the Transylvania Convention in George W. Ranck, *Boonesborough, Its Founding, Pioneer Struggles, Indian Experiences, Transylvania Days, and Revolutionary Annals, Filson Club Publication*, no. 16 (Louisville, Ky., 1901), pp. 196–210.

[5] Christopher Collier, "Roger Sherman and the New Hampshire Grants," *Vermont History*, XXX (July 1962), pp. 211–212; Winn Lowell Taplin, Jr., "The Vermont Problem in the Continental Congress and in Interstate Relations, 1776–1787" (Ph.D. dissertation, University of Michigan, 1956), pp. 17–31, 75–99; and Clinton Williamson, *Vermont in Quandary: 1763–1825* (Montpelier, 1949), pp. 55–56, 77–83.

[6] Carl Bridenbaugh, *Myths and Realities: Societies of the Colonial South* (Baton Rouge, 1952), pp. 155–158; and Lucien E. Roberts, "Sectional Problems in Georgia during the Formative Period, 1776–1798," *Georgia Historical Quarterly*, XVII (September 1934), p. 210.

[7] William A. Schaper, "Sectionalism and Representation in South Carolina," American Historical Association, *Annual Report for 1900* (Washington, 1901), p. 367; Charles Gregg Singer, *South Carolina in the Confederation* (Philadelphia, 1941), p. 9; and Elisha P. Douglass, *Rebels and Democrats, the Struggle for Equal Political Rights and Majority Rule during the American Revolution*, (Chapel Hill, N.C., 1955), pp. 36–37, 42, 44, 130–131.

[8] Thomas Smith to Arthur St. Clair, August 3, 1776, William Henry Smith, ed., *The Life and Public Services of Arthur St. Clair . . . with His Correspondence and Other Papers*, 2 vols. (Cincinnati, 1882), I, 370–371; Brunhouse, *Counter Revolution in Pennsylvania*, 32–34, 36, 54–56; Theodore G. Thayer, *Pennsylvania*

Politics and the Growth of Democracy, 1740–1776 (Harrisburg, 1953), pp. 127–131; and David Hawke, *In the Midst of Revolution* (Philadelphia, 1961), pp. 59–60.

⁹ Stanley F. Horn, "The Cumberland Compact," *Tennessee Historical Quarterly*, III (March 1944), pp. 65–66. For a similar situation in Pennsylvania see John B. Linn, "Indian Land and Its Fair-Play Settlers, 1773–1785," *Pennsylvania Magazine of History and Biography*, VII (1883), pp. 420–425.

¹⁰ Campbell to William Campbell, August 29, 1774, Campbell-Preston Papers, I, doc. 45, Library of Congress, Washington, D.C. See also Bridenbaugh, *Myths and Realities*, pp. 169–171; and Thomas P. Abernethy, *Three Virginia Frontiers* (Baton Rouge, 1940), pp. 59–60. When Botetourt County was created in 1770 Andrew Lewis, Robert Breckinridge, William Preston, William Christian, and William Fleming were among the justices appointed to the county court. William Preston was also escheator and surveyor, and Andrew Lewis was the coroner, James McDowell, the undersheriff, and William Christian and Robert Breckinridge, the ranking militia officers. Preston and Christian were also appointed to high office with the organization of Fincastle County two years later. With them on the county court were Anthony Bledsoe, Arthur Campbell, and William Russell. Christian was deputy clerk of the court, and Preston was surveyor, sheriff, and lieutenant of the county. When Kentucky County was established in 1776, the most prominent, active men, Clark, Benjamin Logan, Isaac Hite, and John Todd, received appointments as justices of the peace. Todd, Logan, John Bowman, and Richard Calloway also sat as the first court of quarter sessions the following year. Calloway represented the county in the state legislature while Bowman was county lieutenant, Anthony Bledsoe, the lieutenant colonel of the militia, and Logan, the sheriff.

¹¹ For a general discussion of the court systems in several colonies and states see Albert Ogden Porter, *County Government in Virginia A Legislative History 1607–1789* (New York, 1947), pp. 15–51; Howard M. Browning, "The Washington County [North Carolina], Court, 1778–1789; A Study in Frontier Administration," *Tennessee Historical Quarterly*, I (December 1942), pp. 328–343; A. B. Reid, "Early Courts, Judges, and Lawyers of Allegheny County," *Western Pennsylvania Historical Magazine*, V (July 1922), pp. 185–202; Alexander S. Guffey, "The First Courts in Western Pennsylvania," *ibid.*, VII (July 1924), pp. 145–177; and Boyd Crumrine, *History of Washington County, Pennsylvania* . . . Philadelphia, 1882), pp. 150–152. In addition to these materials the following discussion is based on the minute books of Botetourt and Fincastle counties, Virginia, printed in Lewis P. Summers, *Annals of Southwest Virginia*, (Abington, Va., 1929); Alvin L. Prichard, ed., "Minute Book A, Jefferson County, Kentucky, March 1781–September, 1783," *Filson Club Quarterly*, III (January–July 1929), pp. 55–83, 121–154, 171–194; Boyd Crumrine, ed., "Minute Book of the Virginia Court Held for Ohio County, Virginia . . . 1774–1780 . . . ," *Annals of the Carnegie Museum*, III (1905–1906), pp. 5–78; Boyd Crumrine, ed., "Minute Book of the Virginia Court Held at Fort Dunmore (Pittsburgh) for the District of West Augusta, 1775–1776," *ibid.*, I (1901–1902), pp. 525–569; Boyd Crumrine, ed., "Minute Book of the Virginia Court Held for Yohogania County . . . 1776–1780," *ibid.*, II (1903–1904), pp. 204–429; and Boyd Crumrine, *County Court for the District of West Augusta, Va., held at Augusta Town* . . . 1776–1777 . . . Washington, Pa., 1905).

¹² Summers, *Annals of Southwest Virginia*, pp. 87, 104, 635.

¹³ Prichard, "Minute Book A. Jefferson County," p. 61; and Crumrine, "Minute Book, Yohogania County," p. 399.

¹⁴ See Ralph Hyden Records, "Land as a Basis for Economic and Social Discontent in Maine and Massachusetts to 1776" (Ph.D. dissertation, University of

Chicago, 1936), pp. 230, 257–258; and Lois K. (Matthews) Rosenberry, *The Expansion of New England* (Boston, 1909), pp. 133–134.

Chapter 12: The Economy and Society of the Back Country

[1] Leo A. Bressler, "Agriculture Among the Germans in Pennsylvania during the Eighteenth Century," *Pennsylvania History*, XXII (April 1955), pp. 107–131; and James Sullivan *et at.*, eds., *The Papers of Sir William Johnson*, 13 vols. (Albany and New York), IV, 348–349, VIII, 182–183.

[2] Percy W. Bidwell and John I. Falconer, *History of Agriculture in the Northern United States, 1620–1860* (Washington, 1925), pp. 115–116; and Hugh T. Lefler and Paul Wagner, eds., *Orange County 1752–1952* (Chapel Hill, N.C., 1953), p. 16.

[3] Wilbur H. Siebert, "Slavery and White Servitude in East Florida, 1726–1785," *Florida Historical Society Quarterly* X (July 1931), January 1932), pp. 3–23, 139–161; Whitfield J. Bell, Jr., "Washington County, Pennsylvania, in the Eighteenth Century Antislavery Movement," *Western Pennsylvania Historical Magazine*, XXV (September-December 1942), pp. 135–142; and Pratt Byrd, "The Kentucky Frontier in 1792," *Filson Club History Quarterly*, XXV (July 1951), p. 190.

[4] Carl Bridenbaugh, *Myths and Realities: Societies of the Colonial South* (Baton Rouge, 1952), pp. 168–169) Lefler and Wager, *Orange County*, p. 16; and J. Reuben Sheeler, "The Negro on the Virginia Frontier," *Journal of Negro History*, XLIII (October 1958), pp. 289–292.

[5] Bidwell and Falconer, *Northern Agriculture*, pp. 77–79, 82, 84; Fletcher, *Pennsylvania Agriculture*, pp. 63–65; Arthur R. Hall, "Soil Erosion and Agriculture in the Southern Piedmont: A History" (Ph.D. dissertation, Duke University, 1948), pp. 75–78; "Journal of General James Whitelaw, Surveyor General of Vermont," *Vermont Historical Society, Proceedings for 1905–1906* (1906), pp. 129–130.

[6] Edward G. Roberts, "The Roads of Virginia, 1607–1840" (Ph.D. dissertation, University of Virginia, 1950), pp. 11, 31–34; Miles S. Malone, "The Distribution of Population on the Virginia Frontier in 1775" (Ph.D. dissertation, Princeton University, 1935), p. 15; and Harry Roy Merrens, *Colonial North Carolina in the Eighteenth Century A Study in Historical Geography* (Chapel Hill, N.C., 1964), p. 144.

[7] Draper Collection, 1AA200, Wisconsin State Historical Society, Madison; Samuel Hazard, ed., *Pennsylvania Archives*, 1st ser. 13 vols. (Philadelphia, 1852–1856), IX, 459, 511; and Howard C. Rice, Jr., "News from the Ohio Valley as Reported by Barthélemi Tardiveau in 1783," Ohio Historical and Philosophical Society, *Bulletin*, XVI (October 1958), pp. 267–292.

[8] Merrens, *Colonial North Carolina*, pp. 144, 153, 159; Miles S. Malone, "Falmouth and the Shenandoah: Trade before the Revolution," *American Historical Review*, XL (July 1935), pp. 693–703; Thayer, *Pennsylvania Politics, 1740–1776*, pp. 127–130; David Hawke, *In the Midst of a Revolution* (Philadelphia, 1961), pp. 70–72.

[9] Wesley Newton Laing, "Cattle in Early Virginia" (Ph.D. dissertation, University of Virginia, 1954), pp. 83, 189–190, 222, 228; Gary S. Dunbar, "Colonial Carolina Cowpens," *Agricultural History*, XXXV (July 1961), pp. 125–128.

[10] See Freeman H. Hart, *The Valley of Virginia in the American Revolution, 1763–1789* (Chapel Hill, N.C., 1942), pp. 8–17.

[11] See H. L. Bourdin and S. T. Williams, eds., "Crèvecoeur on the Susquehanna, 1774–1776," *Yale Review*, new ser., XIV (1925), p. 575.

[12] Joseph R. Nixon, "The German Settlers in Lincoln County and Western North Carolina," University of North Carolina, *The James Sprunt Historical Publications* XI, no. 2 (1912), pp. 34–36; and Alfred P. James, "The First English-Speaking Trans-Appalachian Frontier," *Mississippi Valley Historical Review*, XVII (June 1930), pp. 69–70.

[13] Bridenbaugh, *Myths and Realities*, pp. 130–131, 135–136; and Robert G. Albion and Leonidas Dodson, eds., *Philip Vickers Fithian: Journal, 1775–1776* (Princeton, 1934), pp. 93, 96, 174.

[14] Charles Morse Stotz, *The Early Architecture of Western Pennsylvania* (Pittsburgh, 1936), pp. 12–27.

[15] Rice, "News from the Ohio Valley," p. 287; John Geise, "Household Technology of the Western Frontier," *Western Pennsylvania Historical Magazine*, X (April 1927), pp. 85–101; and William Dana Hoyt, Jr., "Colonel William Fleming on the Virginia Frontier, 1755–1783," (Ph.D. dissertation, Johns Hopkins University, 1940), p. 46.

[16] *The Journal of Nicholas Cresswell, 1774–1777* (New York, 1925), p. 99.

[17] See Harriette Louise (Simpson) Arnow, *Seedtime on the Cumberland* (New York, 1960), p. 427.

[18] James Sterling to John Sterling, October 25, 1762, Sterling Letter Book, p. 83, Clements Library, Ann Arbor, Michigan; and James Sullivan *et al.*, eds., *The Papers of Sir William Johnson*, 13 vols. (Albany and New York, 1921–1962), IV, 876.

[19] Louis B. Wright, *Culture on the Moving Frontier*, Harper Torchbook ed. (New York, 1961), pp. 40–41; Klaus C. Wiest, "The Books of the German Immigrants in the Shenandoah Valley," *Mennonite Quarterly Review*, XXXIII (January 1958), pp. 74–76; and Howard H. Peckham, "Books and Reading on the Ohio Valley Frontier," *Mississippi Valley Historical Review*, XLIV (March 1958), pp. 649–663.

[20] Arnow, *Seedtime on the Cumberland*, p. 426; Walter Brownlow Posey, *The Presbyterian Church in the Old Southwest, 1778–1838* (Richmond, 1952), pp. 5, 54; and Dwight Raymond Guthrie, *John McMillan: the Apostle of Presbyterianism in the West, 1752–1833* (Pittsburgh, 1952), pp. 80–85.

[21] Roy H. Johnson, "Frontier Religion in Western Pennsylvania," *Western Pennsylvania Historical Magazine*, XVI (February 1933), p. 37; Marian Silveus, "Churches and Social Control on the Western Pennsylvania Frontier," *ibid.*, XIX (June 1936), pp. 123–130; Niels Henry Sonne, *Liberal Kentucky, 1780–1828* (New York, 1939), p. 11; and Walter Clark, "The Colony of Transylvania," *North Carolina Booklet; Great Events in North Carolina History*, III, no. 9 (January 1904), pp. 21–22.

[22] Guy S. Klett, ed., *Journals of Charles Beatty, 1762–1769* (University Park, Pa., 1963), p. 50; and Hooker, ed., *Woodmason Journal*, pp. 16–17.

[23] Walter Brownlow Posey, *The Baptist Church in the Lower Mississippi Valley, 1776–1845* (Lexington, 1957), p. 4; and James Allie Davidson, "Baptist Beginnings in western Pennsylvania" (Ph.D. dissertation, Pittsburgh University, 1941), pp. 48–104, 118–120.

[24] Colin B. Goodykoontz, *Home Missions on the American Frontier* (Caldwell, Idaho, 1939), pp. 76–77; Guy S. Klett, "The Presbyterian Church and the Scotch-Irish on the Pennsylvania Colonial Frontier," *Pennsylvania History*, VIII (April 1941), pp. 97–109.

[25] Wright, *Culture on the Moving Frontier*, pp. 15, 30; and Arnow, *Seedtime on the Cumberland*, p. 426.

AN ESSAY ON BIBLIOGRAPHY

Manuscripts

Lyman Copeland Draper gathered a tremendous store of material from the eastern and middle western states. His collection at the Wisconsin State Historical Society is the basic manuscript source for the Revolutionary frontier. A vast amount of material containing the reports of officials in the interior are to be found in the correspondence of British officers in America. Of particular value are the Frederick Haldimand Papers, Add. MSS 21661-21892, the Henry Bouquet Papers, Add. MSS 21631-21660, in the British Museum, London (transcripts in the Public Archives of Canada, Ottawa) and the Colonial Officer papers, series 5, volumes 64–111, Public Record Office, London. The Public Record Office also has the British Army Headquarters Papers (Guy Carleton Papers). Other collections of military and Indian department officials are the Sir Henry Clinton Papers and the Thomas Gage Papers, in the Clements Library, Ann Arbor, Michigan. The Clements Library also holds the Lord George Germain Papers, the Shelburne Papers, and the James Sterling letter book.

The Illinois Historical Survey, Urbana, Illinois, is rich in material, including reproductions from European and American archives and repositories as well as letter books and papers of George Morgan. Additional Morgan material is in the Manuscripts Division, Library of Congress, Washington, D.C. The Library of Congress also has Oliver Pollock Papers, the Preston-Campbell Papers, the Shelby Family Papers, the Cresap Family Papers as well as the Papers of Daniel Brodhead, William Armstrong, and Edward Hand among the Force Transcripts.

Reports and correspondence from officials in the West are also in the Papers of the Continental Congress, National Archives, Washington, D.C. The Edward Ayer Collection in the Newberry Library, Chicago, contains miscellaneous items of interest. Among the very rich holdings of the Historical Society of Pennsylvania in Philadelphia are the George Morgan letter book, the William Irvine Papers, the George Croghan Papers, the Indian Records Collection, the Ohio Company [William Trent] Papers, the Daniel Brodhead letter book, the Gratz Family Papers, the Illinois and Wabash Land Company Minutes, the Wharton Family Papers, and the Papers of the Northumberland County Committee of Safety. The New York City Public Library has the William Edgar Papers, valuable on the fur trade.

Papers of other fur traders, Isidore Chene, Alexander Henry, Alexander Grant, John Askin, James McGill, and Isaac Todd, are in the Burton Historical Collection, Detroit Public Library. The New York Historical Society has the John Lacey Papers and the Papers of the Tryon County, New York, Committee of Safety. In addition to transcripts from the Public Record Office and the

British Museum, the Public Archives of Canada hold the Papers of Daniel Claus and Alexander McKee. Among the holdings in the Southern Historical Collection, University of North Carolina, Chapel Hill, are the Regulator Papers and the James Hogg Papers. Of some interest in the manuscripts of the North Carolina Historical Commission, Raleigh, are the Miscellaneous Papers, the Hayes Collection, the Richard Bennehan Papers, and the Rufus Barringer Papers.

General Documentary Collections

Several extensive published collections are valuable for the frontier during the Revolutionary era. Neville B. Craig, ed., *The Olden Time* . . . , 2 vols. (Cincinnati, 1876) and Peter Force, ed., *American Archives,* 4th and 5th ser., 9 vols. (Washington, 1837–1853) are valuable. Clarence W. Alvord and Clarence E. Carter edited three volumes, X, XI, XVI, of the Illinois Historical Library, *Collections: The Critical Period, 1763–1767* (Springfield, Ill., 1915); *The New Regime, 1765–1767* (Springfield, Ill., 1921); and *Trade and Politics, 1767–1769* (Springfield, Ill., 1921). Alvord edited volumes II and IV, *Cahokia Records, 1778–1790* (Springfield, Ill., 1907) and *Kaskaskia Records, 1778–1790* (Springfield, Ill., 1909). Material on the frontier is also found in various state collections: William L. Saunders, ed., *Colonial Records of North Carolina,* 10 vols. (Raleigh, 1888–1890); Nathaniel Bouton *et al,* eds., *Documents and Records Relating to the Province and State of New Hampshire,* 40 vols. (Concord, N.H., 1867–1940); volumes I and II of the Vermont State Historical Society, *Collections* (Montpelier, 1870–1871); and *State Papers of Vermont,* 9 vols., (Montpelier, 1924–1955). Of particular value are the 1st, 2d, and 4th series of Samuel Hazard *et al.,* eds., *Pennsylvania Archives,* 138 vols. in 9 ser. (Harrisburg and Philadelphia, 1838–1935).

Travel Accounts and Journals

Reuben Gold Thwaites, ed., *Early Western Travels* . . . , 32 vols. (Cleveland, 1904–1907) and Newton D. Mereness, ed., *Travels in the American Colonies, 1690–1783* (New York, 1916) have several valuable accounts. The "Journal of General James Whitelaw . . . ," Vermont Historical Society, *Proceedings* (1905–1906), pp. 121–157 surveys the frontier. For the northern section see the journal of John Montrésor in Clarence J. Webster, "Life of John Montrésor," Royal Society of Canada, *Proceedings,* 3d ser., XXII, sec. 2 (1928), pp. 8–31; Fred Coyne Hamil, ed., "Schenectady to Michilimackinac, 1765 and 1766; journal of John Porteus," Ontario Historical Society, *Papers,* XXXIII (1939), pp. 75–98; and M. Agnes Burton, ed., *Journal of J[ohn] L[ees] of Quebec, Merchant* (Detroit, 1911). Several accounts were left by travelers on the middle borders: Nicholas B. Wainwright, ed., "Turmoil at Pittsburgh, Diary of Augustine Prevost, 1774" *Pennsylvania Magazine of History and Biography,* LXXXV (April 1961), pp. 111–162; John W. Jordan, ed., "Journal of James Kenny, 1761–1763," *ibid.,* XXXVII (January–April 1913), pp. 1–47, 152–201; Francis R. Reese, ed., "Colonel [William] Eyre's Journal of His Trip from New York to Pittsburgh, 1762," *Western Pennsylvania*

Historical Magazine, XXVII (March–June 1944), pp. 37–50; Franklin B. Dexter, ed., *Diary of David McClure* . . . (New York, 1899); Robert G. Albion and Leonidas Dodson, eds., *Philip Vickers Fithian: Journal, 1775–1776* (Princeton, N.J., 1934); *The Journal of Nicholas Cresswell, 1774–1777* (New York, 1924); *David Jones, A Journal of Two Visits Made to Some Nations of Indians* (Burlington, N.J., 1774); and H. L. Bourdin and S. T. Williams, eds., "Crèvecoeur on the Susquehanna, 1774–1776," *Yale Review*, new ser., XIV (April 1925), pp. 552–584. For accounts of the southern back settlements see [Albert C. Bates], ed., *The Two Putnams, Rufus and Israel . . . in the Mississippi River Exploration, 1772–1773* . . . (Hartford, Conn., 1931); William Bartram, "Travels in Georgia and Florida, 1773–1774 . . . ," ed., Francis Harper, American Philosophical Society, *Transactions*, new ser., XXXIII (1942–1943), part. 1; and John Bartram, "Diary of a Journey through the Carolinas, Georgia, and Florida . . . ," ed., Francis Harper, *ibid.*, new ser., XXXIII (1942–1943), part. 1. Lewis H. Kilpatrick, "The Journal of William Caulk, Kentucky Pioneer," *Mississippi Valley Historical Review*, VII (March 1921), pp. 363–377; John Ferdinand Dalziel Smyth, *Tour in the United States of America*, 2 vols. (London, 1784); and Virginius C. Hall, "Journal of Isaac Hite, 1773," Historical and Philosophical Society of Ohio, *Bulletin*, XII (October 1954), pp. 262–282 contain accounts of trips to Kentucky.

Interpretive Works

For views differing from those expressed by Frederick Jackson Turner in *The Frontier in American History* (New York, 1925), and "The Old West," Wisconsin State Historical Society, *Proceedings* (1908), pp. 184–233, the student may consult Thomas P. Abernethy, *Three Virginia Frontiers* (University City, La., 1940); *From Frontier to Plantation in Tennessee* (Chapel Hill, N.C., 1932); "The First Transmontane Advance," in *Humanistic Studies in Honor of John Calvin Metcalf* (Charlottesville, Va., 1941); and "Democracy and the Southern Frontier," *Journal of Southern History*, IV (February 1938), pp. 3–13 as well as Clarence W. Alvord, "The Daniel Boone Myth," Illinois State Historical Society, *Journal*, XIX (April 1926), pp. 16–30. Generally agreeing with Turner are John D. Barnhart, *Valley of Democracy: The Frontier versus the Plantation in the Ohio Valley, 1775–1818* (Bloomington, Ind., 1953) and Philip G. Davidson, "The Southern Back Country on the Eve of the Revolution," in Avery O. Craven, ed., *Essays in Honor of William E. Dodd* (Chicago, 1935), pp. 1–14. For a provocative analysis see the chapter entitled "The Back Settlements," in Carl Bridenbaugh, *Myths and Realities: Societies of the Colonial South* (Baton Rouge, 1952).

General Secondary Accounts

There are several general and regional works dealing with the frontier during the Revolutionary period. John Anthony Caruso's three books, *The Appalachian Frontier: America's First Surge Westward* (Indianapolis, [1959]); *The Great Lakes Frontier: An Epic of the Old Northwest* (Indianapolis, [1961]); and *The Southern Frontier* (Indianapolis, [1963]) are popular, uncritical treatments as are Dale Van Every, *Forth to the Wilderness: The First American Frontier, 1754–1774* (New York, 1961); Archibald Henderson, *The Conquest of the Old Southwest . . . 1740–1790* (New York, 1920); and William Brewster, *The Pennsylvania and New York Frontier from 1720 to the Close of the Revolution* (Philadelphia, 1954). Joseph Doddridge, *Notes on the Settlement and Indian Wars of the Western Parts of Virginia & Pennsylvania, from the Year 1763 until the Year 1783 . . .* (Wellsburgh, Va., 1824) is antiquarian. Good treatments are contained in John R. Alden, *The South in the Revolution, 1763–1789* (Baton Rouge, 1957); Louise P. Kellogg, *The British Regime in Wisconsin and the Northwest* (Madison, Wis., 1905); and Nelson V. Russell, *The British Regime in Michigan and the Old Northwest, 1760–1796* (Northfield, Minn., 1939).

For the New England frontier see Lois H. (Kimball) Matthews (Rosenberry), *Expansion in New England* (Boston, 1909); Lawrence Donald Bridgham, "Maine Public Lands, 1781–1795: Claims, Trespassers, and Sales" (Ph. D. dissertation, Boston University, 1959); and Ralph Hyden Records, "Land As A Basis For Economic and Social Discontent in Maine and Massachusetts to 1776" (Ph.D. dissertation, University of Chicago, 1936). On the many works dealing with Vermont, see especially Chilton Williamson, *Vermont in Quandary: 1763–1825* (Montpelier, 1949); Florence May Woodward, *The Town Proprietors in Vermont: The New England Town Proprietary in Decline* (New York, 1936); Matt Bushnell Jones, *Vermont in the Making, 1750–1777* (Cambridge, Mass., 1939); and Lewis D. Stilwell, "Migration from Vermont (1776–1860)," Vermont Historical Society, *Proceedings*, new ser., V (June 1937), pp. 63–245.

The best work on the New York frontier is Ruth Higgins, *Expansion in New York with Special Reference to the Eighteenth Century* (Columbus, Ohio, 1931). See also Thomas Wood Clarke, *The Bloody Mohawk* (New York, 1940); William W. Campbell, *Annals of Tryon County . . .*, 4th rev. ed. (New York, 1924); and Francis W. Halsey, *The Old New York Frontier* (New York, 1901). P. Duncan Fraser, "Sir John Johnson's Rent Roll of the Kingsborough Patent," *Ontario History*, LIII (September 1960), pp. 176–189 is revealing. The Pennsylvania frontier is best covered in Solon J. and Elizabeth H. Buck, *The Planting of Civilization in Western Pennsylvania* (Pittsburgh, 1939). For local studies see Boyd Crumrine, *History of Washington County, Pennsylvania . . .* (Philadelphia, 1882) and Christian M. Bomberger, *A Short History of Westmoreland County, the First County West of the Appalachians* (Jeanette, Pa., [1941]). The roles of the Virginians and Yankees on the Pennsylvania frontier are treated in Alfred P. James, "The First English-Speaking Trans-Appalachian Frontier," *Mississippi Valley Historical Review*," XVIII (June 1930), pp. 55–71; Charles Miner, *History of Wyoming . . .* (Philadelphia, 1845); and Julian P. Boyd, ed., *The Susquehanna Company Papers*, 4 vols. (Wilkes-Barre, Pa., 1930–1933). Sectional conflicts in Pennsylvania are treated in Brooke Hindle, "The March of the Paxton Boys," *William and Mary Quarterly*, 3d ser., III (October 1946), pp. 461–486 and John R. Dunbar, ed., *The Paxton Papers* (The Hague,

1957), but for a revisionary view see also chapter III, "The Backcountry," in David Hawke, *In the Midst of a Revolution* (Philadelphia, 1961), pp. 59–88. The conflict between Pennsylvania and the Old Dominion for control of the Upper Ohio is treated in Percy B. Caley, "Lord Dunmore and the Pennsylvania-Virginia Boundary Dispute," *Western Pennsylvania Historical Magazine,* XXII (June 1939), pp. 87–100 and Boyd Crumrine, "The Boundary Controversy between Pennsylvania and Virginia, 1748–1785," *Annals of the Carnegie Museum,* I (1901–1902), pp. 505–524.

The Virginia frontier is discussed in Freeman H. Hart, *The Valley of Virginia in the American Revolution, 1763–1769* (Chapel Hill, 1942); Miles S. Malone, "Distribution of Population on the Virginia Frontier in 1775" (Ph. D. dissertation, Princeton University, 1935); and Francis Williard Bliss, "The Tuckahoe in the Valley" (Ph.D. dissertation, Princeton University, 1946). Robert S. Cotterill, *History of Pioneer Kentucky* (Cincinnati, 1917) is the best general work on the subject. See also George W. Ranck, *Boonesborough . . . ,* Filson Club, *Publications, no.* 16 (Louisville, Ky., 1901); William Lester, *The Transylvania Colony* (Spencer, Ind., 1935); and James R. Robertson, "New Light on Early Kentucky," Mississippi Valley Historical Association, *Proceedings,* IX (1918), pp. 90–98. Also valuable are James R. Robertson, *Petitions of the Early Inhabitants of Kentucky to the General Assembly of Virginia 1769 to 1792,* Filson Club, *Publications, no.* 27 (Louisville, Ky., 1914); Samuel Mackay Wilson, *The First Land Court of Kentucky, 1779–1780* (Lexington, 1923); and *The Certificate Book of the Virginia Land Commission of 1779–1780,* Kentucky Historical Society, *Register,* Supplement, XXI (1923).

An excellent, but brief treatment of the North Carolina back country for this period is in Hugh T. Lefler and Paul Wagner, eds., *Orange County, 1752–1952* (Chapel Hill, N.C., 1953). For more extended accounts see John S. Bassett, "The Regulators of North Carolina (1765–1771)," American Historical Association, *Annual Report for 1894* (1895), pp. 141–212 and Elmer D. Johnson, "The War of the Regulation: Its Place in History" (M. A. thesis, University of North Carolina, 1942). Regulator tracts are printed in William K. Boyd, "Some North Carolina Tracts of the 18th Century," *North Carolina Historical Review,* III (January–October 1926), pp. 52–118, 223–362, 457–476, 591–621. Hariette L. S. Arnow, *Seedtime on the Cumberland* (New York, 1960) treats both the North Carolina back country and the Tennessee settlements. Both James G. Ramsey, *The Annals of Tennessee . . . to 1800* (Charleston, 1853) and John Haywood, *The Civil and Political History . . . of Tennessee . . . to . . . 1796* (Knoxville, Tenn., 1823), although antiquarian, are valuable. More recent accounts are Samuel Cole Williams, *Dawn of Tennessee Valley and Tennessee History* (Johnson City, Tenn., 1937) and Thomas P. Abernethy, *From Frontier to Plantation in Tennessee* (Chapel Hill, N.C., 1932).

Unfortunately Robert L. Meriwether's excellent study, *The Expansion of South Carolina, 1726–1765* (Kingsport, Tenn., 1940), does not deal with the entire period under consideration. Two older works are John B. O. Landrum, *Colonial and Revolutionary History of Upper South Carolina* (Greenville, S.C., 1897) and John Henry Logan, *A History of the Upper Country of South Carolina* (Charleston, S.C., 1859). Two recent works are very valuable: Richard M. Brown, *The South Carolina Regulators* (Cambridge, Mass., 1961) and Richard James Hooker, ed., *The Carolina Backcountry on the Eve of the Revolution: The Journal and other writings of Charles Woodmason, Anglican Itinerant* (Chapel Hill, N.C., 1953). Material on the Georgia frontier will be found in Kenneth Coleman, *The American Revolution in Georgia, 1763–1789* (Athens, Ga., 1959); William W. Abbott, *The Royal Governors of Georgia, 1754–1775* (Chapel Hill, N.C., 1959); James Etheridge Callaway, *The Early Settlement of Georgia* (Athens, Ga., 1948); and Lucien E. Roberts, "Sectional Problems in Georgia during the Formative Period, 1776–1798," *Georgia Quarterly*, XVIII (September 1934), pp. 207–227. There are three good studies on the Floridas during this period: Charles Loch Mowat, *East Florida as a British Province, 1763–1784* (Berkeley, Calif., 1943); Cecil Johnson, *British West Florida, 1763–1783* (New Haven, Conn., 1943); and Clinton N. Howard, *The British Development of West Florida, 1763–1769* (Berkeley, Calif., 1947).

Emigration and National Groups

Much research recently has been devoted to emigration. Abbott E. Smith, *Colonists in Bondage; White Servitude and Convict Labor in America, 1607–1776* (Chapel Hill, N.C., 1947); Catherine S. Crary, "The Humble Immigrant and the American Dream: Some Case Histories, 1746–1776," *Mississippi Valley Historical Review*, XLVI (June 1959), pp. 46–66 and Eugene R. Fingerhut, "They Came Last: Immigrants from Great Britain to the Frontier of New York in the Revolutionary Period" (M.A. thesis, Columbia University, 1957) are valuable. Various national groups have recieved special attention. For the Scots see Ian C. C. Graham, *Colonists from Scotland: Emigration to North America, 1707–1783* (Ithaca, N.Y., 1956) and Duane G. Meyer, *The Highland Scots of North Carolina, 1732–1776* (Chapel Hill, N.C., 1962). The Scots-Irish are well treated in James G. Leyburn, *The Scotch-Irish, A Social History* (Chapel Hill, N.C., 1962); Guy S. Klett, *The Scotch-Irish in Pennsylvania* (Gettysburg, Pa., 1948); Wayland F. Dunaway, *The Scotch-Irish of Colonial Pennsylvania* (Chapel Hill, N.C., 1944); Edward R. R. Green, "Queensborough Township: Scotch-Irish Emigration and the Expansion of Georgia, 1763–1776," *William and Mary Quarterly*, 3d ser., XVII (April 1960), pp. 183–199; and E. R. R. Green, "Scotch-Irish Emigration: An Imperial Problem," *Western Pennsylvania Historical Magazine*, XXXV (December 1952), pp. 193–209. For the Germanic element in the back country see Levi Oscar Kuhns, *The German and Swiss Settlements of Colonial Pennsylvania* (New York, 1901); Walter Allen Knittle, *The Early Eighteenth-Century Palatine Emigration* (Philadelphia, 1936); John W. Wayland, *The German Element of the Shenandoah Valley of Virginia* (Charlottesville, Va., 1907); and Percy V. Flippin, "The Dutch Element in Early Kentucky," *Mississippi Valley Historical Association, Proceedings*, IX, part i (1915–1916), pp.

135–150. Migration from southern Europe and England are discussed in E. P. Panagopolous, "The Background of the Greek Settlers in the New Smyrna Colony," *Florida Historical Quarterly*, XXXV (October 1956), pp. 95–115 and Mildred Campbell, "English Emigration on the Eve of the American Revolution," *American Historical Review*, LXI (October 1959), pp. 1–20.

Indian Trade

There are several good works on the traffic in the North: Harold Adams Innis, *The Fur Trade in Canada*, 2d rev. ed. (Toronto, 1956); Murray G. Lawson, *Fur: A Study in English Mercantilism, 1700–1775* (Toronto, 1943); Wayne E. Stevens, *The Northwest Fur Trade, 1763–1800* (Urbana, Ill., 1928); Ida A. Johnson, *The Michigan Fur Trade* (Lansing, Mich., 1919); and Paul C. Phillips, "The Fur Trade in the Maumee-Wabash Country," *Studies in American History Inscribed to James Albert Woodburn . . .* (Bloomington, Ind., 1926), pp. 91–118. Charles A. Hanna, *The Wilderness Trail; or the Ventures and Adventures of the Pennsylvania Traders on the Allegheny Path*, 2 vols. (New York, 1911) contains a wealth of undigested material. For the southern trade see W. Neil Franklin, "Virginia and the Cherokee Indian Trade, 1753–1775," East Tennessee Historical Society, *Publications*, V (January 1933), pp. 22–38; J. A. Brown, "Panton, Leslie and Company: Indian traders of Pensacola and St. Augustine," *Florida Historical Quarterly*, XXXVII (April 1959), pp. 328–336; Alexander Brannon, The Pensacola Indian Trade," *ibid.*, XXXI (July 1952), pp. 1–15; and John H. Goff, "The Path to Oakfuskee: Upper Trading Route in Alabama to the Creek Indians," *Georgia Historical Quarterly*, XXXIX (March, June 1955), pp. 1–36, 152–171.

Governmental Policy for the Frontier

For Indian relations in the North during the British regime see Peter D. Marshall, "The Rise and Fall of Imperial Regulation of American Indian Affairs, 1763–1774" (Ph.D. dissertation, Yale University, 1959) and Jack M. Sosin, *Whitehall and the Wilderness: The Middle West in British Colonial Policy, 1760–1775* (Lincoln, Neb., 1961); for the southern district see John R. Alden, *John Stuart and the Southern Colonial Frontier* (Ann Arbor, Mich., 1944) and Helen Louise Shaw, *British Administration of the Southern Indians, 1756–1783* (Lancaster, Pa., 1931). For Indian relations during the American regimes see Walter Mohr, *Federal Indian Relations, 1774–1788* (Philadelphia, 1933); Homer Bast, "Creek Indian Affairs, 1775–1778," *Georgia Historical Quarterly*, XXXIII (March 1949), pp. 1–25; Kenneth Coleman, Federal Indian Relations in the South, 1781–1789," *Chronicles of Oklahoma*, XXXV (Winter 1957–1958), pp. 435–458; Randolph G. Downes, "Cherokee-American Relations in the Upper Tennessee Valley, 1776–1791," East Tennessee Historical Society, *Publications*, VIII (January 1936), pp. 35–53; and R. C.

Downes, "Creek-American Relations, 1782–1790," *Georgia Historical Quarterly*, XXI (June 1937), pp. 142–184. Some aspects of warfare between whites and Indians are dealt with in John K. Mahon, "Anglo-American Methods of Indian Warfare, 1676–1794," *Mississippi Valley Historical Review*, XLV (September 1958), pp. 254–275; Francis Parkman, *The Conspiracy of Pontiac and the Indian War after the Conquest of Canada*, 2 vols. (Boston, 1882); Howard H. Peckham, *Pontiac and the Indian Uprising* (Princeton, N.J., 1947); Edward G. Williams, ed., "The Orderly Book of Colonel Henry Bouquet's Expedition against the Ohio Indians, 1764," *Western Pennsylvania Historical Magazine*, XLII (March–September 1959), pp. 9–34, 179–200, 283–302; Randolph C. Downes, *Council Fires on the Upper Ohio* (Pittsburgh, 1940); and John P. Brown, *Old Frontiers; The Story of the Cherokee Indians from Earliest Times to the Date of Their Removal to the West, 1838* (Kingsport, Tenn., 1938). Valuable for the efforts toward accommodation with the Indians are Leslie R. and Elma F. Gray, *Wilderness Christians; the Moravian Missions to the Delaware Indians* (Ithaca, N.Y., 1956); and Paul A. W. Wallace, ed., *Thirty Thousand Miles with John Heckewelder* (Pittsburgh, 1958).

British policy for the frontier is discussed in Clarence W. Alvord, *The Mississippi Valley in British Politics*, 2 vols. (Cleveland, 1917) and J. M. Sosin, *Whitehall and the Wilderness;* American policy in Edmund C. Burnett, *The Continental Congress* (New York, 1941); Clarence W. Alvord, *The County of Illinois* (Urbana, 1907); and George A. Cribbs, *The Frontier Policy of Pennsylvania* (Pittsburgh, 1919). On British and colonial land policy see in addition Raymond Arthur Plath, "British Mercantilism and the British Colonial Land Policy in the Eighteenth Century" (Ph.D. dissertation, Wisconsin University, 1939); Manning C. Voorhis, "The Land Grant Policy of Colonial Virginia, 1607–1774" (Ph.D. dissertation, University of Virginia, 1940); Fairfax Harrison, *Virginia Land Grants, A Study in Conveyancing in Relation to Colonial Politics* (Richmond, Va., 1925); and St. George L. Sioussat, "The Breakdown of the Royal Management of Lands in the Southern Provinces, 1773–1775," *Agricultural History*, III (April 1929), pp. 67–98. On land policy under various American regimes see Merrill Jensen, *The Articles of Confederation* (Madison, Wis., 1940); Phyllis Ruth Abbott, "The Development and Operation of an American Land System to 1800" (Ph.D. dissertation, University of Wisconsin, 1959); Marshall D. Harris, *Origin of the Land Tenure System in the United States* (Ames, Iowa, 1953); Rudolph Freund, "Military Bounty Lands and the Origins of the Public Domain," *Agricultural History*, XX (January 1946), pp. 8–18; and Paul V. Lutz, "Land Grants for Service in the Revolution," New York Historical Society, *Quarterly*, XLVIII (July 1964), pp. 221–236.

Land Speculation

An over-all treatment of the subject is Thomas P. Abernethy, *Western Lands and the American Revolution* (New York, 1939). On the situation in several states see Edith M. Fox, *Land Speculation in the Mohawk Country*

(Ithaca, 1949); Edward P. Alexander, *A Revolutionary Conservative: James Duane of New York* (New York, 1938); Norman B. Wilkinson, "Land Policy and Speculation in Pennsylvania, 1779–1800" (Ph.D. dissertation, University of Pennsylvania, 1958); and Archibald Henderson, "The Transylvania Company, a Study in Personnel," *Filson Club History Quarterly*, XXI (January–October 1947), pp. 3–21, 228–242, 327–349. See, in addition, several works on the land companies: Shaw Livermore, *Early American Land Companies: Their Influence on Corporate Development* (New York, 1939); Archibald Henderson, "Dr. Thomas Walker and the Loyal Land Company of Virginia," *American Antiquarian Society, Proceedings*, new ser., XLI (1931), pp. 77–178; Kenneth P. Bailey, *The Ohio Company of Virginia and the Westward Movement, 1748–1792* (Glendale, Calif., 1939); Alfred P. James, *The Ohio Company: Its Inner History* (Pittsburgh, 1959); Kenneth P. Bailey, ed., *The Ohio Company Papers, 1753–1817, Being Primarily Papers of the "Suffering Traders" of Pennsylvania* (Arcata, Calif., [1947]); Lois Mulkearn, ed., *George Mercer Papers Relating to the Ohio Company of Virginia* (Pittsburgh, 1954); George E. Lewis, *The Indiana Company, 1763–1798* (Glendale, Calif.), 1941); and William Lester, *The Transylvania Colony* (Spencer, Ind., 1935).

Whigs and Tories

Of general interest on divisions in the back country during the Revolution are William Nelson, *The American Tory* (New York, 1961); James John Talmon, ed., *Loyalist Narratives from Upper Canada* (Toronto, 1946); and Paul Hubert Smith, *Loyalists and Redcoats: a Study in British Revolutionary Policy* (Chapel Hill, N.C., 1964). The most comprehensive studies, by Wilbur H. Siebert, are in a series of articles too long to be included here, but among the key items are "The Tories of the Upper Ohio," *Ohio Valley Historical Association, Report*, VIII (1915), pp. 38–48; "The Loyalists of Pennsylvania," *Ohio State University Studies, Contributions in History and Political Science*, no. V (Columbus, Ohio, 1920); and "The Loyalists in West Florida and the Natchez District," *Mississippi Valley Historical Review*, II (March 1916), pp. 465–483. On the northern frontier see Mary G. Nye, "Tories in the Champlain Valley," *Vermont Historical Society, Proceedings*, IX (September 1941), pp. 197–203; Richard K. MacMaster, "Parish in Arms: A Study of Father John MacKenna and the Mohawk Valley Loyalists, 1773–1778," *United States Catholic Historical Society, Historical Records and Studies*, XLV (1957), pp. 107–125; and Alexander C. Flick, *Loyalism in New York during the American Revolution* (New York, 1901). For the partisan divisions in the Southern back country see Isaac S. Harrell, *Loyalism in Virginia* (Durham, 1926); Robert O. Demond, *The Loyalists in North Carolina during the Revolution* (Durham, 1940); Robert Woodward Barnwell, Jr., "Loyalism in South Carolina, 1765–1785" (Ph.D. dissertation, Duke University, 1951); Kenneth Coleman, "Restored Colonial Georgia, 1779–1782," *Georgia Historical Quarterly*, XL (March 1956), pp. 1–20; and C. Ashley Ellefson, "Loyalists and Patriots in Georgia during the American Revolution," *Historian*, XXIV (May 1962), pp. 347–356.

The Revolutionary War

There is extensive literature on the war in the West, but from the multitude of works the following items are of particular interest. On the war in the North see Wynn Underwood, "Indian and Tory Raids in the Otter Valley, 1777–1782," *Vermont Quarterly*, new ser., XV (1947), pp. 105–221; Perry Eugene LeRoy, "Sir Guy Carleton as a Military Leader during the American Revolution. Invasion and Repulse, 1775–1776" (Ph.D. dissertation, Ohio State University, 1960); Allen French, *The First Year of the American Revolution* (Boston, 1934); Hoffman Nickerson, *The Turning Point of the Revolution; or, Burgoyne in America* (Boston, 1928); Howard Swiggert, *War Out of Niagara, Walter Butler and the Tory Rangers* (New York, 1933); and Alexander C. Flick, *The Sullivan-Clinton Campaign in 1779* (Albany, 1929). Valuable for the war in the South are John R. Alden, *The South in the Revolution* (Baton Rouge, 1957); John W. Caughey, *Bernardo de Galvez in Louisiana, 1776–1783* (Berkeley, Calif., 1934); and Samuel C. Williams, *Tennessee during the Revolutionary War* (Nashville, Tenn., 1944). Portions of the Haldimand Papers published in vols. IX, X, XI, XIX, XX, and XXIII of the *Michigan Pioneer and Historical Collections* and in volumes XI–XII of the *Wisconsin State Historical Society Collections* relate to the war in Kentucky and the Northwest. A basic collection of documents for the conflict in this region is in Reuben Gold Thwaites and Louise P. Kellogg, eds., *Documentary History of Lord Dunmore's War* (Madison, Wis., 1905); *The Revolution on the Upper Ohio, 1775–1777* (Madison, Wis., 1908); *Frontier Defense on the Upper Ohio, 1777–1778* (Madison, Wis., 1912); *Frontier Advance on the Upper Ohio, 1778–1779* (Madison, Wis., 1916); and *Frontier Retreat on the Upper Ohio, 1779–1781* (Madison, Wis., 1917). See also John D. Barnhart, ed., *Henry Hamilton and George Rogers Clark in the American Revolution* . . . (Crawfordsville, Ind., 1951); Charles G. Talbert, "A Roof for Kentucky," *Filson Club History Quarterly*, XXXIX (April 1955), pp. 145–165; Abraham P. Nasatir, "The Anglo-Spanish Frontier in the Illinois Country during the American Revolution," Illinois State Historical Society, *Journal*, XXXI (1928), pp. 291–358; Lawrence Kinnard, "The Spanish Expedition against Fort St. Joseph in 1781, A New Interpretation," *Mississippi Valley Historical Review*, XIX (September 1932), pp. 173–191; Lois E. Graham, "Fort McIntosh," *Western Pennsylvania Historical Magazine*, XV (May 1932), pp. 93–119; and Randolph G. Downes, "Indian War on the Upper Ohio, 1779–1782," *ibid.*, XVII (June 1934), pp. 93–115.

The West in the Diplomacy of the Revolution

The best works on the subject are Samuel F. Bemis, *Diplomacy of the American Revolution* (New York, 1935); S. F. Bemis, "The Rayneval Memoranda of 1782 on Western Boundaries . . . ," American Antiquarian Society, *Proceedings*, new ser., XLVII (1937), pp. 15–92; Richard B. Morris, *The Peacemakers. The Great Powers and American Independence* (New York, 1965); and Vincent T. Harlow, *The Founding of the Second British Empire,*

1763–1793 (London, 1952). Also valuable are Gerald Stourzh, *Benjamin Franklin and American Foreign Policy* (Chicago, 1954); George Dangerfield, *Chancellor Robert R. Livingston of New York, 1746–1813* (New York, 1960); and Gerald S. Graham, *British Policy and Canada, 1774–1791* (London, 1930). For Congressional opinion see Paul C. Phillips, *The West in the Diplomacy of the American Revolution* (Urbana, Ill., 1913). James A. James, "The Northwest; Gift or Conquest?" *Indiana Magazine of History*, XXX (March 1934), pp. 1–15 argues unconvincingly that Clark's military operations were decisive.

Law and Government

For the political status of the back country communities in the colonial and state governments see Elisha P. Douglass, *Rebels and Democrats, The Struggle for Equal Political Rights and Majority Rule during the American Revolution* (Chapel Hlll, N.C., 1955). Valuable for new governments proposed in the back country are George H. Alden, *New Governments West of the Alleghenies before 1780* (Madison, Wis., 1897); Frederick Jackson Turner, "Western State Making in the Revolutionary Era," *American Historical Review*, I (October 1895, January 1896), pp. 70–87, 251–269; and John Edmund Stealey, III, "French Lick and the Cumberland Compact" *Tennessee Historical Quarterly*, XXII (December 1963), pp. 323–334. On the operation of the county governments and courts see Carl E. Boyd, "The County of Illinois," *American Historical Review*, IV (July 1899), pp. 623–635; A. B. Reid, "Early Courts, Judges and Lawyers of Allegheny County," *Western Pennsylvania Historical Magazine*, V (July 1922), pp. 185–202; Alexander S. Guffey, "The First Courts in Western Pennsylvania," *ibid.*, VII (May 1924), pp. 145–177; Howard M. Browning, "The Washington County Court, 1778–1789: A Study in Frontier Administration," *Tennessee Historical Quarterly*, I (December 1942), pp. 328–343; and Adolph P. Gratiot, "Criminal Justice of the Kentucky Frontier" (Ph.D. dissertation, University of Pennsylvania, 1952). Boyd Crumrine edited the court minute books of several of the northwestern Virginia counties for the *Annals of the Carnegie Museum*, I (1901–1902), pp. 525–569, II (1903–1904), pp. 205–429, III (1905–1906), pp. 5–78.

Frontier Economy

For general agricultural conditions see Percy W. Bidwell and John I. Falconer, *History of Agriculture in the Northern United States, 1620–1860* (Washington, D.C., 1925); Lewis C. Gray, *History of Agriculture in the Southern United States to 1860*, 2 vols. (Washington, D.C., 1933); Arthur R. Hall, "Soil Erosion and Agriculture in the Southern Piedmont: A History" (Ph.D. dissertation, Duke University, 1948); William S. Sachs, "Agricultural Conditions in the Northern Colonies before the Revolution," *Journal of Economic History*, XIII (Summer 1953), pp. 274–290; and Richard H. Shyrock, "British versus German Traditions in Colonial Agriculture," *Mississippi Valley Historical Review*, XXVI (June 1929), pp. 39–54. Valuable specialized and regional studies are Harry Roy Merrens, *Colonial North Carolina in the Eighteenth Century: A Study in Historical Geography* (Chapel Hill, N.C., 1964); Willard Range, "The Agricultural Revolution in Royal Georgia, 1752–1775," *Agricultural History*, XXI (October 1947), pp. 250–255; Chilton Williamson, "New York's Struggle for the Champlain Valley Trade, 1760–1825," *New York History*, XXII (October 1941), pp. 426–436; John G. Gagliardo, "Germans and Agriculture in Colonial Pennsylvania," *Pennsylvania Magazine of History and Biography*, LXXXIII (April 1959), pp. 192–218; and Leo A. Bressler, "Agriculture Among the Germans in Pennsylvania during the Eighteenth Century," *Pennsylvania History*, XXII (April 1955), pp. 103–113. On cattle raising see Gary S. Dunbar, "Colonial Carolina Cowpens," *Agricultural History*, XXV (July 1961), pp. 125–130; and Wesley Newton Laing, "Cattle in Early Virginia" (Ph.D. dissertation, University of Virginia, 1954). Of interest for merchants and marketing are Miles S. Malone, "Falmouth and the Shenandoah: Trade before the Revolution," *American Historical Review*, XL (July 1935), pp. 693–703; Charles M. Thomas, "Successful and Unsuccessful Merchants in the Illinois Country," Illinois State Historical Society, *Journal*, XXX (January 1938), pp. 429–440; and Howard C. Douds, "Merchants and Merchandising in Pittsburgh, 1759–1800," *Western Pennsylvania Historical Magazine*, XX (June 1937), pp. 123–132.

Religion

Of general interest for the religious organizations on the frontier are Marian Silveus, "Churches and Social Control on the Western Pennsylvania frontier," *Western Pennsylvania Historical Magazine*, XXIX (June 1936), pp. 123–134; Roy H. Johnson, "Frontier Religion in Western Pennsylvania," *ibid.*, XVI (February 1933), pp. 23–37; and Colin B. Goodykoontz, *Home Missions on the American Frontier* (Caldwell, Idaho, 1939). For the Presbyterians see Guy S. Klett, "The Presbyterian Church and the Scotch-Irish on the Pennsylvania Colonial Frontier," *Pennsylvania History*, VIII (April 1951), pp. 97–190; Robert F. Scott, "Colonial Presbyterianism in the Valley of Virginia, 1727–1775," Presbyterian Historical Society, *Journal*, XXXV (June, September 1957), pp. 71–92, 171–192; and Walter Browlow Posey, *The Presbyterian Church in the Old Southwest, 1778–1838* (Richmond, 1952). Valuable for the Baptists are Walter Brownlow Posey, *The Baptist Churches in the Lower Mississippi Valley, 1776–1845* (Lexington, Ky., 1957); and James Allie Davidson, "Baptist Beginnings in Western Pennsylvania" (Ph.D. dissertation, University of Pittsburgh, 1941).

Back Country Society

For various evaluations, at times conflicting, of frontier cultural achievements see Arthur K. Moore, *The Frontier Mind; a Cultural Analysis of the Kentucky Frontiersman* (Lexington, Ky., 1957); Howard Henry Sonne, *Liberal Kentucky, 1780–1828* (New York, 1928); Louis B. Wright, *Culture on the Moving Frontier* (Bloomington, Ind., 1955); and Howard H. Peckham,

"Books and Reading on the Ohio Valley Frontier," *Mississippi Valley Historical Review*, XLIV (March 1958), pp. 649–663. For frontier life and manners see Everett Dick, *The Dixie Frontier* (New York, 1948); Stevenson Whitcomb Fletcher, *Pennsylvania Agriculture and Country Life, 1640–1840* (Harrisburg, 1950); James P. Wright and Doris S. Corbett, *Pioneer Life in Western Pennsylvania* (Pittsburgh, 1940); and James I. Robertson, Jr., "Frolics, Fights, and Firewater in Frontier Tennessee," *Tennessee Historical Quarterly*, XVII (June 1958), pp. 97–111. For an institution not commonly associated with the frontier see J. Reuben Sheeler, "The Negro on the Virginia Frontier," *Journal of Negro History*, XLIII (October 1958), pp. 279–297; Kenneth Wiggins Porter, "Negroes on the Southern Frontier, 1670–1763, *ibid.*, XXXIII (January 1948), pp. 53–78; and Edward M. Burns, "Slavery in Western Pennsylvania," *Western Pennsylvania Historical Magazine*, VIII (October 1925), pp. 204–211.

Biographical Studies and Writings

Publications on leading figures on the northern frontier include John Pell, *Ethan Allen* (Boston, 1929); James Benjamin Wilbur, *Ira Allen, Founder of Vermont, 1751–1815*, 2 vols. (Boston and New York, 1928); Milo M. Quaife, ed., *The John Askin Papers, 1747–1820*, 2 vols. (Detroit, 1928–1931); Marc Jack Smith, "Joseph Brant, a Mohawk Statesmen" (Ph.D. dissertation, University of Wisconsin 1946); Harvey Chalmers and Ethel Brant Monture, *Joseph Brant: Mohawk* (East Lansing, Mich., 1955); Orville John Haebker, "Henry Hamilton: British Soldier and Colonial Governor" (Ph. D. dissertation, Indiana University, 1954); Arthur Pound, *Johnson of the Mohawks* (New York, 1930); James Sullivan *et al.*, eds., *The Papers of Sir William Johnson*, 13 vols. (Albany and New York, 1921–1962); Milton W. Hamilton, "Myths and Legends of Sir William Johnson," *New York History*, XXXIV (January 1953), pp. 3–26; Mabel G. Walker, "Sir John Johnson, Loyalist," *Mississippi Valley Historical Review*, III (December 1916), pp. 318–346; Peter H. Bryce, "Sir John Johnson, Baronet; Superintendent-General of Indian Affairs, 1743–1830," New York State Historical Association, *Journal*, IX (July 1928), pp. 233–271; Walter R. Hoberg, "Early History of Colonel Alexander McKee," *Pennsylvania Magazine of History and Biography*, LVIII (January 1934), pp. 26–36; W. R. Hoberg, "A Tory [Alexander McKee] in the Northwest," *ibid.*, LIX (January 1935), pp. 32–41; and John Pell, "Philip Skene of Skenesborough," New York State Historical Association, *Journal*, IX (January 1928), pp. 27–44.

Among the biographical studies and writings for influential figures on the Pennsylvania, Ohio, and Kentucky frontiers are Guy S. Klett, ed., *Journals of Charles Beatty, 1762–1769* (University Park, Pa., [1963]); G. S. Klett, "Charles Beatty, Wilderness Churchman," Presbyterian Historical Society, *Journal*, XXXII (September 1954), pp. 143–159; John Bakeless, *Daniel Boone* (New York, 1939); Lilly L. Nixon, *James Burd, Frontier Defender, 1726–1793* (Philadelphia 1941); John Bakeless, *Background to Glory; the Life of George Rogers Clark* (Philadelphia, 1957); James A. James, *The Life of George*

Rogers Clark (Chicago, 1928); James A. James, ed., *George Rogers Clark Papers, 1771–1784*, 2 vols. (Springfield, Ill., 1912–1916); Percy B. Caley "The Life Adventures of . . . John Connolly . . . ," *Western Pennsylvania Historical Magazine*, XI (January–October 1928), pp. 10–49, 76–111, 144–179, 225–259; Consul W. Butterfield, ed., *Washington-Crawford Letters. Being the correspondence between George Washington and William Crawford . . . concerning western lands* (Cincinnati 1877); Brantz Mayer, *Tah-Gah-Jute; or Logan and [Michael] Cresap, an Historical Essay* (Albany, 1867); John J. Jacob, . . . *the Life of the Late Capt. Michael Cresap* (Cumberland, Md., 1826); Kenneth P. Baily, *Thomas Cresap, Maryland Frontiersmen* (Boston, 1944); Nicholas B. Wainwright, *George Croghan, Wilderness Diplomat* (Chapel Hill, N.C., 1959); Percy B. Caley, "Dunmore, Colonial Governor, New York and Virginia, 1770–1782" (Ph.D. dissertation, University of Pittsburgh, 1940); Consul W. Butterfield, *History of the Girtys* (Cincinnati, 1890); Kathryn Harrod Mason, *James Harrod of Kentucky* (Baton Rouge, 1951); Dwight Raymond Guthrie, *John McMillan: the Apostle of Presbyterianism in the West, 1752–1833* (Pittsburgh, 1952); Charles Gano Talbert, *Benjamin Logan, Kentucky Frontiersman* (Lexington, Ky., 1962); Max Savelle, *George Morgan, Colony Builder* (New York, 1932); Patricia Jahns, *The Violent Years, Simon Kenton and the Ohio-Kentucky Frontier* (New York, 1962); Ellis Beals, "Arthur St. Clair, Western Pennsylvania's Leading Citizen, 1764–1818," *Western Pennsylvania Historical Magazine*, XII (April, July 1929), pp. 75–96, 175–196; William Henry Smith, ed., *The Life and Public Services of Arthur St. Clair . . . with His Correspondence*, 2 vols. (Cincinnati, 1882); Sewall E. Slick, *William Trent and the West* (Harrisburg, 1947); Clarence Brent Allman, *Lewis Wetzel, Indian Fighter, the Life and Times of a Frontier Hero* (New York, 1961); and John Gerald Patterson, "Ebenezar Zane, Frontiersman," *West Virginia History*, XIII (October 1950), pp. 4–45.

For some leading personalities in the southern back country see William H. Masterson, *William Blount* (Baton Rouge, 1954); William Dana Hoyt, Jr., "Colonel William Fleming on the Virginia Frontier, 1775–1783" (Ph.D. dissertation, The Johns Hopkins University, 1940); Mary Elinor Lazenby, *Herman Husband, a Story of His Life, 1724–1795* (Washington, D.C., 1940); Alice Noble Waring, *The Fighting Elder Andrew Pickens (1739–1817)* (Columbia., S.C., 1963); R. B. Marston, "Colonel William Preston," *The John P. Branch Historical Papers of Randolph-Macon College*, IV, no. 3 (June 1915), pp. 257–346; Carl S. Driver, *John Sevier, Pioneer of the Old Southwest* (Chapel Hill, N.C., 1932); and John R. Alden, *John Stuart and the Southern Colonial Frontier* (Ann Arbor, Mich., 1944).

INDEX

225

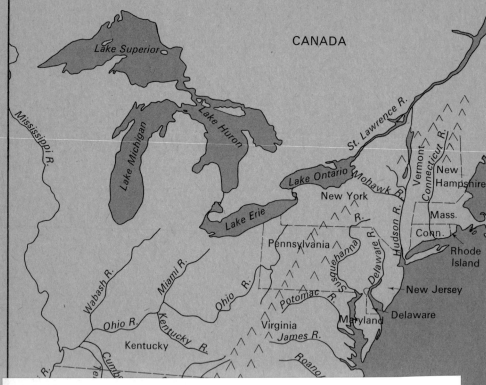

The United States in 1783

MILES

50   0   100   200   300

– – – – – State Boundaries

∧ ∧ ∧ ∧ ∧ Mountain Ranges

CANADA

Lake Superior

Mississippi R.

Lake Michigan

Lake Huron

St. Lawrence R.

Lake Ontario

Mohawk R.

New York

Lake Erie

Vermont

New Hampshire

Connecticut R.

Hudson R.

Mass.

Conn.

Pennsylvania

Susquehanna R.

Delaware R.

Rhode Island

New Jersey

Wabash R.

Miami R.

Ohio R.

Delaware

Ohio R.

Kentucky R.

Potomac R.

Maryland

Virginia

James R.

Kentucky

Roano

Cumb

Te